EVERYDAY & DIET-SMART BREAD MACHINE COOKBOOK

Easy-to-Make Sourdough, Gluten-Free, Keto, Vegan, and More Delicious Bread Machine Recipes

William James Wheatley

Table of Contents

CHAPTER 12: DIET-FRIENDLY RECIPES: WHOLE GRAIN BREAD   157

WHOLE GRAIN BREAD FOR BREAD MACHINES: BILL'S TIPS   157

HOW TO BAKE PUMPKIN BREAD IN A BREAD MACHINE: BILL'S TIPS 163

CHAPTER 13:DIET-FRIENDLY RECIPES: VEGAN BREAD   164

VEGAN BREAD FOR BREAD MACHINES: BILL'S TIPS   164

CHAPTER 14: DIET-FRIENDLY RECIPES: DIABETIC-FRIENDLY BREAD (With Low-Sodium Bread)   175

DIABETIC-FRIENDLY BREAD FOR BREAD MACHINES: BILL'S TIPS   175

CHAPTER 15: DIET-FRIENDLY RECIPES: KETO & LOW-CARB BREADS   186

KETO BREADS FOR BREAD MACHINES: BILL'S TIPS   186

LOW-CARB BREAD BREADS FOR BREAD MACHINES: BILL'S TIPS   191

CHAPTER 16: DOUGH RECIPES   197

PRACTICALITY OF BREAD MACHINES FOR KNEADING DOUGH   197

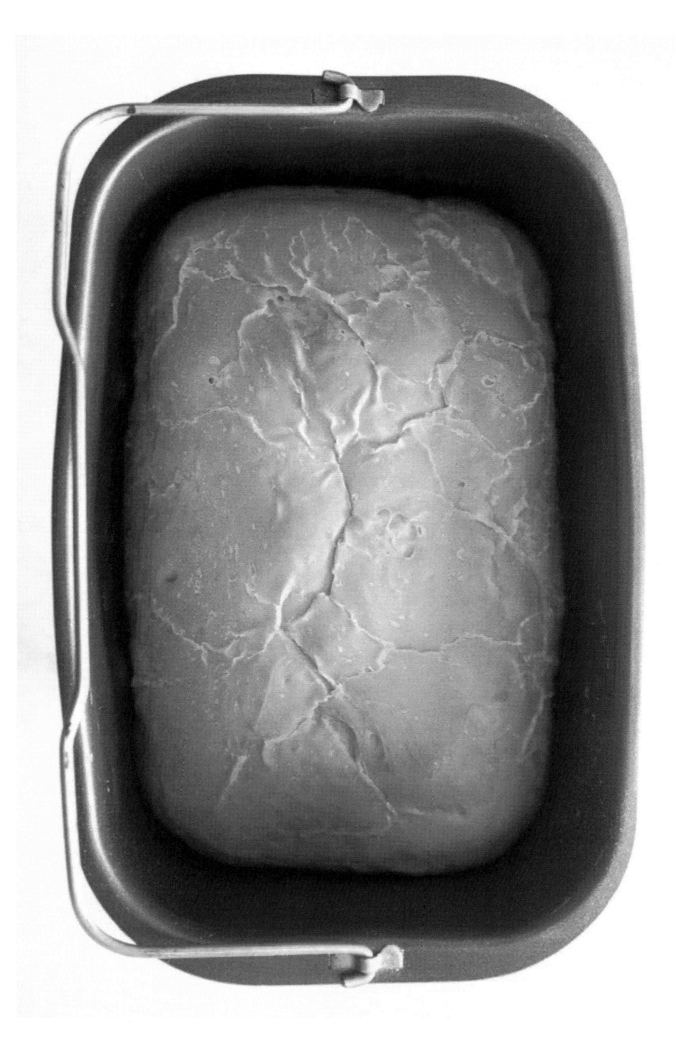

INTRODUCTION

There's something truly magical about waking up to the aroma of freshly baked bread filling your home. It's a simple pleasure that sets the tone for the day, whether from an early morning visit to a bakery or the warm surprise from your kitchen. But imagine achieving this delight with your bread machine, readying your bread just as you start your day.

As a traditional baker and owner of small bakeries, I confidently endorse bread machines. They allow everyone to enjoy fresh bread whenever they want, using their favorite ingredients or adhering to any desired diet. When reliable bakeries are not an option, baking at home becomes an excellent alternative, and a bread machine is the perfect tool. Over the years, I've worked with traditional recipes, explored new ones, and tested them in various bread machines. Not just any machines—I specifically used different models with the same recipes to ensure perfect results every time.

We've refined these recipes through countless trials to bring out the best in your bread machine. We've adapted sourdough starters for machine use and crafted various recipes to accommodate different dietary needs, including gluten-free, sugar-free, low-carb, keto, and more. And it doesn't end with bread—this book is packed with recipes for everything your machine can handle, from yogurt and jam to soups and pilafs.

So, whether you're here for the perfect loaf of bread or to discover the full range of your bread machine's capabilities, you're in for a treat. I'm excited to share these recipes with you and hope they bring as much joy to your kitchen as they have to mine.

Your friend,
Bill

HOW TO USE THIS BOOK

This book is designed so anyone, from beginners to experienced bakers, can easily find inspiration and recipes that suit their needs. We even cover how to get started with your bread machine (perfect for beginners) and discuss common issues that might arise during baking.

The book is divided into chapters, each focusing on a specific type of recipe: from classic bread and sourdough to desserts, doughs, international dishes, diet-friendly options, and more unconventional recipes. This structure lets you quickly find the perfect recipe based on your mood or dietary requirements.

We've included a difficulty index for sourdough recipes. This helps novices and seasoned bakers choose recipes that match their skill level.

Each recipe includes tips on enhancing your baking, making it versatile and easily adaptable to your specific setup. We've also provided ingredient substitutions to meet various dietary preferences, such as plant-based alternatives for dairy or different oil replacements.

Special chapters explore gluten-free baking or working with sourdough in detail. They provide thorough guidance on ingredient selection, preventing cross-contamination, and using different types of flour and starters.

This book goes beyond traditional bread making. It includes recipes for yogurt, jams, soups, and even pilaf, helping you unlock the full potential of your bread machine as a multifunctional kitchen tool.

To make your experience even more enjoyable, every recipe is accompanied by preparation times, nutritional information, and dietary considerations. This ensures you can easily choose the recipe for you and your family.

9

CHAPTER 1:

BASICS
OF BREAD MACHINE

BASICS OF BREAD MACHINE OPERATION

Understanding the fundamentals of bread machine operation reveals this kitchen appliance's convenience and versatility. Here are the core functions and features typically available to the user:

Dough Kneading Function: The bread machine automatically mixes the ingredients and kneads the dough, saving you from the manual labor of doing it yourself. This function is particularly useful for those who prefer to avoid mess and effort while ensuring perfectly kneaded dough every time.

Dough Rising Function: This feature controls the temperature and timing for optimal fermentation. The bread machine creates ideal conditions for the dough to rise, which is crucial for yeast breads. This helps the dough rise evenly and achieve the perfect texture.

Baking Function: After the kneading and rising stages are complete, the baking function activates the heating elements to bake the bread. You can choose the crust darkness level (light, medium, or dark) to achieve the desired result.

Delay Timer: The delay timer lets you schedule a precise start time for the baking process. This feature is perfect for anyone who wants to wake up to the aroma of freshly baked bread or come home to a loaf that's ready to enjoy. Automatic Ingredient Dispenser: Some models, like Panasonic, come equipped with dispensers that automatically add yeast, nuts, raisins, or other ingredients at the appropriate time during the baking process. This simplifies the process and ensures even distribution of ingredients.

Variety of Programs: Bread machines offer various programs, such as "White Bread," "Whole Wheat Bread," "Gluten-Free Bread," "Pizza Dough," "French Bread," and more. These programs automatically adjust the kneading, rising, and baking times to deliver perfect results.

Dough and Pastry Settings: The dough kneading function also allows you to prepare dough for various items, such as pizza, rolls, croissants, and more. The bread machine will knead and rise the dough, which can then be baked in a conventional oven.

Additional Functions: Some models have extra features, such as making jam, yogurt, or soup. These expand the bread machine's capabilities, turning it into a multifunctional kitchen appliance.

Automatic Keep Warm: After baking, most bread machines automatically switch to a "keep warm" mode, keeping your bread warm and fresh until you're ready to enjoy it.

Custom Settings: Some bread machines, like those from Zojirushi or Panasonic, allow you to manually adjust various stages of the baking process, such as kneading, rising, and baking times. This feature offers greater control over the final product, allowing you to experiment with various recipes to create the perfect loaf.

Opportunities for the User:

Time and Effort Savings: The bread machine automates baking, allowing you to enjoy fresh bread with minimal effort.

Recipe Variety: With various programs and features, you can experiment with different types of bread, dough, and even non-bread recipes.

Ingredient Control: Users can select high-quality ingredients, avoid artificial additives, and create bread that suits their dietary preferences (such as gluten-free or low-carb).

Convenience: The bread machine enables you to bake bread at a time that suits you, including using the delay timer to have bread ready for breakfast or dinner.

These features and capabilities make the bread machine an indispensable kitchen tool, perfect for beginners and experienced bakers.

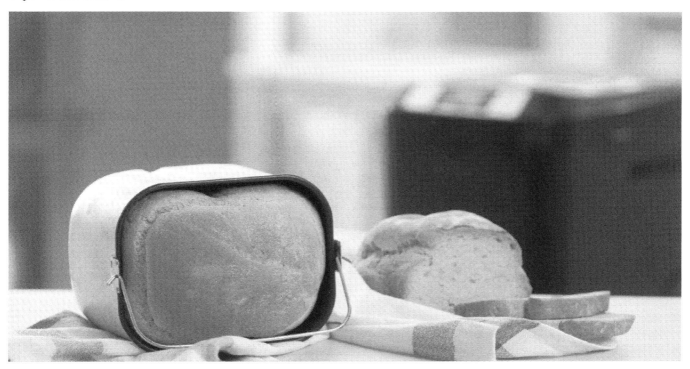

INGREDIENT SELECTION TIPS

Fresh Yeast: Using fresh yeast is essential for successful bread baking. Over time, yeast can lose its potency, leading to insufficient dough rise and a dense texture. To ensure the best results, purchase yeast in small quantities and store it in the refrigerator to extend its shelf life.

High-Quality Flour: Flour is the foundation of any bread, and its quality directly impacts the final product. Opt for flour with a high protein content, especially for bread, as it helps create a better structure and texture. Many bakers prefer organic flour free from pesticides and other chemicals.

Natural Sweeteners: Natural sweeteners like honey, maple syrup, or organic sugar can enhance the flavor and texture of bread, making it more wholesome and nutritious. They often contain more nutrients than refined sugar.

Organic Ingredients: Choosing organic ingredients, such as flour, milk, and butter, can make your bread not only more flavorful but also healthier. By selecting organic products, you avoid additives, pesticides, and GMOs, which is particularly important for those mindful of their health.

Additional Tips: The dedicated sections of this book guide on selecting gluten-free and dietary ingredients, such as sugar or flour substitutes. These recommendations will help you tailor recipes to your nutritional needs and preferences.

CHAPTER 2:

GETTING STARTED

‖‖

INTRODUCTION TO WORKING WITH A BREAD MACHINE: MAIN FUNCTIONS AND PROGRAMS

KNEADING DOUGH

Standard Function: The bread machine automatically mixes the ingredients and kneads the dough, sparing the user from the laborious and messy process of hand mixing.

Bill's Tip:
Use Room-Temperature Ingredients: If the ingredients are too cold or hot, they can affect the kneading process and the final result.

Don't Overload the Pan: Excessing the recommended amounts of flour and liquid is crucial to ensure even kneading. Adjust the liquid or flour to achieve consistency if the dough seems too stiff or loose.

DOUGH RISING

Standard Function: The bread machine automatically maintains the optimal temperature for dough rising, ensuring even fermentation.

Bill's Tip:
Use Fresh Yeast: Old yeast may not perform well, leading to poor dough rise. Always use fresh yeast, especially with complex doughs like whole grain.

Add Moisture: If the dough seems too dry, lightly dampen the surface to improve the rise. This is particularly helpful when using whole wheat or rye flour.

BAKING

Standard Function: After kneading and rising, the bread machine automatically bakes the bread at the correct temperature. Users can choose the crust color—light, medium, or dark.

Bill's Tip:
Customize the Crust: If you prefer a crispier crust, select the dark crust setting, but be mindful not to dry out the bread.

Remove the Paddle: If your machine allows, remove the kneading paddle after the final rise to avoid leaving a large hole at the bottom of the finished loaf.

DELAY TIMER

Standard Function: The delay timer allows you to set the bread machine to begin baking at a chosen time.

Bill's Tip:
Use Fresh Ingredients: When using the delay timer, it's essential that the ingredients, especially yeast and dairy, are fresh to prevent issues with dough rise.

Adjust for Room Conditions: Humidity and temperature can affect the dough's rise, particularly with long delays. In hot weather, reduce the delay time to prevent over proofing.

AUTOMATIC INGREDIENT DISPENSER

Standard Function: Some models, like Panasonic, include a dispenser for automatically adding extra ingredients (e.g., yeast, nuts, raisins) at the right moment.

Bill's Tip:
Preserve Texture: The automatic ingredient dispenser ensures even distribution without damaging delicate items during kneading, which is crucial for nuts, dried fruits, or chocolate chips.

Experiment with Combinations: Add nuts, dried fruits, or spices to your bread to create varied flavors and textures.

KEEP WARM MODE

Standard Function: The bread machine automatically switches to a keep-warm mode after baking.

Bill's Tip:
Avoid Overusing: While the keep-warm mode is convenient, leaving the bread in the machine too long can result in an overly hard crust. Removing the bread promptly after baking is best, allowing it to cool on a rack.
Reheat Soups or Dishes: Some bread machines can warm other dishes, such as soups or porridges.

MAINTENANCE AND CLEANING TIPS

Standard Guidance: Regular maintenance and cleaning of your bread machine are essential to keep it in good working order and ensure consistent baking results. The instruction manual usually provides a basic outline for cleaning, but there are a few additional tips to keep in mind.

Bill's Tip:
Clean After Every Use:
Why It Matters: Residual dough and ingredients left in the pan or on the kneading paddle can harden and affect future baking cycles. These leftovers can also harbor bacteria, leading to unpleasant odors or contamination.

Bill's Tip:
After each baking session, remove the baking pan and kneading paddle for thorough cleaning. Clean the components using warm, soapy water and a non-abrasive sponge to avoid damage. Make sure to dry everything completely before reassembling.

Check the Seals and Gaskets:
Why It Matters: Over time, the seals and gaskets on the bread pan and around the paddle shaft can wear out or collect residue, leading to leaks or compromised performance.

Bill's Tip:
Inspect the seals regularly for signs of wear or cracking. If they start to show wear, replace them promptly to avoid potential leaks. Wipe these areas with a damp cloth to keep them clean after every use.

Prevent Mold and Odors:
Why It Matters: Bread machines can develop mold or odors if not properly ventilated or cleaned after use, especially in humid environments.

Bill's Tip:
Leave the bread machine's lid open for a few hours after use to allow any moisture to evaporate. Wipe the interior with vinegar and water for persistent odors, then leave it open to air out.

Remove and Clean the Dispenser Trays:
Why It Matters: If your bread machine has an automatic ingredient dispenser, ingredients can sometimes get stuck or spill, leading to mold or buildup.

Bill's Tip:
Remove the dispenser trays regularly and clean them thoroughly. Check for leftover ingredients and make sure the mechanism is free of blockages. This is particularly important if you use sticky ingredients like dried fruits or nuts.

Descale and De-gunk:
Why It Matters: Over time, mineral deposits from water or ingredient residue can accumulate on the heating element or other internal parts.

Bill's Tip:
Periodically run a cleaning cycle or a simple mix of water and vinegar through the machine to descale the interior. Follow this by running a plain water cycle to ensure no vinegar taste remains. Clean out any buildup around the kneading paddle shaft to prevent it from getting stuck.

Protect Non-stick Coatings:
Why It Matters: Many bread pans and paddles are coated with non-stick materials, which can be easily scratched or damaged.

Bill's Tip:
Avoid using metal utensils or abrasive cleaners on these surfaces. Opt for silicone or wooden utensils when removing bread and a soft sponge for cleaning. If the non-stick coating begins to peel or wear off, consider replacing the pan or paddle to maintain the quality of your bread.

Store Your Machine Properly:
Why It Matters: Dust and debris can accumulate in and around your bread machine when unused, affecting performance.

Bill's Tip:
When not in use, cover the bread machine with a clean cloth or store it in a dry, dust-free area. If you're storing it for an extended period, thoroughly clean before and after storage to ensure it's ready to use.
By following these tips, you can keep your bread machine in top condition, extend its lifespan, and ensure you always get the best results from your baking efforts.

TIPS FOR STORING AND USING BREAD FROM YOUR BREAD MACHINE WITH BILL'S RECOMMENDATIONS

STORING BREAD
Standard Practice: Fresh bread is ideally stored in an airtight container or a paper bag to maintain its softness and prevent it from drying out.

Bill's Tip:
Never store bread in the refrigerator, as it accelerates the staling process. Instead, keep it at room temperature in a cool, dry place. If you won't eat the entire loaf within a few days, slice it and freeze the portions in freezer bags. This way, you can thaw just the amount you need.

USING BREAD

Standard Practice: Bread from the bread machine can be enjoyed fresh or reheated in a toaster or oven.

Bill's Tip:

Reheat bread in the oven at a low temperature (around 300°F or 150°C) for a few minutes to refresh its taste and texture. You can lightly mist the crust with water before reheating to achieve a crispier finish. Any leftover slices can be repurposed into croutons or breadcrumbs or used for bread pudding.

EXTENDING BREAD FRESHNESS

Standard Practice: Proper storage is key to keeping bread fresh, but it may still stale quickly.

Bill's Tip:

If your bread starts to stale, don't toss it. Use it for making French toast, bread pudding, or homemade breadcrumbs. Another way to extend its freshness is to wrap the bread in a cloth napkin before placing it in the bread box. This helps regulate moisture and keeps the bread fresh longer.

TIPS ON PREVENTING MOLD IN BREAD

Standard Practice: Mold can develop on bread due to moisture and improper storage, especially in warm orhumid environments.

Bill's Tip:

To prevent mold, always store bread in a cool, dry place, preferably in a breathable container like a paper or cloth bag that allows some air circulation. Avoid storing bread in plastic bags at room temperature, as they trap moisture, which can promote mold growth. If you live in a humid area, slicing and freezing your bread and thawing slices as needed is better. Adding a slice of apple or parchment paper sprinkled with salt into the storage bag can help absorb excess moisture and delay mold formation.

HANDLING DIFFERENT TYPES OF BREAD

Sourdough Bread: Bill's Tip: Sourdough bread, made with natural fermentation, tends to have a longer shelf life due to its lower pH, which inhibits mold growth. Store it at room temperature, loosely wrapped in a cloth or paper bag. If the crust becomes too hard, lightly mist it with water and reheat it in the oven to refresh it.

Whole Grain Bread: Bill's Tip: Whole grain bread, being more dense and containing more natural oils from the grains, can stale faster and is more prone to developing an off taste if not stored properly. It's best kept in a bread box or a paper bag at room temperature. For longer storage, slice and freeze it, then toast or reheat slices as needed.

Standard Bread:
Bill's Tip:

Standard white or sandwich bread should be stored in an airtight container at room temperature for short-term use. To extend its freshness, you can freeze the bread. When freezing, ensure the bread is well wrapped to prevent freezer burn. Thaw it at room temperature or reheat it directly from the freezer in a toaster or oven.

These tips will help you get the most out of your homemade bread, ensuring it stays fresh and delicious for as long as possible.

BREAD MACHINE BASICS: FLOUR & YEAST

Bread machines are a game-changer, but they need the right ingredients to deliver that perfect loaf every time. Let's break it down:

FLOUR: GET IT RIGHT, EVERY TIME

Bread Flour is King: For most bread machine recipes, bread flour is your go-to. It's high in protein, which means better gluten development and a stronger, more elastic dough. This translates to a tall, chewy loaf—just what you want.

Bill's Tip:
Try a mix of bread and all-purpose bread for softer, fluffier bread. Just remember, it's all about balance.

Whole Wheat Flour: Whole wheat flour adds a hearty flavor and more nutrients but is denser and can produce a heavier loaf. For the best results, mix it with bread flour or add vital wheat gluten to boost the dough.

Bill's Tip:
Add a tablespoon of honey or molasses if your whole wheat bread isn't rising like you'd hoped. It helps feed the yeast and keeps your loaf soft.

Gluten-Free Blends: Bread machines can handle gluten-free flours like champs, but these doughs require different handling. Look for blends that include rice, tapioca, or potato starch. They mimic the elasticity of gluten.

Bill's Tip:
Gluten-free doughs tend to be stickier, so don't be afraid to add more flour or reduce the liquid. Also, always scrape down the sides during the kneading cycle.

SPECIALTY FLOURS:

When working with specialty flours, remember that each has unique properties that can affect your bread's texture, flavor, and rise. While we've detailed the specific roles and tips for these flours in the corresponding recipes, don't hesitate to experiment on your own. Following the advice will get you started, but the best results often come from a bit of trial and error—so don't be afraid to make each recipe your own! Yeast: The Rise of Great Bread

Instant Yeast for the Win: Instant yeast (also known as bread machine yeast) is made for these machines. It's finely ground and activates quickly. Just toss it in with the dry ingredients—no proofing needed.

Bill's Tip:
Want a more robust flavor? Use active dry yeast instead for a longer rise. Remember to proof it first in warm water—about 110°F should do the trick.

Measuring Matters: Yeast is potent, but too much or too little can throw off your loaf. Measure carefully—typically, 2 teaspoons of instant yeast per 4 cups of flour is the sweet spot.

Bill's Tip:
Yeast can act up if you live in a humid climate. Reduce the liquid slightly and keep an eye on the dough during kneading to ensure it's not too wet.

Storage Solutions: Keep yeast in the fridge or freezer to maintain potency. Always check the expiration date—expired yeast equals flatbread.

Bill's Tip:
Store your yeast in an airtight container and let it come to room temperature before using it. Cold yeast can slow down the rise.

FINAL FLOUR & YEAST CHECKLIST

Mix Smart: Blend your flours for texture and flavor.

Keep It Fresh: Fresh ingredients yield the best results.

Measure Precisely: Bread machines are precise, so be precise with your measurements.

Adjust for Success: Don't be afraid to tweak your recipe based on climate and altitude—bread making is part science, part art.

HOW TO ADAPT RECIPES TO YOUR BREAD MACHINE

Adapting recipes to your specific bread machine can greatly enhance the quality of your bread and make the baking process more seamless. Here are some key steps to follow:

UNDERSTAND YOUR BREAD MACHINE'S CAPACITY:

Check the Manual: First, review your bread machine's manual to determine its maximum capacity for flour and liquid. This is crucial to prevent overflows or dense, undercooked bread.

Adjust Quantities: If a recipe makes a larger loaf than your machine can handle, reduce the quantities of all ingredients proportionally.

SEQUENCE OF INGREDIENTS:

Layering: Bread machines generally require adding ingredients in a specific order. Liquids are typically added first, dry ingredients are added last, and yeast is added later. Be sure to adjust the recipe's instructions to follow this order. Salt and Yeast Placement: Before mixing, place the salt and yeast in separate corners of the bread pan to prevent yeast activation.

ADJUSTING FOR DIFFERENT FLOURS:

Whole Grain Flour: If using whole grain flour, you may need to increase the amount of liquid by 1-2 tablespoons, as these flours absorb more moisture.

Gluten-Free Flour: When using gluten-free flour, extra binding agents like xanthan gum or psyllium husk are often necessary to ensure the dough holds together.

ADJUST THE RISING TIME:

Machine Settings: Different bread machines have varying rising times. If your bread is over or under-proofed, try adjusting the dough cycle or selecting a different program.

Environmental Factors: Room temperature can affect rising time. In a warm room, the dough may rise faster; in a cooler room, it may need more time.

CRUST CONTROL:

Crust Settings: Many machines offer light, medium, or dark crust options. Experiment with these settings to match the recipe's intended crust color and texture.

Manual Adjustments: If your bread machine doesn't have customizable settings, consider stopping the machine early or restarting the bake cycle to achieve the desired crust.

TESTING AND TASTING:

Small Batches: When adapting a new recipe, make a smaller loaf first to ensure correct proportions and baking times.

Taste and Texture: After baking, evaluate the taste and texture. If adjustments are needed, note them for future attempts.

USING PRE-PROGRAMMED SETTINGS:

Select the Right Program: Different types of bread require different settings (e.g., whole wheat, French, or sweet bread). Select the program that best matches the recipe you're adapting.

Custom Programs: If your bread machine allows custom programming, use this feature to fine-tune the baking process.

TWEAKING LIQUIDS AND FLOUR:

Flour and Humidity: Depending on your local climate, you might need to slightly adjust the liquid or flour amount. If the dough seems too wet or dry during the first kneading cycle, add more flour or liquid a tablespoon at a time until the consistency is right.

DEALING WITH ADD-INS:

Nuts, Seeds, and Dried Fruits: If your recipe includes these, add them at the beep (or during the "Add" cycle) to prevent them from getting too crushed during kneading.

Cheese and Chocolate: For melt ingredients, consider freezing them before adding them to the dough to prevent them from melting too early.

NOTE ADJUSTMENTS FOR FUTURE USE:

Record Changes: Record any adjustments you make to the recipe. This approach will help you replicate successful results more easily in the future.

LIST OF USEFUL KITCHEN GADGETS FOR BAKING

Digital Kitchen Scale: For precise measurement of ingredients, essential for consistent results.

Silicone Spatula: This is used for scraping down bowls and ensuring no ingredient is left behind.

Dough Scraper/Bench Knife: Ideal for handling sticky dough and keeping your work surface clean.

Instant-Read Thermometer: To check the internal temperature of your bread, ensuring it's perfectly baked.

Measuring Cups and Spoons: A must-have for accurately measuring wet and dry ingredients.

Silicone Baking Mats or Parchment Paper: To prevent sticking and make cleanup easier.

Proofing Basket (Banneton): Useful for shaping and proofing artisan-style loaves.

Cooling Rack: Allows air around the bread, preventing a soggy bottom.

Bread Lame or Sharp Knife: This tool scores the dough before baking, controlling how the bread expands in the oven.

Spray Bottle: For misting the dough with water to create steam, which helps with crust development.

Stand Mixer with Dough Hook: A stand mixer with a dough hook can be helpful when working with bread machines for a few reasons. It's great for pre-kneading dense or sticky doughs that might be challenging for the bread machine, ensuring ingredients are well mixed and gluten is developed. Additionally, it's useful for larger batches of dough or for recipes that require a more precise kneading process, like brioche or panettone.

Oven Thermometer: This helps verify that your oven is at the correct temperature since built-in thermometers can often be inaccurate.

WORKING WITH THE BANNETON

Place the banneton on a clean surface. Make sure it does not stick to the table or substrate.

Sprinkle the inside of the banneton with flour. This will help keep the dough from sticking.

Place the dough in the banneton. The top of the dough should be on the bottom.

Use plastic wrap or a fresh towel to cover the dough. This will help prevent crusting on the surface of the dough.

Leave the dough in the banneton and watch it. It will rise and take shape.

Turn the banneton over so that the dough is on top.

Carefully remove the dough from the banneton and transfer it to a bread machine or oven.

CHAPTER 3 :

BREAD BASICS

Sometimes, you might notice differences in ingredient quantities for the same recipe. This can happen due to several reasons:

Taste Preferences: Recipes are sometimes tailored to specific taste preferences, including more sugar, salt, or yeast than recipes from other regions.

Ingredient Handling: Different bread machines handle ingredients differently. Some machines might be more efficient with smaller amounts of yeast or salt, which can influence the overall recipe.

Model Specifications: Due to their specific programming, some machines' automatic programs often require fewer ingredients. These settings might be optimized for smaller or more precise quantities.

Recipe Recommendations: Bread machine manufacturers sometimes recommend ingredient quantities to achieve the best results with their models. These recommendations might differ from traditional recipes.

SCALING YOUR LOAF: ADJUSTING RECIPES FOR L AND XL SIZES

When baking the perfect loaf, size matters—but don't worry, we've got you covered. Each recipe provided is designed for an M-size loaf, but with a simple adjustment, you can easily scale it up to L or XL. Follow the multipliers (L x 1.5 | XL x 2) to increase the ingredients proportionally. Whether baking for a cozy family dinner or a large gathering, this approach ensures that your bread will turn out just as delicious, regardless of size. Happy baking, and remember, sometimes bigger is better!

CLASSIC WHITE BREAD

(L x 1.5 | XL x 2)

Ingredients:

- 3 cups (360 g) bread flour
- 1½ teaspoons (7.5 g) salt
- 1 tablespoon (12 g) sugar
- 1 tablespoon (14 g) unsalted butter, softened
- 1¼ cups (300 ml) warm water
- 1½ teaspoons (4.5 g) active dry yeast

Nutritional Information:
(per slice, based on 12 slices)

*120 kcal, 2g fat, 1g sat fat,
5mg cholesterol, 210mg sodium,
22g carbs, 1g fiber, 2g sugar, 4g protein.*

Instructions:

Mixing Ingredients: Add the warm water (110°F/43°C) to the bread pan. Ensure it is not too hot to avoid killing the yeast. Add the flour, salt, sugar, and softened butter to the pan. The dry ingredients should create a barrier between the yeast and water.

Adding Yeast: Make a small well in the center of the dry ingredients and add the active dry yeast.

Kneading and Rising: Select the "Basic" or "White Bread" setting on your bread machine. Choose the crust color according to your preference (light, medium, or dark). The machine will knead, rise, and bake the dough in about 3 hours.

Baking: Allow the bread machine to complete its baking cycle. Once baking is complete, take the bread out of the pan. Allow it to cool on a wire rack for at least 30 minutes before slicing.

Bill's Tip:

To achieve the perfect crust, consider removing the dough after the last kneading cycle and removing the kneading paddle. This way, you'll avoid having a large hole at the bottom of your loaf. Additionally, lightly brush the top of the dough with melted butter just before the baking cycle begins for a golden, tender crust.

WHITE BREAD SESAME SEEDS

(L x 1.5 | XL x 2)

Ingredients:

- 3 cups (360 g) bread flour
- 1½ teaspoons (7.5 g) salt
- 1 tablespoon (12 g) sugar
- 1 tablespoon (14 g) unsalted butter, softened
- 1¼ cups (300 ml) warm water
- 1½ teaspoons (4.5 g) active dry yeast
- 3 tablespoons (25 g) sesame seeds

Nutritional Information:

*125 kcal, 3g fat, 1g sat fat,
5mg cholesterol, 210mg sodium,
23g carbs, 1g fiber, 2g sugar, 4g protein.*

Instructions:

Mixing Ingredients: Add the warm water (110°F/43°C) to the bread pan. Add flour, salt, sugar, butter, and sesame seeds. Make a well in the flour and add yeast.

Kneading and Rising: Select the «Basic» or «White Bread» setting on your machine, medium crust.

Baking: Let the bread machine complete its baking cycle. Once baking is complete, take the bread out of the pan. Allow it to cool on a wire rack for at least 30 minutes before slicing.

Bill's Tip:

Toast sesame seeds before adding them for a richer flavor.

HONEY WHITE BREAD

(L x 1.5 | XL x 2)

Ingredients:

- 3 cups (360 g) bread flour
- 1½ teaspoons (7.5 g) salt
- 2 tablespoons (30 g) honey
- 1 tablespoon (14 g) unsalted butter, softened
- 1¼ cups (300 ml) warm water
- 1½ teaspoons (4.5 g) active dry yeast

Nutritional Information:

130 kcal, 2g fat, 1g sat fat,
5mg cholesterol, 200mg sodium,
24g carbs, 1g fiber, 4g sugar, 4g protein.

Instructions:

Mixing Ingredients: Add the warm water (110°F/43°C) to the bread pan. Ensure it is not too hot to avoid killing the yeast. Add the flour, salt, sugar, and softened butter to the pan. The dry ingredients should create a barrier between the yeast and water.

Adding Yeast: Make a small well in the center of the dry ingredients and add the active dry yeast.

Kneading and Rising: Select the «Basic» or «White Bread» setting on your bread machine. Choose the crust color according to your preference (light, medium, or dark). The machine will knead, rise, and bake the dough in about 3 hours.

Baking: Allow the bread machine to complete its baking cycle. Once baking is complete, take the bread out of the pan. Allow it to cool on a wire rack for at least 30 minutes before slicing

Bill's Tip:

Add an extra spoon of honey for a sweeter, richer bread.

MILK BREAD

(L x 1.5 | XL x 2)

Ingredients:

- 3 cups (360 g) bread flour
- 1½ teaspoons (7.5 g) salt
- 1 tablespoon (12 g) sugar
- 2 tablespoons (28 g) unsalted butter, softened
- 1¼ cups (300 ml) warm milk
- 1½ teaspoons (4.5 g) active dry yeast

Nutritional Information:

135 kcal, 4g fat, 2g sat fat,
10mg cholesterol, 220mg sodium,
23g carbs, 1g fiber, 3g sugar, 5g protein.

Instructions:

Mixing Ingredients: Add the warm water (110°F/43°C) to the bread pan. Ensure it is not too hot to avoid killing the yeast. Add the flour, salt, sugar, and softened butter to the pan. The dry ingredients should create a barrier between the yeast and water.

Adding Yeast: Make a small well in the center of the dry ingredients and add the active dry yeast.

Kneading and Rising: Select the «Basic» or «White Bread» setting on your bread machine. Choose the crust color according to your preference (light, medium, or dark). The machine will knead, rise, and bake the dough in about 3 hours.

Baking: Allow the bread machine to complete its baking cycle. Once baking is complete, take the bread out of the pan. Allow it to cool on a wire rack for at least 30 minutes before slicing

Bill's Tip:

Use whole milk for a richer flavor.

GARLIC HERB BREAD

(L x 1.5 | XL x 2)

Ingredients:

- 3 cups (360 g) bread flour
- 1½ teaspoons (7.5 g) salt
- 1 tablespoon (12 g) sugar
- 1 tablespoon (14 g) unsalted butter, softened
- 1¼ cups (300 ml) warm water
- 1½ teaspoons (4.5 g) active dry yeast

Nutritional Information:

130 kcal, 2g fat, 1g sat fat,
5mg cholesterol, 220mg sodium,
23g carbs, 1g fiber, 2g sugar, 4g protein.

Instructions:

Mixing Ingredients: Add the warm water (110°F/43°C) to the bread pan. Ensure it is not too hot to avoid killing the yeast. Add the flour, salt, sugar, and softened butter to the pan. The dry ingredients should create a barrier between the yeast and water.

Adding Yeast: Make a small well in the center of the dry ingredients and add the active dry yeast.

Kneading and Rising: Select the «Basic» or «White Bread» setting on your bread machine. Choose the crust color according to your preference (light, medium, or dark). The machine will knead, rise, and bake the dough in about 3 hours.

Baking: Allow the bread machine to complete its baking cycle. Once baking is complete, take the bread out of the pan. Allow it to cool on a wire rack for at least 30 minutes before slicing

Bill's Tip:

Add fresh garlic and herbs for a stronger flavor.

WHEAT-RYE BREAD

(L x 1.5 | XL x 2)

Ingredients:

- 2 cups (240 g) bread flour
- 1 cup (120 g) rye flour
- 1½ teaspoons (7.5 g) salt
- 1 tablespoon (12 g) sugar
- 1 tablespoon (14 g) unsalted butter, softened
- 1¼ cups (300 ml) warm water
- 1½ teaspoons (4.5 g) active dry yeast

Nutritional Information:

130 kcal, 2g fat, 1g sat fat,
5mg cholesterol, 210mg sodium,
24g carbs, 2g fiber, 2g sugar, 4g protein.

Instructions:

Mixing Ingredients: Add the warm water (110°F/43°C) to the bread pan. Ensure it is not too hot to avoid killing the yeast. Add the flour, salt, sugar, and softened butter to the pan. The dry ingredients should create a barrier between the yeast and water.

Adding Yeast: Make a small well in the center of the dry ingredients and add the active dry yeast.

Kneading and Rising: Select the «Basic» or «White Bread» setting on your bread machine. Choose the crust color according to your preference (light, medium, or dark). The machine will knead, rise, and bake the dough in about 3 hours.

Baking: Allow the bread machine to complete its baking cycle. Once baking is complete, take the bread out of the pan. Allow it to cool on a wire rack for at least 30 minutes before slicing

Bill's Tip:

Mix in some caraway seeds for a traditional taste.

GRAHAM BREAD

(L x 1.5 | XL x 2)

Ingredients:

- 3 cups (360 g) Graham flour
  If unavailable, substitute with either:
- 2 cups (240 g) all-purpose flour and 1 cup (120 g) rye flour, or
- 2 cups (240 g) all-purpose flour with ½ cup (60 g) bran flour and ½ cup (60 g) rye flour1½ teaspoons (7.5 g) salt
- 2 tablespoons (24 g) sugar
- 1 tablespoon (14 g) unsalted butter, softened
- 1¼ cups (300 ml) warm water
- 1½ teaspoons (4.5 g) active dry yeast

Nutritional Information:

140 kcal, 3g fat, 1g sat fat,
5mg cholesterol, 200mg sodium,
25g carbs, 2g fiber, 3g sugar, 5g protein.

Instructions:

Mixing Ingredients: Add the warm water (110°F/43°C) to the bread pan. Ensure it is not too hot to avoid killing the yeast. Add the flour, salt, sugar, and softened butter to the pan. The dry ingredients should create a barrier between the yeast and water.

Adding Yeast: Make a small well in the center of the dry ingredients and add the active dry yeast.

Kneading and Rising: Select the "Basic" or "White Bread" setting on your bread machine. Choose the crust color according to your preference (light, medium, or dark). The machine will knead, rise, and bake the dough in about 3 hours.

Baking: Let the bread machine complete its baking cycle. Once baking is complete, take the bread out of the pan. Allow it to cool on a wire rack for at least 30 minutes before slicing.

Bill's Tip:

Use dark graham flour for a deeper flavor.

BUTTER WHITE BREAD

(L x 1.5 | XL x 2)

Ingredients:

- 3 cups (360 g) bread flour
- 1½ teaspoons (7.5 g) salt
- 1 tablespoon (12 g) sugar
- 2 tablespoons (28 g) unsalted butter, softened
- 1¼ cups (300 ml) warm water
- 1½ teaspoons (4.5 g) active dry yeast

Nutritional Information:

140 kcal, 4g fat, 2g sat fat,
10mg cholesterol, 220mg sodium,
23g carbs, 1g fiber, 2g sugar, 4g protein.

Instructions:

Mixing Ingredients: Add the warm water (110°F/43°C) to the bread pan. Ensure it is not too hot to avoid killing the yeast. Add the flour, salt, sugar, and softened butter to the pan. The dry ingredients should create a barrier between the yeast and water.

Adding Yeast: Make a small well in the center of the dry ingredients and add the active dry yeast.

Kneading and Rising: Select the «Basic» or «White Bread» setting on your bread machine. Choose the crust color according to your preference (light, medium, or dark). The machine will knead, rise, and bake the dough in about 3 hours.

Baking: Allow the bread machine to complete its baking cycle. Once baking is complete, take the bread out of the pan. Allow it to cool on a wire rack for at least 30 minutes before slicing

Bill's Tip:

Add a tablespoon of butter for a richer buttery loaf.

TRADITIONAL RYE BREAD

(L x 1.5 | XL x 2)

Ingredients:

- 1½ cups (180 g) rye flour
- 1½ cups (180 g) whole wheat flour
- 1½ teaspoons (7.5 g) salt
- 1 tablespoon (12 g) sugar
- 1 tablespoon (14 g) unsalted butter, softened
- 1¼ cups (300 ml) warm water
- 1½ teaspoons (4.5 g) active dry yeast
- 2 tablespoons (30 g) molasses

Nutritional Information:

145 kcal, 3g fat, 1g sat fat,
5mg cholesterol, 210mg sodium,
26g carbs, 3g fiber, 4g sugar, 4g protein.

Instructions:

Mixing Ingredients: Pour the warm water (110°F/43°C) into the bread pan. Add the softened butter, rye flour, salt, sugar, and molasses. Make a small well in the flour and add the active dry yeast.

Adding Yeast: Make a small well in the center of the dry ingredients and add the active dry yeast.

Kneading and Rising: Your bread machine should have the «Whole Wheat» or «Whole Grain/Rye» setting, accommodating the denser texture of rye bread.

Baking: Press start to begin the kneading, rising, and baking process. The total time will vary depending on the machine used. After the baking cycle finishes, carefully remove the bread from the pan. Place the bread on a wire rack and let it cool completely before slicing.

Bill's Tip:

Combine rye and whole wheat flour to enhance the texture and flavor and create a denser loaf.

RYE BREAD WITH CARAWAY SEEDS

(L x 1.5 | XL x 2)

Ingredients:

- 1½ cups (180 g) rye flour
- 1½ cups (180 g) whole wheat flour
- 1½ teaspoons (7.5 g) salt
- 1 tablespoon (12 g) sugar
- 1 tablespoon (14 g) unsalted butter, softened
- 1¼ cups (300 ml) warm water
- 1½ teaspoons (4.5 g) active dry yeast
- 2 teaspoons (4 g) caraway seeds

Nutritional Information:

140 kcal, 3g fat, 1g sat fat,
5mg cholesterol, 210mg sodium, 25g carbs,
2g fiber, 3g sugar, 4g protein.

Instructions:

Use the «Whole Wheat» or «Whole Grain/Rye» setting on your bread machine, following the program's specific instructions for kneading, rising, and baking.

Bill's Tip:

Toast caraway seeds before adding them to enhance their flavor.

RYE BREAD WITH HONEY

(L x 1.5 | XL x 2)

Ingredients:

- Rye Flour: 1 ½ cups (180g)
- Whole Wheat Flour: 1 ½ cups (180g)
- Salt: 1 ½ tsp (7.5g)
- Honey: 2 tbsp (30g)
- Unsalted Butter, softened: 1 tbsp (14g)
- Warm Water: 1 ¼ cups (300ml)
- Active Dry Yeast: 1 ½ tsp (4.5g)

Instructions:

Use the «Whole Wheat» or «Whole Grain/Rye» setting on your bread machine, following the program's specific instructions for kneading, rising, and baking.

Nutritional Information:

145 kcal, 3g fat, 1g sat fat,
5mg cholesterol, 210mg sodium,
26g carbs, 2g fiber, 4g sugar, 4g protein.

Bill's Tip:

Combine honey and molasses for a deeper sweetness.

WHOLE WHEAT BREAD

(L x 1.5 | XL x 2)

Ingredients:

- 3 cups (360 g) whole wheat flour
- 1½ teaspoons (7.5 g) salt
- 1 tablespoon (12 g) honey
- 1 tablespoon (14 g) unsalted butter, softened
- 1¼ cups (300 ml) warm water
- 1½ teaspoons (4.5 g) active dry yeast

Instructions:

Use the «Whole Wheat» or «Whole Grain/Rye» setting on your bread machine, following the program's specific instructions for kneading, rising, and baking.

Nutritional Information:

130 kcal, 2g fat, 1g sat fat,
5mg cholesterol, 210mg sodium,
23g carbs, 2g fiber, 2g sugar, 4g protein.

Bill's Tip:

To make the bread fluffier, replace 1/4 cup of the flour with vital wheat gluten.

26

WHOLE WHEAT BREAD 75%

Ingredients:

(L x 1.5 | XL x 2)

Instructions:

- 2¼ cups (270 g) whole wheat flour
- ¾ cup (90 g) bread flour
- 1½ teaspoons (7.5 g) salt
- 1 tablespoon (12 g) honey
- 1 tablespoon (14 g) unsalted butter, softened
- 1¼ cups (300 ml) warm water
- 1½ teaspoons (4.5 g) active dry yeast

Use the «Whole Wheat» or «Whole Grain/Rye» setting on your bread machine, following the program's specific instructions for kneading, rising, and baking.

Nutritional Information:

130 kcal, 2g fat, 1g sat fat,
5mg cholesterol, 210mg sodium,
24g carbs, 2g fiber, 2g sugar, 4g protein.

Bill's Tip:

The bread flour mix helps balance the texture while keeping it mostly whole grain.

WHOLE WHEAT BREAD 50%

Ingredients:

(L x 1.5 | XL x 2)

Instructions:

- 1½ cups (180 g) whole wheat flour
- 1½ cups (180 g) bread flour
- 1½ teaspoons (7.5 g) salt
- 1 tablespoon (12 g) honey
- 1 tablespoon (14 g) unsalted butter, softened
- 1¼ cups (300 ml) warm water
- 1½ teaspoons (4.5 g) active dry yeast

Use the «Whole Wheat» or «Whole Grain/Rye» setting on your bread machine, following the program's specific instructions for kneading, rising, and baking.

Nutritional Information:

130 kcal, 2g fat, 1g sat fat,
5mg cholesterol, 210mg sodium,
24g carbs, 2g fiber, 2g sugar, 4g protein.

Bill's Tip:

This version is a great compromise for those who prefer softer bread but still want whole-grain goodness.

27

WHOLE WHEAT BREAD WITH YOGURT

(L x 1.5 | XL x 2)

Ingredients:

- 3 cups (360 g) whole wheat flour
- 1½ teaspoons (7.5 g) salt
- 1 tablespoon (12 g) honey
- 1 tablespoon (14 g) unsalted butter, softened
- 1¼ cups (300 ml) warm plain yogurt
- 1½ teaspoons (4.5 g) active dry yeast

Nutritional Information:

140 kcal, 3g fat, 2g sat fat,
10mg cholesterol, 210mg sodium,
24g carbs, 2g fiber, 3g sugar, 5g protein.

Instructions:

Use the «Whole Wheat» or «Whole Grain/Rye» setting on your bread machine, following the program's instructions for kneading, rising, and baking, but replace warm water with warm yogurt.

Bill's Tip:

Yogurt adds a subtle tang to bread, making it perfect for savory spreads. When choosing yogurt for baking, opt for plain yogurt. It should be free of added sugars or flavors to ensure your bread has a balanced taste and texture. If you prefer a thicker texture, Greek yogurt is a great option, but always go for the unsweetened variety.

WHOLE WHEAT BREAD WITH PECANS AND FIGS

(L x 1.5 | XL x 2)

Ingredients:

- 3 cups (360 g) whole wheat flour
- 1½ teaspoons (7.5 g) salt
- 1 tablespoon (12 g) honey
- 1 tablespoon (14 g) unsalted butter, softened
- 1¼ cups (300 ml) warm water
- 1½ teaspoons (4.5 g) active dry yeast
- ½ cup (60 g) chopped pecans
- ½ cup (75 g) dried figs, chopped

Nutritional Information:

160 kcal, 5g fat, 1g sat fat, 5mg cholesterol,
220mg sodium, 26g carbs, 3g fiber, 4g sugar,
5g protein.

Instructions:

Use the «Whole Wheat» or «Whole Grain/Rye» setting on your bread machine, following the program's specific instructions for kneading, rising, and baking. Add pecans and figs during the kneading cycle.

Bill's Tip:

To make the figs softer and more flavorful, soak them in warm water for 10 minutes before incorporating them into the dough.

AMARANTH BREAD

Ingredients:

- 2 cups (240 g) whole wheat flour
- 1 cup (120 g) bread flour
- ⅔ cup (80 g) amaranth flour
- 1 teaspoon (5 g) salt
- 1 tablespoon (12 g) sugar
- 1½ tablespoons (21 g) unsalted butter, softened
- 1 cup (240 ml) warm water
- 1½ teaspoons (4.5 g) active dry yeast

Nutritional Information:

(per slice, based on a 1.5 lb loaf)
140 kcal, 2.5g fat, 1g sat fat,
5mg cholesterol, 210mg sodium,
24g carbs, 3g fiber, 4g sugar, 5g protein.

(L x 1.5 | XL x 2)

Instructions:

Mixing Ingredients: Pour the warm water (110°F/43°C) into the bread pan. Add the softened butter, rye flour, salt, sugar, and molasses. Make a small well in the flour and add the active dry yeast.

Adding Yeast: Make a small well in the center of the dry ingredients and add the active dry yeast.

Kneading and Rising: Choose the «Whole Wheat» or «Whole Grain/Rye» setting on your bread machine, which accommodates the denser texture of rye bread. Opt for the medium loaf size (1.5 lbs) and select your preferred crust setting (light, medium, or dark).

Baking: Press start to begin the kneading, rising, and baking process. The total time will vary depending on the machine used. After the baking cycle finishes, carefully remove the bread from the pan. Place the bread on a wire rack and let it cool completely before slicing.

Bill's Tip:

Amaranth flour adds a distinct, nutty flavor and a nutritional boost. Monitor the dough during the kneading phase and adjust moisture levels as needed. Add a tablespoon of water if the dough feels too dry, adjusting until the desired consistency is achieved. Continue adding until the dough reaches the desired consistency.

CINNAMON RAISIN BREAD

Ingredients:

- 2½ cups (300 g) bread flour
- 1 teaspoon (5 g) salt
- ¼ cup (50 g) sugar
- 2 teaspoons (4 g) ground cinnamon
- 2 tablespoons (28 g) unsalted butter, softened
- ½ cup (80 g) raisins
- 1 cup (240 ml) warm water
- 1½ teaspoons (4.5 g) active dry yeast

Nutritional Information:
(per slice, based on a 1.5 lb loaf)
180 kcal, 3g fat, 1.5g sat fat,
10mg cholesterol, 250mg sodium,
31g carbs, 1g fiber, 15g sugar, 4g protein.

(L x 1.5 | XL x 2)

Instructions:

Mixing Ingredients: Pour warm water (110°F/43°C) into the bread pan. Add bread flour, salt, sugar, and ground cinnamon. Add the softened butter and raisins. Finally, add the yeast, ensuring it doesn't come into direct contact with the liquid until mixing starts.

Adding Yeast: Make a small well in the center of the dry ingredients and add the active dry yeast.

Kneading and Rising: Choose the Basic or Sweet Bread program on your bread machine. Opt for the medium loaf size (1.5 lbs) and select your preferred crust setting (light, medium, or dark).

Baking: Press start to begin the kneading, rising, and baking cycle. The total time will depend on the machine used.
Cooling: After the baking cycle finishes, carefully remove the bread from the pan. Place the bread on a wire rack and let it cool completely before slicing.

Bill's Tip:

For an extra cinnamon flavor, sprinkle additional cinnamon sugar on top of the dough before the baking cycle starts. Mix the raisins thoroughly during the initial kneading phase to ensure they are evenly distributed throughout the dough.

CHAPTER 4:

SWEET ROLLS AND PIES

CLASSIC CINNAMON ROLLS WITH CREAM CHEESE FROSTING

Ingredients:

Dough:
- 1 cup warm milk (240ml)
- 2 large eggs (100g)
- ⅓ cup melted butter (75g)
- 4½ cups bread flour (540g)
- 1 teaspoon salt (5g)
- ½ cup sugar (100g)
- 2¼ teaspoons yeast (7g)

Filling:
- ½ cup softened butter (113g)
- 1 cup brown sugar (200g)
- 2½ tablespoons ground cinnamon (20g)

Cream Cheese Frosting:
- 4 oz cream cheese, softened (115g)
- ¼ cup butter, softened (56g)
- 1½ cups powdered sugar (180g)
- ½ teaspoon vanilla extract (2.5ml)

Nutritional Information:
(per roll)

Approx. 300 kcal, 18g fat,
65mg cholesterol, 320mg sodium,
45g carbs, 2g fiber, 20g sugar, 5g protein

Instructions:

Prepare Dough: In your bread machine, place the warm milk, eggs, melted butter, bread flour, salt, sugar, and yeast in the order recommended by the manufacturer. Choose the "Dough" cycle and let the machine handle the process.

Make the Filling: While the dough is being prepared, mix the softened butter, brown sugar, and ground cinnamon in a bowl until well combined.

Roll the Dough: When the dough cycle is complete, move the dough to a floured surface.
Roll it out into a large rectangle, approximately 16x21 inches. Evenly spread the cinnamon filling across the dough.

Shape the Rolls: Roll up the dough tightly from one long edge to the other, then cut it into 12 equal-sized rolls. Place the rolls into a greased bread machine pan or an oven-safe dish that fits inside the machine.

Second Rise: Let the rolls rise in the machine for about 30 minutes until they double in size.

Bake: Select the "Bake" cycle on your bread machine and bake for 20-25 minutes or until golden brown.

Prepare Frosting: While the rolls are baking, mix the softened cream cheese, butter, powdered sugar, and vanilla extract until smooth.

Finish: Spread the cream cheese frosting over the warm rolls after baking the rolls.

Bill's Tip:

Drizzle a small amount of heavy cream over the rolls for a gooey texture. Then, bake as directed. This will make them extra soft and indulgent, perfect for a sweet morning treat!

MAPLE PECAN STICKY BUNS

Ingredients:

Dough:
- 1 cup warm milk (240ml)
- 2 large eggs (100g)
- ⅓ cup melted butter (75g)
- 4½ cups bread flour (540g)
- 1 teaspoon salt (5g)
- ½ cup sugar (100g)
- 2¼ teaspoons yeast (7g)

Filling:
- ½ cup softened butter (113g)
- 1 cup brown sugar (200g)
- 2 tablespoons ground cinnamon (15g)
- ½ cup chopped pecans (50g)

Topping:
- ½ cup unsalted butter (113g)
- ½ cup brown sugar (100g)
- ¼ cup maple syrup (60ml)
- ¾ cup chopped pecans (75g)

Nutritional Information:
(per sticky bun)

Approx. 400 kcal, 25g fat,
80mg cholesterol, 320mg sodium,
55g carbs, 2g fiber, 30g sugar, 5g protein

Instructions:

Prepare Dough: Add warm milk, eggs, melted butter, bread flour, salt, sugar, and yeast to your bread machine, following the manufacturer's recommended order. Then, choose the «Dough» cycle to start the process.

Make the Filling: While the dough is being prepared, mix the softened butter, brown sugar, ground cinnamon, and chopped pecans in a bowl.

Prepare the Topping: Melt the butter in a small saucepan over medium heat. Incorporate the brown sugar and maple syrup until smooth. Place the mixture into the bottom of the bread machine pan or an oven-safe dish that fits inside. Evenly sprinkle the chopped pecans over the syrup.

Shape the Buns: Once the dough cycle is complete, move the dough to a floured surface. Roll it out into a large rectangle, approximately 16x21 inches. Spread the filling over the dough. Roll the dough tightly from one long edge to the opposite edge. Cut it into 12 equal-sized buns.

Second Rise: Place the buns cut-side down on the pecan topping in the bread machine pan. Allow the buns to rise for about 30 minutes until they've doubled in size.

Bake: Select the «Bake» cycle on your bread machine and bake for 20-25 minutes until golden brown.

Finish: Once baked, carefully invert the pan onto a serving plate so the pecan topping is on top.

Bill's Tip:

For extra indulgence, sprinkle a pinch of sea salt over the sticky buns before serving. The salt complements the sweetness and enhances the maple-pecan flavor.

31

BLUEBERRY LEMON ROLLS

Ingredients:

Dough:
- 1 cup warm milk (240ml)
- 2 large eggs (100g)
- ⅓ cup melted butter (75g)
- 4½ cups bread flour (540g)
- 1 teaspoon salt (5g)
- ½ cup sugar (100g)
- 2¼ teaspoons yeast (7g)

Filling:
- 1 cup fresh blueberries (150g)
- ½ cup sugar (100g)
- Zest of 1 lemon
- 2 tablespoons lemon juice (30ml)
- ¼ cup softened butter (57g)

Glaze:
- 1 cup powdered sugar (125g)
- 2 tablespoons lemon juice (30ml)
- Zest of 1 lemon

Nutritional Information:
(per roll)

Approx. 330 kcal, 15g fat,
45mg cholesterol, 200mg sodium,
55g carbs, 1g fiber, 35g sugar, 4g protein

Instructions:

Prepare Dough: In the bread machine, place the warm milk, eggs, melted butter, bread flour, salt, sugar, and yeast in the order recommended by the manufacturer. Select the «Dough» cycle.

Make the Filling: While the dough is being prepared, mix the sugar, lemon zest, lemon juice, and softened butter in a bowl. Gently fold in the fresh blueberries.

Shape the Rolls: Once the dough cycle is complete, move the dough to a floured surface. Roll it out into a large rectangle, approximately 16x21 inches. Spread the lemon-sugar mixture evenly over the dough. Carefully distribute the blueberries on top.

Roll and Cut: Roll up the dough tightly from one long edge to the other, then cut it into 12 equal-sized rolls. Place the rolls into a greased bread machine pan or an oven-safe dish that fits inside the machine.

Second Rise: Let the rolls rise for about 30 minutes or until they have doubled.

Bake: Select the «Bake» cycle on your bread machine and bake for 20-25 minutes until golden brown.

Glaze: As the rolls bake, whisk together powdered sugar, lemon zest, and juice to create a glaze. Once the rolls are baked and warm, drizzle the glaze generously over them.

Bill's Tip:

Add a few drops of pure lemon extract to the glaze for extra flavor. This will intensify the lemony freshness that pairs perfectly with the sweet blueberries.

PUMPKIN SPICE SWIRL BREAD

Ingredients:

Dough:
- 1 cup warm milk (240ml)
- 2 large eggs (100g)
- ⅓ cup melted butter (75g)
- 4½ cups bread flour (540g)
- 1 teaspoon salt (5g)
- ½ cup sugar (100g)
- 2¼ teaspoons yeast (7g)

Filling:
- ½ cup pumpkin puree (120g)
- ½ cup brown sugar (100g)
- 1 tablespoon ground cinnamon (8g)
- ½ teaspoon ground nutmeg (1g)
- ¼ teaspoon ground cloves (0.5g)
- ¼ teaspoon ground ginger (0.5g)

Glaze:
- ½ cup powdered sugar (62g)
- 1 tablespoon milk (15ml)
- ½ teaspoon vanilla extract (2.5ml)

Nutritional Information:
(per slice)

Approx. 250 kcal, 10g fat,
35mg cholesterol, 150mg sodium,
42g carbs, 1g fiber, 22g sugar, 5g protein

Instructions:

Prepare Dough: In the bread machine, place the warm milk, eggs, melted butter, bread flour, salt, sugar, and yeast in the order recommended by the manufacturer. Select the «Dough» cycle.

Make the Filling: In a bowl, mix the pumpkin puree, brown sugar, and spices until smooth.

Shape the Bread: Once the dough cycle is complete, move the dough to a floured surface. Roll it out into a large rectangle, approximately 16x21 inches. Evenly spread the pumpkin filling across the dough. Roll and Cut: Roll up the dough tightly from one long edge to the other. Place the rolled dough into a greased bread machine pan.

Second Rise: Let the bread rise for approximately 25 minutes or until it has doubled.

Bake: Select the «Bake» cycle on your bread machine and bake for 25-30 minutes until golden brown.

Glaze: As the bread bakes, prepare the glaze by mixing powdered sugar, milk, and vanilla extract until smooth. Drizzle over the warm bread.

Bill's Tip:

Sprinkle some toasted pecans over the glaze for added crunch and flavor. The nuttiness pairs wonderfully with the spiced pumpkin filling.

33

APPLE CINNAMON ROLLS WITH CARAMEL DRIZZLE

Ingredients:

Dough:
- 1 cup warm milk (240ml)
- 2 large eggs (100g)
- ⅓ cup melted butter (75g)
- 4½ cups bread flour (540g)
- 1 teaspoon salt (5g)
- ½ cup sugar (100g)
- 2¼ teaspoons yeast (7g)

Filling:
- 2 large apples, peeled, cored, and diced (approximately 300g)
- ½ cup brown sugar (100g)
- 1 tablespoon ground cinnamon (8g)
- ¼ cup softened butter (56g)

Caramel Drizzle:
- ½ cup brown sugar (100g)
- ¼ cup butter (56g)
- ¼ cup heavy cream (60ml)
- ½ teaspoon vanilla extract (2.5ml)

Nutritional Information:

(per roll)

*Approx. 340 kcal, 15g fat,
45mg cholesterol, 200mg sodium,
55g carbs, 1g fiber, 35g sugar, 4g protein*

Instructions:

Prepare Dough: In the bread machine, place the warm milk, eggs, melted butter, bread flour, salt, sugar, and yeast in the order recommended by the manufacturer. Select the «Dough» cycle.

Make the Filling: While the dough is being prepared, mix the diced apples, brown sugar, and ground cinnamon in a bowl.

Shape the Rolls: Once the dough cycle is complete, move the dough to a floured surface. Roll it out into a large rectangle, approximately 16x21 inches. Evenly coat the dough with softened butter, then sprinkle the apple mixture.

Roll and Cut: Roll up the dough tightly from one long edge to the other, then cut it into 12 equal-sized rolls. Place the rolls into a greased bread machine pan or an oven-safe dish that fits inside the machine.

Second Rise: Let the rolls rise for about 30 minutes or until they have doubled.

Bake: Select the «Bake» cycle on your bread machine and bake for 20-25 minutes until golden brown.

Caramel Drizzle: While the rolls are baking, prepare the caramel drizzle in a small saucepan. In a medium saucepan, melt the butter over medium heat. Stir in the brown sugar and heavy cream, and cook the mixture, stirring constantly, until it reaches a gentle boil. Cook for 3–4 minutes, or until thickened, then remove from heat and stir in the vanilla extract. Drizzle over the warm rolls.

Bill's Tip:

Top each roll with a sprinkle of sea salt before serving for an extra-special touch. The combination of sweet caramel and salty finish makes these rolls irresistible.

34

ORANGE CRANBERRY ROLLS

Ingredients:

Dough:
- 1 cup warm milk (240ml)
- 2 large eggs
- ⅓ cup melted butter (75g)
- 4 ½ cups bread flour (540g)
- 1 teaspoon salt (5g)
- ½ cup sugar (100g)
- 2 ¼ teaspoons yeast (7g)

Filling:
- ½ cup softened butter (115g)
- ½ cup brown sugar (100g)
- Zest of 1 orange
- ½ cup dried cranberries (60g)
- ½ teaspoon ground cinnamon (1g)

Orange Glaze:
- 1 cup powdered sugar (125g)
- 2 tablespoons fresh orange juice (30ml)
- Zest of 1 orange

Nutritional Information:
(per slice)

Approx. 320 kcal, 14g fat,
45mg cholesterol, 200mg sodium,
45g carbs, 1g fiber, 30g sugar, 4g protein

Instructions:

Prepare Dough: In the bread machine, place the warm milk, eggs, melted butter, bread flour, salt, sugar, and yeast in the order recommended by the manufacturer. Select the «Dough» cycle.

Make the Filling: Mix the softened butter, brown sugar, orange zest, dried cranberries, and ground cinnamon in a bowl.

Shape the Rolls: Once the dough cycle is complete, move the dough to a floured surface. Roll it out into a large rectangle, approximately 16x21 inches. Spread the filling evenly over the dough.

Roll and Cut: Roll up the dough tightly from one long edge to the other, then cut it into 12 equal-sized rolls. Place the rolls into a greased bread machine pan or an oven-safe dish that fits inside the machine.

Second Rise: Let the rolls rise for approximately 30 minutes or until they have doubled.

Bake: Select the «Bake» cycle on your bread machine and bake for 20-25 minutes until golden brown.

Glaze: As the rolls bake, prepare a glaze by combining powdered sugar, fresh orange juice, and zest. Drizzle over the warm rolls.

Bill's Tip:

Add a few chopped fresh cranberries to the filling for a fresh flavor. They'll add a nice tartness that complements the sweetness of the orange glaze.

CHOCOLATE CHIP BRIOCHE ROLLS

Ingredients:

Dough:
- ¼ cup warm milk (60ml)
- 4 large eggs
- ¼ cup sugar (50g)
- 1 teaspoon salt (5g)
- 1 cup softened butter (240g)
- 4 cups bread flour (480g)
- 2 ¼ teaspoons yeast (7g)

Filling:
- 1 cup semi-sweet chocolate chips (175g)
- ¼ cup softened butter (60g)

Egg Wash:
- 1 beaten egg
- 1 tablespoon water

Nutritional Information:
(per roll)

Approx. 320 kcal, 22g fat,
80mg cholesterol, 300mg sodium,
35g carbs, 1g fiber, 15g sugar, 6g protein

Instructions:

Prepare Dough: In the bread machine, place the warm milk, eggs, sugar, salt, softened butter, bread flour, and yeast in the order recommended by the manufacturer. Select the «Dough» cycle.

Shape the Rolls: Once the dough cycle is complete, move the dough to a floured surface. Roll it out into a large rectangle, approximately 16x21 inches. Spread the softened butter evenly over the dough, then scatter the chocolate chips.

Roll and Cut: Roll up the dough tightly from one long edge to the other, then cut it into 12 equal-sized rolls. Place the rolls into a greased bread machine pan or an oven-safe dish that fits inside the machine.

Second Rise: Allow the bread to rise for about 30 minutes. It should double in size during this time.

Egg Wash: Brush the rolls with the egg wash mixture before baking.

Bake: Select the «Bake» cycle on your bread machine and bake for 20-25 minutes until golden brown.

Bill's Tip:

Serve these brioche rolls warm with a dusting of powdered sugar for a classic touch, or drizzle with a simple vanilla glaze for added sweetness.

36

BANANA NUT ROLLS WITH HONEY GLAZE

Ingredients:

Dough:
- ½ cup warm milk (120ml)
- 2 large eggs
- ½ cup mashed ripe banana (120g)
- ¼ cup melted butter (60g)
- 4 ½ cups bread flour (540g)
- 1 teaspoon salt (5g)
- ½ cup sugar (100g)
- 2 ¼ teaspoons yeast (7g)

Filling:
- ½ cup softened butter (115g)
- ½ cup brown sugar (100g)
- 1 tablespoon ground cinnamon (8g)
- ½ cup chopped walnuts (60g)

Honey Glaze:
- ½ cup honey (170g)
- 2 tablespoons melted butter (30g)
- ¼ teaspoon vanilla extract

Nutritional Information:
(per slice)

*Approx. 350 kcal, 18g fat,
55mg cholesterol, 220mg sodium,
50g carbs, 2g fiber, 25g sugar, 4g protein*

Instructions:

Prepare Dough: In the bread machine, place the warm milk, eggs, mashed banana, melted butter, bread flour, salt, sugar, and yeast in the order recommended by the manufacturer. Select the «Dough» cycle.

Make the Filling: While the dough is being prepared, mix the softened butter, brown sugar, ground cinnamon, and chopped walnuts in a bowl.

Shape the Rolls: Once the dough cycle is complete, move the dough to a floured surface. Roll it out into a large rectangle, approximately 16x21 inches. Spread the filling evenly over the dough.

Roll and Cut: Roll up the dough tightly from one long edge to the other, then cut it into 12 equal-sized rolls. Place the rolls into a greased bread machine pan or an oven-safe dish that fits inside the machine.

Second Rise: Allow the bread to rise for about 30 minutes. It should double in size during this time.

Bake: Select the «Bake» cycle on your bread machine and bake for 20-25 minutes until golden brown.

Glaze: While the rolls are baking, mix the honey, melted butter, and vanilla extract to create a glaze. Drizzle over the warm rolls.

Bill's Tip:

Try adding a few chopped dried bananas to the filling for an extra layer of banana flavor and texture.

RAISIN AND WALNUT CINNAMON BREAD

Ingredients:

Dough:
- 1 cup warm milk (240ml)
- 2 large eggs
- ¼ cup melted butter (60g)
- 4 ½ cups bread flour (540g)
- 1 teaspoon salt (5g)
- ½ cup sugar (100g)
- 2 ¼ teaspoons yeast (7g)

Filling:
- ½ cup softened butter (115g)
- ½ cup brown sugar (100g)
- 1 tablespoon ground cinnamon (8g)
- ½ cup raisins (80g)
- ½ cup chopped walnuts (60g)

Egg Wash:
- 1 beaten egg (approximately 50g)
- 1 tablespoon water

Nutritional Information:
(per slice)

*Approx. 270 kcal, 11g fat,
50mg cholesterol, 250mg sodium,
39g carbs, 2g fiber, 20g sugar, 5g protein*

Instructions:

Prepare Dough: In the bread machine, place the warm milk, eggs, melted butter, bread flour, salt, sugar, and yeast in the order recommended by the manufacturer. Select the «Dough» cycle.

Make the Filling: While the dough is being prepared, mix the softened butter, brown sugar, ground cinnamon, raisins, and chopped walnuts in a bowl.

Shape the Bread: Once the dough cycle is complete, move the dough to a floured surface. Roll it out into a large rectangle, approximately 16x21 inches. Spread the filling evenly over the dough.

Roll and Place: Roll up the dough tightly from one long edge to the other. Place the rolled dough into a greased bread machine pan.

Second Rise: Allow the bread to rise for about 30 minutes. It should double in size during this time.

Egg Wash: Before baking, brush the top of the bread with the egg wash mixture.

Bake: Select the «Bake» cycle on your bread machine and bake for 25-30 minutes until golden brown.

Bill's Tip:

For a delightful crunch, sprinkle extra chopped walnuts on top of the egg wash before baking.

LEMON POPPY SEED SWEET ROLLS

Ingredients:

Dough:
- 1 cup warm milk (240ml)
- 2 large eggs
- ¼ cup melted butter (60g)
- 4 ½ cups bread flour (540g)
- 1 teaspoon salt (5g)
- ½ cup sugar (100g)
- 2 ¼ teaspoons yeast (7g)

Filling:
- ½ cup softened butter (115g)
- ½ cup sugar (100g)
- Zest of 2 lemons
- 2 tablespoons poppy seeds (16g)

Lemon Glaze:
- 1 cup powdered sugar (120g)
- 2 tablespoons fresh lemon juice (30ml)
- Zest of 1 lemon

Nutritional Information:

(per roll)

Approx. 290 kcal, 11g fat,
40mg cholesterol, 210mg sodium,
43g carbs, 1g fiber, 22g sugar, 4g protein

Instructions:

Prepare Dough: In the bread machine, place the warm milk, eggs, melted butter, bread flour, salt, sugar, and yeast in the order recommended by the manufacturer. Select the «Dough» cycle.

Make the Filling: While the dough is being prepared, mix the softened butter, sugar, lemon zest, and poppy seeds in a bowl.

Shape the Rolls: Once the dough cycle is complete, move the dough to a floured surface. Roll it out into a large rectangle, approximately 16x21 inches. Spread the filling evenly over the dough.

Roll and Cut: Roll up the dough tightly from one long edge to the other, then cut it into 12 equal-sized rolls. Place the rolls into a greased bread machine pan or an oven-safe dish that fits inside the machine.

Second Rise: Allow the rolls to rise for about 30 minutes or until they have doubled.

Bake: Select the «Bake» cycle on your bread machine and bake for 20-25 minutes until golden brown.

Glaze: While the rolls are baking, mix the powdered sugar, fresh lemon juice, and lemon zest to create a glaze. Drizzle over the warm rolls.

Bill's Tip:

For an extra lemony punch, brush the rolls with lemon syrup (made from lemon juice and sugar) right after baking, then add the glaze.

CHAPTER 5:

CHEESE AND SAVORY BREADS

CHEDDAR GARLIC BREAD

Ingredients:

Dough:
- 1 cup warm water (240ml)
- 2 tablespoons melted butter (30g)
- 3 cups bread flour (360g)
- 1 teaspoon salt (5g)
- 2 tablespoons sugar (25g)
- 2¼ teaspoons yeast (7g)
- 1½ cups shredded cheddar cheese (180g)
- 2 cloves garlic, minced

Topping:
- ¼ cup melted butter (60g)
- 1 clove garlic, minced
- 2 tablespoons shredded cheddar cheese (15g)

Instructions:

Prepare Dough: In the bread machine, add the warm water, melted butter, bread flour, salt, sugar, yeast, shredded cheddar cheese, and minced garlic in the order recommended by the manufacturer. Select the «Dough» cycle.

Shape the Bread: Once the dough cycle is complete, turn it onto a floured surface and shape it into a loaf.

Second Rise: Place the dough into a greased bread machine pan. Allow the bread to rise for about 30 minutes. It should double in size during this time.

Top and Bake: Mix the melted butter and minced garlic, then brush over the top of the loaf. Sprinkle with additional shredded cheddar cheese. Select the «Bake» cycle on your bread machine and bake for 25-30 minutes until golden brown.

Nutritional Information:
(per slice)

Approx. 210 kcal, 11g fat,
30mg cholesterol, 330mg sodium,
24g carbs, 1g fiber, 3g sugar, 7g protein

Bill's Tip:

For extra garlic flavor, add a few cloves of roasted garlic into the dough before baking.

JALAPEÑO CHEDDAR CORNBREAD

Ingredients:

Dough:
- 1 cup buttermilk (240ml)
- 2 large eggs
- ¼ cup melted butter (60g)
- 1½ cups cornmeal (240g)
- 1 cup all-purpose flour (120g)
- 2 teaspoons baking powder (10g)
- 1 teaspoon salt (5g)
- ½ teaspoon baking soda (2.5g)
- 1 cup shredded cheddar cheese (120g)
- 1-2 jalapeños, diced (seeds removed for less heat)

Instructions:

Prepare Dough: In the bread machine, place the buttermilk, eggs, melted butter, cornmeal, all-purpose flour, baking powder, salt, baking soda, shredded cheddar cheese, and diced jalapeños in the order recommended by the manufacturer. Select the «Quick Bread» or «Bake» cycle.

Bake: Place the cornbread in the bread machine and bake for 55-65 minutes, or until a toothpick inserted into the center comes clean.

Nutritional Information:
(per serving)

Approx. 230 kcal, 13g fat,
60mg cholesterol, 410mg sodium,
22g carbs, 2g fiber, 2g sugar, 6g protein

Bill's Tip:

For a hint of sweetness, incorporate a tablespoon of honey into the dough mixture before baking.

PARMESAN HERB BREAD

Ingredients:

Dough:
- 1 cup warm water (240ml)
- 2 tablespoons olive oil (30ml)
- 3 cups bread flour (360g)
- 1 teaspoon salt (5g)
- ½ teaspoon sugar (2.5g)
- 2¼ teaspoons yeast (7g)
- ½ cup grated Parmesan cheese (50g)
- 2 tablespoons chopped fresh herbs (such as rosemary, thyme, or basil) (6g)

Instructions:

Prepare Dough: In the bread machine, add warm water, olive oil, bread flour, salt, sugar, yeast, grated Parmesan cheese, and chopped herbs in the order recommended by the manufacturer. Select the «Dough» cycle.

Shape the Bread: Once the dough cycle is complete, turn it onto a floured surface and shape it into a loaf.

Second Rise: Place the dough into a greased bread machine pan. Allow the bread to rise for about 30 minutes. It should double in size during this time.

Bake: Select the «Bake» cycle on your bread machine and bake for 25-30 minutes until golden brown.

Nutritional Information:
(per serving)

Approx. 180 kcal, 7g fat,
10mg cholesterol, 320mg sodium,
22g carbs, 1g fiber, 1g sugar, 5g protein

Bill's Tip:

Mix dried and fresh herbs in the dough for a more intense herb flavor.

CHEESE AND CHIVE SCONES

Ingredients:

Dough:
- ½ cup cold butter, cubed (115g)
- 2½ cups all-purpose flour (300g)
- 1 tablespoon baking powder (15g)
- 1 teaspoon salt (5g)
- 1 cup shredded cheddar cheese (100g)
- ¼ cup chopped fresh chives (15g)
- ¾ cup buttermilk (180ml)
- 1 large egg

Instructions:

Prepare Dough: In the bread machine, add the cold butter, all-purpose flour, baking powder, salt, shredded cheddar cheese, and chopped chives. Add the buttermilk and egg. Select the «Dough» cycle.

Shape the Scones: Once the dough cycle is complete, turn it onto a floured surface and pat it into a 1-inch-thick round. Cut into 8 wedges.

Bake: Place the scones onto a greased baking sheet and bake in a warm oven at 375°F (190°C) for 15-20 minutes until golden brown.

Nutritional Information:
(per scone)

Approx. 260 kcal, 16g fat,
60mg cholesterol, 410mg sodium,
22g carbs, 1g fiber, 2g sugar, 6g protein

Bill's Tip:

Brush the scones with a little buttermilk before baking for a crispy top.

CLASSIC CHEDDAR AND BACON BREAD

Ingredients:

Dough:
- 1 cup warm water (240ml)
- 2 tablespoons melted butter (28g)
- 3 cups bread flour (360g)
- 1 teaspoon salt (5g)
- ½ teaspoon sugar (2.5g)
- 2 ¼ teaspoons yeast (7g)
- 1 cup shredded cheddar cheese (113g)
- ½ cup cooked and crumbled bacon (75g)

Instructions:

Prepare Dough: In the bread machine, add the warm water, melted butter, bread flour, salt, sugar, yeast, shredded cheddar cheese, and cooked bacon in the order recommended by the manufacturer. Select the «Dough» cycle.

Shape the Bread: Once the dough cycle is complete, turn it onto a floured surface and shape it into a loaf.

Second Rise: Place the dough into a greased bread machine pan. Allow the bread to rise for about 30 minutes. It should double in size during this time.

Bake: Select the «Bake» cycle on your bread machine and bake for 25-30 minutes until golden brown.

Nutritional Information:
(per serving)

Approx. 250 kcal, 10g fat,
25mg cholesterol, 350mg sodium,
32g carbs, 1g fiber, 1g sugar, 10g protein.

Bill's Tip:

Sprinkle extra cheddar on top of the loaf before baking for a cheesy crust.

SPINACH AND FETA STUFFED BREAD

Ingredients:

Dough:
- 1 cup warm water (240ml)
- 2 tablespoons olive oil (30ml)
- 3 cups bread flour (360g)
- 1 teaspoon salt (5g)
- ½ teaspoon sugar (2.5g)
- 2 ¼ teaspoons yeast (7g)

Filling:
- 1 cup cooked spinach, drained and chopped (240g)
- ½ cup crumbled feta cheese (75g)
- 1 clove garlic, minced
- 1 tablespoon olive oil (15ml)

Instructions:

Prepare Dough: Add warm water, olive oil, bread flour, salt, sugar, and yeast to the bread machine pan in the order specified by the manufacturer. Select the Dough cycle to mix and knead the ingredients. Allow the machine to complete the cycle, preparing the dough for the next steps.

Make the Filling: In a bowl, mix the cooked spinach, crumbled feta, minced garlic, and olive oil.

Shape and Fill the Bread: Once the dough cycle is complete, turn the dough onto a floured surface and roll it out into a large rectangle. Spread the filling over the dough, then roll it up tightly. Place the rolled dough into a greased bread machine pan.

Second Rise: Allow the bread to rise for about 30 minutes. It should double in size during this time.

Bake: Select the «Bake» cycle on your bread machine and bake for 25-30 minutes until golden brown.

Nutritional Information:
(per serving)

Approx. 210 kcal, 8g fat,
10mg cholesterol, 400mg sodium,
28g carbs, 2g fiber, 1g sugar, 7g protein.

Bill's Tip:

For a more robust flavor, add a handful of sun-dried tomatoes to the filling.

45

THREE CHEESE PULL-APART BREAD

Ingredients:

Dough:
- 1 cup warm water (240ml)
- 2 tablespoons melted butter (30g)
- 3 cups bread flour (360g)
- 1 teaspoon salt (5g)
- ½ teaspoon sugar (2.5g)
- 2 ¼ teaspoons yeast (7g)

Cheese Mix:
- ½ cup shredded mozzarella cheese (60g)
- ½ cup shredded cheddar cheese (60g)
- ½ cup grated Parmesan cheese (50g)
- 1 tablespoon chopped parsley (4g)
- 2 tablespoons melted butter (30g)

Instructions:

Prepare Dough: In the bread machine, add the warm water, melted butter, bread flour, salt, sugar, and yeast in the order recommended by the manufacturer. Select the «Dough» cycle.

Make Cheese Mix: In a bowl, mix the mozzarella, cheddar, Parmesan, chopped parsley, and melted butter.

Shape the Bread: Once the dough cycle is complete, turn the dough onto a floured surface and divide it into small pieces. Roll each piece in the cheese mix and stack them into a greased bread machine pan.

Second Rise: Allow the bread to rise for about 30 minutes. It should double in size during this time.

Bake: Select the «Bake» cycle on your bread machine and bake for 25-30 minutes until golden brown and bubbly.

Nutritional Information:
(per serving)

Approx. 220 kcal, 10g fat,
20mg cholesterol, 360mg sodium,
26g carbs, 1g fiber, 1g sugar, 8g protein.

Bill's Tip:

Serve this pull-apart bread warm with a side of marinara sauce for dipping.

46

RICOTTA AND HERB BREAD

Ingredients:

Dough:
- 1 cup warm water (240ml)
- 2 tablespoons olive oil (28ml)
- 3 cups bread flour (360g)
- 1 teaspoon salt (5g)
- ½ teaspoon sugar (2.5g)
- 2 ¼ teaspoons yeast (7g)
- ½ cup ricotta cheese (120g)
- 2 tablespoons chopped fresh herbs (such as parsley, basil, or thyme) (6g)

Instructions:

Prepare Dough: In the bread machine, add warm water, olive oil, bread flour, salt, sugar, yeast, ricotta cheese, and chopped herbs in the order recommended by the manufacturer. Select the «Dough» cycle.

Shape the Bread: Once the dough cycle is complete, turn it onto a floured surface and shape it into a loaf.

Second Rise: Place the dough into a greased bread machine pan. Allow the bread to rise for about 30 minutes. It should double in size during this time.

Bake: Select the «Bake» cycle on your bread machine and bake for 25-30 minutes until golden brown.

Nutritional Information:
(per erving)

Approx. 200 kcal, 8g fat,
20mg cholesterol, 300mg sodium,
26g carbs, 1g fiber, 2g sugar, 7g protein.

Bill's Tip:

To make the bread more aromatic, incorporate a bit of garlic powder or minced garlic into the dough.

TOMATO BASIL CHEESE BREAD

Ingredients:

Dough:
- 1 cup warm tomato juice (240ml)
- 2 tablespoons olive oil (28ml)
- 3 cups bread flour (360g)
- 1 teaspoon salt (5g)
- 2 tablespoons sugar (25g)
- 2 ¼ teaspoons yeast (7g)
- ½ cup shredded mozzarella cheese (60g)
- 2 tablespoons chopped fresh basil (6g)

Instructions:

Prepare Dough: In the bread machine, add the warm tomato juice, olive oil, bread flour, salt, sugar, yeast, shredded mozzarella cheese, and chopped basil in the order recommended by the manufacturer. Select the «Dough» cycle.

Shape the Bread: Once the dough cycle is complete, turn it onto a floured surface and shape it into a loaf.

Second Rise: Place the dough into a greased bread machine pan. Allow the bread to rise for about 30 minutes. It should double in size during this time.

Bake: Select the «Bake» cycle on your bread machine and bake for 25-30 minutes until golden brown.

Nutritional Information:
(per serving)

Approx. 210 kcal, 7g fat,
15mg cholesterol, 350mg sodium,
30g carbs, 1g fiber, 4g sugar, 8g protein.

Bill's Tip:

Use sun-dried tomato paste instead of juice for a more intense flavor.

CREAM CHEESE AND CHIVE BREAD

Ingredients:

Dough:
- 1 cup warm water (240ml)
- 2 tablespoons melted butter (28g)
- 3 cups bread flour (360g)
- 1 teaspoon salt (5g)
- 2 tablespoons sugar (25g)
- 2 ¼ teaspoons yeast (7g)
- ½ cup cream cheese, softened (120g)
- ¼ cup chopped fresh chives (10g)

Instructions:

Prepare Dough: In the bread machine, add warm water, melted butter, bread flour, salt, sugar, yeast, cream cheese, and chopped chives in the order recommended by the manufacturer. Select the «Dough» cycle.

Shape the Bread: Once the dough cycle is complete, turn it onto a floured surface and shape it into a loaf.

Second Rise: Place the dough into a greased bread machine pan. Allow the bread to rise for about 30 minutes. It should double in size during this time.

Bake: Select the «Bake» cycle on your bread machine and bake for 25-30 minutes until golden brown.

Nutritional Information:
(per serving)

Approx. 250 kcal, 9g fat,
30mg cholesterol, 350mg sodium,
36g carbs, 1g fiber, 5g sugar, 7g protein.

Bill's Tip:

Add grated Parmesan cheese to the dough mixture for a richer flavor.

CHAPTER 6:

PIES AND CAKES

APPLE CINNAMON STREUSEL CAKE

Ingredients:

Dough:
- ½ cup unsalted butter, softened (115g)
- 1 cup granulated sugar (200g)
- 2 large eggs
- 1 teaspoon vanilla extract (5ml)
- 1½ cups all-purpose flour (180g)
- 1 teaspoon baking powder (4g)
- ½ teaspoon baking soda (2g)
- ¼ teaspoon salt (1.5g)
- ½ cup sour cream (120g)
- 1 apple, peeled and diced (approximately 150g)
- 1 teaspoon ground cinnamon (2.5g)

Streusel Topping:
- ½ cup all-purpose flour (60g)
- ¼ cup brown sugar (50g)
- ¼ cup unsalted butter, cold and cubed (57g)
- ½ teaspoon ground cinnamon (1g)

Nutritional Information:
(per serving)

Approx. 360 kcal, 20g fat,
85mg cholesterol, 180mg sodium,
44g carbs, 1g fiber, 30g sugar, 3g protein.

Instructions:

Prepare Dough: Cream the butter and sugar in a bowl, then add the eggs individually. Stir in the vanilla extract. Combine the flour, baking powder, baking soda, and salt in a separate bowl. Gradually incorporate the dry ingredients into the wet mixture. Alternate adding the dry ingredients with the sour cream. Fold in the diced apple and ground cinnamon.

Prepare Streusel: In a separate bowl, mix the flour, brown sugar, and cinnamon. Cut in the cold butter until the mixture resembles coarse crumbs.

Bake: Pour the cake batter into the bread machine pan, then sprinkle the streusel topping over the batter. Select the «Cake» or «Quick Bread» cycle. Check for doneness with a toothpick.

Bill's Tip: *Add a handful of chopped pecans to the streusel topping for an extra flavor.*

PUMPKIN SPICE CAKE

Ingredients:

Dough:
- ½ cup vegetable oil (120ml)
- 1 cup granulated sugar (200g)
- 2 large eggs
- 1 cup canned pumpkin puree (240g)
- 1 teaspoon vanilla extract (5ml)
- 1½ cups all-purpose flour (180g)
- 1 teaspoon baking powder (4g)
- ½ teaspoon baking soda (2g)
- ½ teaspoon salt (1.5g)
- 1 teaspoon ground cinnamon (2.5g)
- ½ teaspoon ground ginger (1g)
- ¼ teaspoon ground cloves (0.5g)

Nutritional Information:
(per serving)

Approx. 290 kcal, 15g fat,
40mg cholesterol, 150mg sodium,
35g carbs, 1g fiber, 20g sugar, 3g protein.

Instructions:

Prepare Dough: Mix the oil and sugar in a bowl until well combined. Add the eggs one at a time, then stir in the pumpkin puree and vanilla extract. Whisk together the flour, baking powder, baking soda, salt, cinnamon, ginger, and cloves in a separate bowl. Add the dry ingredients to the wet mixture, mixing until just combined.

Bake: Pour the batter into the bread machine pan and select the «Cake» or «Quick Bread» cycle. Check for doneness by inserting a toothpick into the center of the cake; it should come out clean when fully baked.

Bill's Tip:

For added richness, stir in ½ cup of chocolate chips or chopped nuts before baking.

CLASSIC CHOCOLATE CHIP CAKE

Ingredients:

Dough:
- ½ cup unsalted butter, softened (115g)
- ¾ cup granulated sugar (150g)
- 2 large eggs
- 1 teaspoon vanilla extract (5ml)
- 1½ cups all-purpose flour (180g)
- 1 teaspoon baking powder (4g)
- ½ teaspoon baking soda (2g)
- ¼ teaspoon salt (1.5g)
- ½ cup sour cream (120ml)
- 1 cup semisweet chocolate chips (175g)

Instructions:

Prepare Dough: Cream the butter and sugar in a bowl. Add the eggs one at a time, followed by the vanilla extract. Mix the flour, baking powder, baking soda, and salt in a separate bowl. Add the dry ingredients to the wet mixture, alternating with sour cream. Stir in the chocolate chips.

Bake: Pour the batter into the bread machine pan and select the «Cake» or «Quick Bread» cycle. Check for doneness by inserting a toothpick into the center of the loaf; it should come out clean when fully baked.

Nutritional Information:
(per serving)

Approx. 350 kcal, 20g fat,
60mg cholesterol, 180mg sodium,
40g carbs, 1g fiber, 25g sugar, 4g protein.

Bill's Tip:

Drizzle melted chocolate over the cooled cake before serving for an extra chocolatey treat.

52

LEMON POUND CAKE

Ingredients:

Dough:
- 1 cup unsalted butter, softened (230g)
- 1¼ cups granulated sugar (250g)
- 4 large eggs
- 1 teaspoon vanilla extract (5ml)
- 1 tablespoon lemon zest (6g)
- ¼ cup lemon juice (60ml)
- 2 cups all-purpose flour (240g)
- 1 teaspoon baking powder (4g)
- ¼ teaspoon salt (1.5g)

Instructions:

Prepare Dough: Cream the butter and sugar together until light and fluffy. Add the eggs one at a time, beating well after each addition. Stir in the vanilla extract, lemon zest, and lemon juice. Mix the flour, baking powder, and salt in a separate bowl. Gradually add the dry ingredients to the wet mixture.

Bake: Pour the batter into the bread machine pan and select the «Cake» or «Quick Bread» cycle. Check for doneness with a toothpick.

Nutritional Information:

(per serving)

Approx. 420 kcal, 24g fat,
95mg cholesterol, 200mg sodium,
50g carbs, 1g fiber, 30g sugar, 4g protein.

Bill's Tip:

Drizzle a lemon glaze over the warm cake for an extra lemony finish.

CARROT CAKE WITH NUTS

Ingredients:

Dough:
- ½ cup vegetable oil (120ml)
- 1 cup granulated sugar (200g)
- 2 large eggs
- 1 teaspoon vanilla extract (5ml)
- 1½ cups all-purpose flour (180g)
- 1 teaspoon baking soda (4g)
- ½ teaspoon baking powder (2g)
- ½ teaspoon salt (3g)
- 1 teaspoon ground cinnamon (2.6g)
- ¼ teaspoon ground nutmeg (0.5g)
- 1½ cups grated carrots (180g)
- ½ cup chopped walnuts or pecans (60g)

Nutritional Information:
(per serving)

Approx. 340 kcal, 22g fat,
40mg cholesterol, 180mg sodium,
35g carbs, 2g fiber, 23g sugar, 4g protein.

Instructions:

Prepare Dough: Mix the oil and sugar in a bowl, then add the eggs individually. Stir in the vanilla extract. Whisk together the flour, baking soda, baking powder, salt, cinnamon, and nutmeg in a separate bowl. Add the dry ingredients to the wet mixture, then fold the grated carrots and chopped nuts.

Bake: Pour the batter into the bread machine pan and select the «Cake» or «Quick Bread» cycle. Check for doneness with a toothpick.

Bill's Tip:

Top the cooled cake with a cream cheese frosting for a classic touch.

BLUEBERRY COFFEE CAKE

Ingredients:

Dough:
- ½ cup unsalted butter, softened (115g)
- 1 cup granulated sugar (200g)
- 2 large eggs
- 1 teaspoon vanilla extract (5ml)
- ½ cup milk (120ml)
- 2 cups all-purpose flour (240g)
- 1 teaspoon baking powder (4g)
- ½ teaspoon baking soda (2g)
- ¼ teaspoon salt (1.5g)
- 1 cup fresh or frozen blueberries (150g)

Instructions:

Prepare Dough: Cream the butter and sugar in a bowl. Add the eggs one at a time, followed by the vanilla extract. Mix the flour, baking powder, baking soda, and salt in a separate bowl. Add the dry ingredients to the wet mixture, alternating with the milk. Gently fold in the blueberries.

Bake: Pour the batter into the bread machine pan and select the «Cake» or «Quick Bread» cycle. Check for doneness with a toothpick.

Nutritional Information:
(per serving)

Approx. 310 kcal, 15g fat,
55mg cholesterol, 200mg sodium,
40g carbs, 1g fiber, 22g sugar, 3g protein.

Bill's Tip:

For a crumbly topping, mix 1/4 cup sugar, 1/4 cup flour, and 2 tablespoons butter, and sprinkle over the batter before baking.

ZUCCHINI BREAD WITH WALNUTS

Ingredients:

Dough:
- ½ cup vegetable oil (120ml)
- 1 cup granulated sugar (200g)
- 2 large eggs
- 1 teaspoon vanilla extract (5ml)
- 1 ½ cups all-purpose flour (180g)
- 1 teaspoon baking soda (4g)
- ½ teaspoon baking powder (2g)
- ½ teaspoon salt (3g)
- 1 teaspoon ground cinnamon (2g)
- 1 cup grated zucchini (120g)
- ½ cup chopped walnuts (60g)

Nutritional Information:
(per slice)

Approx. 270 kcal, 14g fat,
40mg cholesterol, 180mg sodium,
32g carbs, 1g fiber, 20g sugar, 4g protein.

Instructions:

Prepare Dough: Mix the oil and sugar in a bowl, then add the eggs individually. Stir in the vanilla extract. Whisk together the flour, baking soda, baking powder, salt, and cinnamon in a separate bowl. Add the dry ingredients to the wet mixture, then fold the grated zucchini and chopped walnuts.

Bake: Pour the batter into the bread machine pan and select the «Cake» or «Quick Bread» cycle. Check for doneness with a toothpick.

Bill's Tip:

For added texture, sprinkle some walnuts on top before baking.

56

BANANA CAKE WITH CREAM CHEESE FROSTING

Ingredients:

Dough:
- ½ cup unsalted butter, softened (115g)
- 1 cup granulated sugar (200g)
- 2 large eggs
- 1 teaspoon vanilla extract (5ml)
- 1 cup mashed ripe bananas (about 2 large bananas) (240g)
- 1 ½ cups all-purpose flour (180g)
- 1 teaspoon baking powder (4g)
- ½ teaspoon baking soda (2g)
- ¼ teaspoon salt (1.5g)

Frosting:
- ½ cup cream cheese, softened (115g)
- ¼ cup unsalted butter, softened (57g)
- 1 teaspoon vanilla extract (5ml)
- 2 cups powdered sugar (240g)

Nutritional Information:

(per serving, including frosting)

Approx. 350 kcal, 20g fat,
60mg cholesterol, 250mg sodium,
42g carbs, 1g fiber, 30g sugar, 4g protein.

Instructions:

Prepare Dough: Cream the butter and sugar in a bowl, then add the eggs individually. Stir in the vanilla extract and mashed bananas. Mix the flour, baking powder, baking soda, and salt in a separate bowl. Add the dry ingredients to the wet mixture.

Bake: Pour the batter into the bread machine pan and select the «Cake» or «Quick Bread» cycle. Check for doneness with a toothpick.

Frosting: While baking the cake, prepare the frosting by mixing the cream cheese, butter, vanilla extract, and powdered sugar until smooth. Once the cake is cooled, frost and serve.

Bill's Tip:

Add a splash of banana extract to the frosting for an extra banana flavor.

CINNAMON APPLE BREAD

Ingredients:

Dough:
- ½ cup unsalted butter, softened (115g)
- 1 cup granulated sugar (200g)
- 2 large eggs
- 1 teaspoon vanilla extract (5ml)
- 1 ½ cups all-purpose flour (180g)
- 1 teaspoon baking powder (4g)
- ½ teaspoon baking soda (2g)
- ¼ teaspoon salt (1.5g)
- ½ cup milk (120ml)
- 1 apple, peeled and diced (about 180g)
- 1 teaspoon ground cinnamon (2g)

Nutritional Information:
(per serving)

Approx. 320 kcal, 16g fat,
55mg cholesterol, 200mg sodium,
40g carbs, 1g fiber, 28g sugar, 3g protein.

Instructions:

Prepare Dough: Cream the butter and sugar in a bowl, then add the eggs individually. Stir in the vanilla extract. Mix the flour, baking powder, baking soda, and salt in a separate bowl. Add the dry ingredients to the wet mixture, alternating with the milk. Fold in the diced apple and ground cinnamon.

Bake: Pour the batter into the bread machine pan and select the «Cake» or «Quick Bread» cycle. Bake until a toothpick inserted into the center comes out clean.

Bill's Tip:

Add a streusel topping for an extra crunch.

58

PUMPKIN RAISIN BREAD

Ingredients:

Dough:
- ½ cup vegetable oil (120ml)
- 1 cup granulated sugar (200g)
- 2 large eggs
- 1 cup canned pumpkin puree (240ml)
- 1 teaspoon vanilla extract (5ml)
- 1 ½ cups all-purpose flour (180g)
- 1 teaspoon baking soda (4g)
- ½ teaspoon baking powder (2g)
- ½ teaspoon salt (3g)
- 1 teaspoon ground cinnamon (2g)
- ½ teaspoon ground ginger (1g)
- ¼ teaspoon ground cloves (0.5g)
- ½ cup raisins (80g)

Nutritional Information:
(per serving)

Approx. 310 kcal, 15g fat,
55mg cholesterol, 180mg sodium,
40g carbs, 1g fiber, 25g sugar, 3g protein.

Instructions:

Prepare Dough: Mix the oil and sugar in a bowl, then add the eggs individually. Stir in the pumpkin puree and vanilla extract. Whisk together the flour, baking soda, baking powder, salt, cinnamon, ginger, and cloves in a separate bowl. Add the dry ingredients to the wet mixture, then fold the raisins.

Bake: Pour the batter into the bread machine pan and select the «Cake» or «Quick Bread» cycle. Bake until a toothpick inserted into the center comes out clean.

Bill's Tip:

For a festive touch, add chopped pecans or walnuts to the batter.

59

CHAPTER 7:

COTTAGE CHEESE BREADS

COTTAGE CHEESE HERB BREAD

Ingredients:

- 1 cup cottage cheese (240g)
- ¼ cup warm water (60ml)
- 1 large egg
- 2 tablespoons olive oil (28ml)
- 3 cups bread flour (360g)
- 1 teaspoon salt (5g)
- 1 tablespoon sugar (12g)
- 2¼ teaspoons yeast (7g)
- 2 tablespoons fresh herbs (like dill, parsley, or thyme), finely chopped (about 6g)

Instructions:

Prepare Dough: Add cottage cheese, warm water, egg, and olive oil to your bread machine pan. Layer the bread flour, salt, sugar, and yeast on top.

Mix in Herbs: Add the finely chopped herbs to ensure they're evenly distributed once the initial mix starts.

Bake: Select the «Basic» or «White Bread» cycle with a medium crust setting.

Baking Tips: If your bread machine has a "Mix-in" option, use it to add the herbs at the appropriate time for even distribution. Finish: Let the bread cool slightly before slicing.

Nutritional Information:
(per serving)

Approx. 190 kcal, 7g fat,
35mg cholesterol, 320mg sodium,
35g carbs, 2g fiber, 3g sugar, 10g protein.

Bill's Tip:

This bread pairs wonderfully with creamy herb butter. Spread it on a warm slice for a delicious, fragrant treat!

GARLIC AND COTTAGE CHEESE BREAD

Ingredients:

- 1 cup cottage cheese (240g)
- ¼ cup warm water (60ml)
- 2 tablespoons butter (28g)
- 3 cups bread flour (360g)
- 1 teaspoon salt (5g)
- 1 tablespoon sugar (12g)
- 2¼ teaspoons yeast (7g)
- 3 garlic cloves, minced (about 9g)
- 1 tablespoon garlic powder (optional, for extra flavor) (8g)

Instructions:

Prepare Dough: Add cottage cheese, warm water, and butter to your bread machine pan. Layer the bread flour, salt, sugar, and yeast on top.

Add Garlic: Add minced garlic early in the dough cycle.

Bake: Use the «French» or «Garlic Bread» cycle with a medium crust setting.

Baking Tips: Add garlic powder to the dry ingredients for a stronger flavor.

Finish: Cool slightly before serving, and enjoy with some garlic butter for an extra kick!

Nutritional Information:
(per serving)

Approx. 190 kcal, 8g fat,
35mg cholesterol, 350mg sodium,
36g carbs, 2g fiber, 2g sugar, 11g protein.

Bill's Tip:

Rub a cut clove of garlic on the crust after baking for an extra flavor.

COTTAGE CHEESE AND CHIVE BREAD

Ingredients:

- 1 cup cottage cheese (240g)
- ¼ cup warm water (60ml)
- 1 large egg
- 2 tablespoons butter, melted (28g)
- 3 cups bread flour (360g)
- 1 teaspoon salt (5g)
- 1 tablespoon sugar (12g)
- 2¼ teaspoons yeast (7g)
- ¼ cup fresh chives, chopped (about 6g)

Instructions:

Prepare Dough: Add cottage cheese, warm water, egg, and melted butter to your bread machine pan. Layer the bread flour, salt, sugar, and yeast on top.

Mix in Chives: Add the chopped chives during the mixing cycle.

Bake: Choose the «Basic» or «Whole Wheat» cycle with a medium crust setting.

Baking Tips: Monitor the dough's consistency during the initial mix. Add a tablespoon of water or flour as needed.

Finish: Let the bread cool slightly before slicing.

Nutritional Information:
(per serving)

Approx. 220 kcal, 8g fat, 35mg cholesterol, 360mg sodium, 37g carbs, 2g fiber, 2g sugar, 12g protein.

Bill's Tip:

Serve this bread with cream cheese spread for a savory breakfast or snack!

62

COTTAGE CHEESE AND SPINACH BREAD

Ingredients:

- 1 cup cottage cheese (240g)
- ¼ cup warm water (60ml)
- 1 large egg
- 2 tablespoons olive oil (28ml)
- 3 cups bread flour (360g)
- 1 teaspoon salt (5g)
- 1 tablespoon sugar (12g)
- 2¼ teaspoons yeast (7g)
- ½ cup spinach, wilted and drained (about 15g)

Instructions:

Prepare Dough: Add cottage cheese, warm water, egg, and olive oil to your bread machine pan. Layer the bread flour, salt, sugar, and yeast on top.

Mix in Spinach: Add the wilted spinach after the initial mixing cycle starts.

Bake: Select the «Basic» or «White Bread» cycle with a medium crust setting.

Baking Tips: Ensure the spinach is well-drained to prevent excess moisture in the dough.

Finish: Cool slightly before serving.

Nutritional Information:
(per serving)

Approx. 215 kcal, 6g fat, 30mg cholesterol, 320mg sodium, 33g carbs, 2g fiber, 2g sugar, 11g protein.

Bill's Tip:

This bread pairs excellently with a bowl of warm soup for a comforting meal!

63

COTTAGE CHEESE AND SUN-DRIED TOMATO BREAD

Ingredients:

- 1 cup cottage cheese (240g)
- ¼ cup warm water (60ml)
- 1 large egg
- 2 tablespoons olive oil (28ml)
- 3 cups bread flour (360g)
- 1 teaspoon salt (5g)
- 1 tablespoon sugar (12g)
- 2¼ teaspoons yeast (7g)
- ¼ cup sun-dried tomatoes, chopped (about 30g)

Instructions:

Prepare Dough: Add cottage cheese, warm water, egg, and olive oil to your bread machine pan. Layer the bread flour, salt, sugar, and yeast on top.

Mix in Sun-Dried Tomatoes: Add the chopped sun-dried tomatoes during the mixing cycle.

Bake: Choose the «Basic» or «French» cycle with a medium crust setting.

Baking Tips: Rehydrate the sun-dried tomatoes in warm water before adding them to enhance the flavor.

Finish: Let the bread cool before slicing.

Nutritional Information:
(per serving)

Approx.200 kcal, 4.5g fat,
30mg cholesterol, 139mg sodium,
33g carbs, 2g fiber, 4g sugar, 4.4g protein.

Bill's Tip:

Serve this Mediterranean-inspired bread with olive oil and balsamic vinegar for dipping!

COTTAGE CHEESE AND CHEDDAR BREAD

Ingredients:

- 1 cup cottage cheese (240g)
- ¼ cup warm water (60ml)
- 1 large egg
- 2 tablespoons butter, melted (28g)
- 3 cups bread flour (360g)
- 1 teaspoon salt (5g)
- 1 tablespoon sugar (12g)
- 2¼ teaspoons yeast (7g)
- 1 cup sharp cheddar cheese, shredded (115g)

Instructions:

Prepare Dough: Add cottage cheese, warm water, egg, and melted butter to your bread machine pan. Layer the bread flour, salt, sugar, and yeast on top.

Mix in Cheddar: Add the shredded cheese during the mixing cycle.

Bake: Select the «Cheese» or «Basic» cycle with a medium crust setting.

Baking Tips: Monitor the dough's consistency during the initial mix. Add a tablespoon of water or flour as needed.

Finish: Let the bread cool slightly before slicing.

Nutritional Information:
(per serving)

*Approx. 225 kcal, 7.5g fat,
40mg cholesterol, 148mg sodium,
33g carbs, 1g fiber, 4g sugar, 6.9g protein.*

Bill's Tip:

This bread is perfect for grilled cheese sandwiches or as a side to a hearty soup!

COTTAGE CHEESE AND CARAMELIZED ONION BREAD

||||||||||||||||||||||||||||||||||||||||||||||||||||||||||||||||||||||||||||||||||||||||||||||||||||||||||||||||||

Ingredients:

- 1 cup cottage cheese (240g)
- ¼ cup warm water (60ml)
- 1 large egg
- 2 tablespoons butter, melted (28g)
- 3 cups bread flour (360g)
- 1 teaspoon salt (5g)
- 1 tablespoon sugar (12g)
- 2¼ teaspoons yeast (7g)
- ½ cup caramelized onions (75g)

Instructions:

Prepare Dough: Add cottage cheese, warm water, egg, and butter to your bread machine pan. Layer the bread flour, salt, sugar, and yeast on top.

Mix in Onions: Add the caramelized onions during the mixing cycle.

Bake: Select the «Basic» or «Whole Wheat» cycle with a medium crust setting.

Baking Tips: Ensure the onions are fully cooled before adding them to the dough to avoid yeast activation issues.

Finish: Let the bread cool before slicing.

Nutritional Information:
(per serving)

Approx. 190 kcal, 4.3g fat,
40mg cholesterol, 79mg sodium,
51g carbs, 1g fiber, 5g sugar, 4.3g protein.

Bill's Tip:

This bread makes an excellent base for savory sandwiches or a delicious side to a roast dinner!

66

SWEET COTTAGE CHEESE BREAD

Ingredients:

- 1 cup cottage cheese (240g)
- ¼ cup warm water (60ml)
- ¼ cup honey (85g)
- 1 large egg
- 2 tablespoons butter, melted (28g)
- 3 cups bread flour (360g)
- 1 teaspoon salt (5g)
- 2¼ teaspoons yeast (7g)
- 1 teaspoon vanilla extract (5ml)

Instructions:

Prepare Dough: Add cottage cheese, warm water, honey, egg, butter, and vanilla extract to your bread machine pan. Layer the bread flour, salt, and yeast on top.

Bake: Select the «Sweet» or «Basic» cycle with a medium crust setting.

Baking Tips: Sprinkle a little sugar before baking for an extra sweet touch.

Finish: Let the bread cool slightly before serving.

Nutritional Information:
(per serving)

Approx. 205 kcal, 3.88g fat,
40mg cholesterol, 79mg sodium,
11g carbs, 1g fiber, 7g sugar, 4.2g protein.

Bill's Tip:

This bread is delicious with a dollop of whipped cream or a drizzle of honey for a sweet treat!

COTTAGE CHEESE AND JALAPEÑO BREAD

Ingredients:

- 1 cup cottage cheese (240g)
- ¼ cup warm water (60ml)
- 1 large egg
- 2 tablespoons butter, melted (28g)
- 3 cups bread flour (360g)
- 1 teaspoon salt (5g)
- 2¼ teaspoons yeast (7g)
- ½ cup chopped jalapeños, fresh or pickled (60g)

Instructions:

Prepare Dough: Add the cottage cheese, warm water, egg, and butter to your bread machine pan. Then, layer the bread flour, salt, and yeast on top.

Add Jalapeños: Add the chopped jalapeños to the dough once the initial mixing begins. The bread machine will mix them evenly throughout the dough.

Bake: Select the «Basic» or «Whole Wheat» cycle with a medium crust setting.

Baking Tips: If you prefer more heat, include the jalapeños' seeds or use a hotter pepper variety.

Finish: Allow the bread to cool slightly before slicing.

Nutritional Information:
(per serving)

*Approx. 180 kcal, 3.88g fat,
40mg cholesterol, 79mg sodium,
4.1g carbs, 1g fiber, 2g sugar,
4.28g protein.*

Bill's Tip:

This bread adds a spicy twist to any meal, making it a great accompaniment to soups, stews, or even grilled meats.

68

COTTAGE CHEESE AND PUMPKIN BREAD

Ingredients:

- 1 cup cottage cheese (240g)
- ¼ cup warm water (60ml)
- ½ cup canned pumpkin puree (120g)
- 1 large egg
- 2 tablespoons butter, melted (28g)
- 3 cups bread flour (360g)
- 1 teaspoon salt (5g)
- 2¼ teaspoons yeast (7g)
- ½ teaspoon ground cinnamon (1g)
- ¼ teaspoon ground nutmeg (0.5g)

Instructions:

Prepare Dough: Add cottage cheese, warm water, pumpkin puree, egg, and butter to your bread machine pan. Layer the bread flour, salt, cinnamon, nutmeg, and yeast on top.

Bake: Select the «Sweet» or «Basic» cycle with a medium crust setting.

Baking Tips: For added texture, mix in a handful of chopped nuts or dried cranberries during the mixing cycle.

Finish: Let the bread cool before slicing.

Nutritional Information:
(per serving)

*Approx. 180 kcal, 3.93g fat,
40mg cholesterol, 79mg sodium,
4g carbs, 1g fiber, 4g sugar, 4.3g protein.*

Bill's Tip:

Serve this bread with a smear of cream cheese or a drizzle of maple syrup for a perfect autumn treat!

69

CHAPTER 8:

INTERNATIONAL FLAVORS

POPULAR EUROPEAN RECIPES

GERMAN RYE BREAD (ROGGENBROT)

Ingredients:

- 1 ½ cups warm water (360ml)
- 2 tablespoons molasses or honey (30ml)
- 1 ½ cups rye flour (180g)
- 1 ½ cups whole wheat flour (180g)
- 1 ½ teaspoons salt (8g)
- 2 teaspoons caraway seeds (optional) (4g)
- 2¼ teaspoons active dry yeast (7g)
- 2 tablespoons apple cider vinegar (30ml)

Instructions:

Prepare Dough: Add warm water, molasses (or honey), and apple cider vinegar to your bread machine pan. Layer the rye flour, whole wheat flour, salt, and caraway seeds (if using) on top. Finally, add the yeast, ensuring it doesn't come directly with the liquid before mixing.

Bake: Select the "Whole Wheat" cycle on your bread machine and choose the medium crust setting. This cycle allows for the longer rise time needed for rye bread.

Check the Dough: About 10 minutes into the kneading process, check the dough's consistency. It should be slightly sticky but not overly wet. If it's too sticky, add a tablespoon of bread flour at a time until it reaches the desired consistency.

Baking: Let the bread machine complete the cycle. Once done, let the bread cool slightly in the pan before transferring it to a wire rack to cool completely.

Nutritional Information:
(per slice, assuming 12 slices)

Approx. 160 kcal, 1.8g fat,
0mg cholesterol, 320mg sodium,
32g carbs, 3g fiber, 5g sugar, 5g protein

Bill's Tip:

Rye bread benefits from resting. Let the loaf sit for a few hours or overnight before slicing to allow the flavors to develop fully. If you like extra texture, add a tablespoon of whole caraway or sunflower seeds to the dough for a traditional touch. This bread is excellent with hearty soups or as a base for open-faced sandwiches.

BORODINSKY BREAD

Ingredients:

- 1 ½ cups warm water (360ml)
- 2 tablespoons molasses (30ml)
- 2 tablespoons apple cider vinegar (30ml)
- 1 cup rye flour (120g)
- 2 cups bread flour (240g)
- 1 ½ teaspoons salt (8g)
- 2 tablespoons whole coriander seeds (crushed slightly) (12g)
- 1 teaspoon ground coriander (2g)
- 2 tablespoons dark malt powder (30g)
- 2¼ teaspoons active dry yeast (7g)

Nutritional Information:
(per slice, assuming 12 slices)

Approx. 170 kcal, 2g fat, 0mg cholesterol, 320mg sodium, 32g carbs, 3g fiber, 8g sugar, 5g protein

Instructions:

Prepare Dough: Add warm water, molasses, and apple cider vinegar to your bread machine pan. Layer the rye flour, bread flour, salt, ground coriander, crushed coriander seeds, and dark malt powder. Finally, add the yeast, ensuring it doesn't touch the liquid before mixing.

Bake: Select the «Whole Wheat» or «Basic» cycle on your bread machine with a medium crust setting. This will allow the bread to develop its rich flavor and deep color.

Check the Dough: About 10 minutes into the kneading process, check the dough. It should be slightly sticky but should hold its shape. If needed, adjust by adding a tablespoon of bread flour at a time.

Baking: Let the bread machine complete the cycle. After baking, take the bread out of the pan and place it on a wire rack. Allow it to cool completely before slicing.

Bill's Tip:

Borodinsky bread is known for its unique flavor profile, thanks to the coriander and dark malt combination. For an authentic touch, sprinkle a few more crushed coriander seeds on top of the loaf before baking. This bread pairs wonderfully with pickled vegetables, smoked meats, and strong cheeses. Let it rest overnight before slicing to allow the flavors to mature.

FRENCH BAGUETTE

Ingredients:

- 1 ½ cups warm water (360ml)
- 2 ¼ teaspoons active dry yeast (7g)
- 3 ¼ cups bread flour (390g)
- 2 teaspoons salt (10g)
- 1 teaspoon sugar (4g)

Instructions:

Prepare Dough: Add warm water and yeast to your bread machine pan. Let it sit for about 5 minutes until the yeast begins to foam. Then, add the bread flour, salt, and sugar.
Bake: Select your bread machine's «Dough» cycle. This cycle will knead the dough and allow it to rise.

Shape the Baguettes: Once the dough cycle is complete, remove it from the pan and place it on a lightly floured surface. Divide the dough into two equal parts. Shape each part into a long baguette, about 12-14 inches (30-35cm). Line a baking sheet with parchment paper. Place the dough on top. Leave enough space between each piece to allow for expansion during baking.

Final Rise: Cover the baguettes with a clean kitchen towel. Allow them to rise for 30-45 minutes until they double in size.

Preheat Oven: Preheat your oven to 450°F (230°C). Place an empty baking dish on the bottom rack of the oven while it preheats.

Bake: Before placing the baguettes in the oven, use a sharp knife to make 3-4 diagonal slashes across the top of each baguette. This ensures that the bread has enough room to expand properly. Place the baking sheet in the oven. Pour one cup of hot water into the baking dish on the bottom rack to create steam. This will give the baguettes their characteristic crispy crust. Bake for 15-20 minutes.

Cool: Let the baguettes cool on a wire rack before slicing.

Nutritional Information:
(per slice, assuming 16 slices per baguette)
Approx. 150 kcal, 0.5g fat,
0mg cholesterol, 280mg sodium,
30g carbs, 1g fiber, 1g sugar, 5g protein

Bill's Tip:

For an extra crispy crust, mist the baguettes with water using a spray bottle before baking. Serve these baguettes warm with butter, or use them for sandwiches. They're also great with a hearty soup or salad.

72

IRISH SODA BREAD

Ingredients:

- 4 cups all-purpose flour (480g)
- 1 teaspoon baking soda (4g)
- 1 teaspoon baking powder (4g)
- 1 teaspoon salt (5g)
- 2 tablespoons sugar (25g)
- 1 large egg
- 1 ¾ cups buttermilk (420ml)
- 2 tablespoons unsalted butter, melted (28g)
- 1 cup raisins or currants (optional) (150g)

Nutritional Information:
(per slice, assuming 12 slices per loaf)

Approx. 190 kcal, 7g fat, 30mg cholesterol, 340mg sodium, 27g carbs, 1g fiber, 7g sugar, 4g protein

Instructions:

Prepare Dough: Mix all-purpose flour and soda in a bowl. Add baking powder, salt, and sugar. In another bowl, whisk the buttermilk. Add the melted butter and egg. Add the wet ingredients to the dry mixture and stir until just combined. If you're adding raisins or currants, fold them in now.

Bake: Transfer the dough mixture to your bread machine pan. Set your bread machine to the «Quick Bread» or «Cake» cycle. If your machine allows, choose the medium crust setting.

Start the Machine: Begin the cycle. The dough will have a dense consistency typical for soda bread. Allow the machine to complete the cycle, which includes mixing, kneading, and baking.

Check for Doneness: Once the cycle is finished, check for doneness with a toothpick.

If not, continue baking on the «Bake Only» setting for 5-10 minutes.

Cool: After baking, remove the bread from the pan and place it on a wire rack. Allow it to cool completely before slicing.

Bill's Tip:

Soda bread is best enjoyed fresh, but if you have leftovers, it makes excellent toast the next day. Try it with a spread of butter and a touch of jam or alongside a hearty soup. Add a tablespoon of sugar and some dried cranberries or orange zest if you prefer a slightly sweeter bread.

73

DANISH RUGBRØD (RYE BREAD)

Ingredients:

Dough:
- 1 ½ cups warm water (360ml)
- 1 cup buttermilk (240ml)
- 2 tablespoons honey or molasses (30ml)
- 2 cups rye flour (240g)
- 2 cups whole wheat flour (240g)
- 1 cup bread flour (120g)
- 1 cup cracked rye or rye flakes (150g)
- ½ cup sunflower seeds (70g)
- ½ cup pumpkin seeds (70g)
- 1 teaspoon salt (5g)
- 2 teaspoons active dry yeast (7g)

Nutritional Information:
(per slice, assuming 12 slices per loaf)

Approx. 220 kcal, 7g fat, 10mg cholesterol, 250mg sodium, 35g carbs, 5g fiber, 4g sugar, 6g protein.

Instructions:

Preparation:
Add warm water, buttermilk, and honey (or molasses) to the bread machine pan. Add the rye flour, whole wheat flour, bread flour, cracked rye (or rye flakes), sunflower, and pumpkin seeds.
Sprinkle the salt along one side of the pan and the yeast along the other, ensuring they do not touch directly.

Bake: Select the Whole Wheat or Rye bread cycle if available. If not, use the Basic or White Bread cycle. Choose a dark crust setting if your machine has one. Set the loaf size to 2 lbs (or M size if your machine uses these terms)

Cooling & Serving: After baking, remove the bread from the pan and place it on a wire rack. Allow it to cool completely before slicing. Danish Rugbrød is best served after resting for a few hours or the next day. Slice thin and enjoy with butter, cheese, or smoked fish.

Bill's Tip:

After a truly authentic Rugbrød, leave the bread in the machine with the lid closed for 15 minutes after the baking cycle finishes. This helps set the dense crumb.

SWEDISH LIMPA BREAD

Ingredients:

Dough:
- 1 cup warm milk (240ml)
- ¼ cup molasses (60ml)
- ¼ cup orange juice (60ml)
- 2 tablespoons unsalted butter, melted (28g)
- 2 cups rye flour (240g)
- 2 cups bread flour (240g)
- 2 teaspoons ground anise seeds (4g)
- 1 teaspoon ground fennel seeds (2g)
- 1 teaspoon salt (5g)
- 2 ¼ teaspoons active dry yeast (7g)

Nutritional Information:
(per slice, assuming 12 slices per loaf)

Approx. 200 kcal, 5g fat, 15mg cholesterol, 280mg sodium, 34g carbs, 3g fiber, 10g sugar, 5g protein.

Instructions:

Preparation:
Pour the warm milk, molasses, orange juice, and melted butter into the bread machine pan.

Add the rye flour and bread flour on top. Sprinkle the anise seeds, fennel seeds, and salt over the flour.

Finally, add the yeast, ensuring it does not come into direct contact with the liquid at this stage.

Bake: Select the Whole Wheat or Basic bread cycle. Choose a medium crust setting. Set the loaf size to 2 lbs (or M size if your machine uses these terms).

Cooling & Serving: After baking, take the bread out of the pan and place it on a wire rack. Allow it to cool completely before slicing. This bread pairs wonderfully with butter and jam, or enjoy it alongside a hearty stew.

Bill's Tip:

For a slightly sweeter flavor, incorporate 1 tablespoon of brown sugar with the other dry ingredients.
Consider using the "Add Ingredients" feature (if your machine has one) to sprinkle additional anise seeds or orange zest during the kneading process for extra flavor.

UKRAINIAN SOURDOUGH BREAD

Ingredients:

Dough:
- ½ cup active sourdough starter (120g)
- 1 cup warm water (240ml)
- 2 ½ cups bread flour (300g)
- 1 cup rye flour (120g)
- 1 ½ teaspoons salt (8g)
- 1 tablespoon honey (21g)
- 2 tablespoons unsalted butter, melted (28g)
- 1 teaspoon caraway seeds (optional) (2g)
- 2 ¼ teaspoons active dry yeast (7g)

Nutritional Information:
(per slice, assuming 12 slices per loaf)

Approx. 180 kcal, 4g fat, 15mg cholesterol, 300mg sodium, 32g carbs, 2g fiber, 5g sugar, 5g protein.

Instructions:

Preparation:
Add the active sourdough starter and warm water to the bread machine pan. Add the bread flour and rye flour on top. Sprinkle the salt, honey, melted butter, and caraway seeds (if using) over the flour. Add the yeast last, ensuring it does not directly touch the liquid.

Bake: First, select the Dough or Manual setting to allow for an extended rise. After the dough cycle is complete, shape the dough inside the pan or remove it to shape by hand. Let it rise again in the bread machine pan until it doubles. Select the Sourdough or French cycle for the final bake.

Cooling & Serving: After baking, take the bread out of the pan and place it on a wire rack. Allow it to cool completely before slicing.

Bill's Tip:

If you have time, let the dough rest in the fridge overnight for a deeper flavor. Just bring it back to room temperature before the final rise. If you prefer a more rustic look, sprinkle extra rye flour on top before the final rise and bake.

PASCA (UKRAINIAN EASTER BREAD)

Ingredients:

- 4 cups bread flour (480g)
- ¾ cup warm milk (180ml)
- 3 large eggs (150g)
- ⅓ cup unsalted butter, melted (75g)
- ½ cup sugar (100g)
- 1 teaspoon salt (5g)
- 2 ¼ teaspoons active dry yeast (7g)
- 1 teaspoon vanilla extract (5ml)
- ½ cup raisins (75g)
- Zest of 1 lemon

Nutritional Information:

(per slice, assuming 12 slices per loaf)

Approx. 230 kcal, 7g fat, 50mg cholesterol, 200mg sodium, 36g carbs, 1g fiber, 10g sugar, 5g protein

Instructions:

Preparation:

Warm Ingredients: Start by warming the milk slightly. This will activate the yeast and create a nice rise for the bread.

Mixing: Place warm milk in the bread maker bowl. Add eggs and melted butter. Also, add sugar, salt, and vanilla extract. Add the bread flour on top, ensuring it covers the liquid ingredients. Make a small well in the flour and add the yeast.

Bread Machine Setting: Depending on your model, set your bread machine to the «Sweet» or «Basic» cycle with a medium crust setting.

Adding Raisins: Add the raisins and lemon zest when your machine beeps for additional ingredients.

Baking: Allow the machine to complete the cycle. The result should be a beautifully golden, slightly sweet bread perfect for Easter celebrations.

Bill's Tip:

To achieve plumper raisins, soak them in warm water or rum for approximately 15 minutes before incorporating them into the dough.

77

AUSTRIAN KAISER ROLLS

Ingredients:

- 4 cups bread flour (480g)
- 1 ½ teaspoons salt (8g)
- 2 teaspoons sugar (8g)
- 2 ¼ teaspoons active dry yeast (7g)
- 1 ¼ cups warm water (300ml)
- 2 tablespoons unsalted butter, softened (28g)
- 1 egg, beaten (for egg wash)

Nutritional Information:
(per roll, assuming 8 rolls)

Approx. 220 kcal, 5g fat, 20mg cholesterol, 400mg sodium, 38g carbs, 2g fiber, 1g sugar, 7g protein

Instructions:

Preparation:
Combine Ingredients: Add the warm water and softened butter to the bread machine pan. Then, add the bread flour, salt, and sugar. Make a small well in the flour and add the yeast.

Dough Setting: Select your bread machine's «Dough» cycle and let it work. The dough should become smooth and elastic.

Shape Rolls: After the dough cycle finishes, remove the dough from the machine and divide it into 8 equal portions for shaping. Form each piece into a ball, then flatten slightly. Create the signature Kaiser roll pattern with your fingers or a Kaiser roll stamp.

Second Rise: Place the rolls on a baking sheet lined with parchment paper. Cover with a clean kitchen towel. Let them rise for 30-4 minutes or until doubled in size.

Egg Wash: Preheat your oven to 425°F (220°CBrush the tops of the buns with beaten egg for a nice crust.

Bake: Bake for 15 to 18 minutes or until buns are golden brown.

Bill's Tip:

Steam Bake: Place a small pan of water in the oven while baking. This will make the crust crispier, mimicking the professional bakery environment.

Freeze Dough: To save time, you can freeze the shaped rolls before the second rise. Thaw and allow them to rise before baking.

ENGLISH OATMEAL BREAD

Ingredients:

- 1 cup warm milk (240ml)
- ¼ cup warm water (60ml)
- 2 tablespoons unsalted butter, softened (28g)
- ¼ cup honey (85g)
- 1 teaspoon salt (5g)
- 3 cups bread flour (360g)
- 1 cup old-fashioned rolled oats (90g)
- 2 ¼ teaspoons active dry yeast (7g)

Instructions:

Preparation:
Layer Ingredients: Pour the warm milk, warm water, and softened butter into your bread machine pan. Add the honey and salt. Then, add the bread flour and rolled oats. Finally, make a small well in the flour and add the yeast.

Select Settings: Choose the «Basic» or «White Bread» setting on your bread machine. Select the desired crust color (light, medium, or dark) and set the loaf size to 1.5 pounds (M-size).

Start Baking: Start the machine. The bread machine will knead the dough, allow it to rise, and bake it.

Cool Down: After baking, remove the bread from the pan and place it on a wire rack. Allow it to cool completely before slicing.

Nutritional Information:

(per slice, assuming 12 slices per loaf)

Approx. 170 kcal, 4g fat, 10mg cholesterol, 220mg sodium, 30g carbs, 2g fiber, 6g sugar, 5g protein

Bill's Tip:

Oat Topping: *For an extra touch, sprinkle some oats on top of the dough before baking for a rustic finish.*

Honey Substitute: *You can replace honey with maple syrup or brown sugar.*

JAPANESE MILK BREAD

Ingredients:

- ¾ cup warm milk (180ml)
- ¼ cup heavy cream (60ml)
- 1 large egg
- ¼ cup sugar (50g)
- 1 teaspoon salt (5g)
- 3 cups bread flour (360g)
- 2 ¼ teaspoons active dry yeast (7g)
  Tangzhong:
- 3 tablespoons bread flour (24g)
- ½ cup water (120ml)
- ¼ cup milk (60ml)

Instructions:

Make the Tangzhong: In a small saucepan, whisk together the flour, water, and milk for the tangzhong. Cook over medium heat, stirring constantly. The mixture should thicken to a paste-like consistency. Then, let the mixture cool to room temperature.

Layer Ingredients: Add the tangzhong to your bread mac hine pan. Then, pour the warm milk, heavy cream, egg, sugar, and salt. Add the bread flour, making a small well in the flour, and add the yeast.

Select Settings: Choose the «Basic» or «White Bread» setting on your bread machine. Select the desired crust color (light, medium, or dark) and set the loaf size to 1.5 pounds (M-size).

Start Baking: Start the machine. The bread machine will knead the dough, allow it to rise, and bake it.

Cool Down: After baking, remove the bread from the pan and place it on a wire rack. Allow it to cool completely before slicing.

Nutritional Information:

(per slice, assuming 12 slices per loaf)

Approx. 190 kcal, 7g fat,
30mg cholesterol, 210mg sodium,
29g carbs, 1g fiber, 6g sugar, 5g protein

Bill's Tip:

To enhance the flavor, replace some milk with additional heavy cream or use whole milk instead of skim for a richer taste.

CHINESE STEAMED BUNS (MANTOU)

Ingredients:

- 1 cup warm water (240ml)
- 2 tablespoons sugar (25g)
- 1 teaspoon salt (5g)
- 2 teaspoons active dry yeast (7g)
- 3 ½ cups all-purpose flour (420g)
- 2 tablespoons vegetable oil (30ml)

Nutritional Information:
(per bun, assuming 12 buns per batch)

Approx. 120 kcal, 2g fat, 0mg cholesterol, 170mg sodium, 22g carbs, 1g fiber, 2g sugar, 3g protein

Instructions:

Preparation:

Activate Yeast: In a small bowl, mix the warm water, sugar, and yeast. Let it sit for about 5 minutes until it becomes frothy.

Layer Ingredients: Add flour and salt to your bread machine pan. Pour in the yeast mixture. Add the vegetable oil.

Select Dough Setting: Start your bread machine and select the «Dough» setting. The machine will knead the dough and complete the first rise (which should take about 1.5 hours)

Shape the Buns: Once the cycle is complete, remove the dough and place it on a lightly floured surface. Knead it for a few minutes, then divide it into 10-12 equal portions. Form each portion into a smooth ball or flat cake for traditional mantou.

Second Rise: Place the shaped buns on small squares of parchment paper. Arrange them in a steamer basket, leaving a little space between each bun. Cover and let rise for another 30-45 minutes.

Steam the Buns: Fill a pot with water and bring it to a boil. Place the steamer basket over boiling water. Cover with a lid. Steam the buns over medium heat for 10 minutes. Turn off the heat and leave the buns in the steamer for 2 minutes before removing the lid to prevent them from shrinking.

Bill's Tip:

Extra Softness: Add 1 tablespoon of milk powder to the dough for even softer buns.

Perfect Steaming: Make sure the water in the steamer doesn't touch the buns, as direct water contact can cause the buns to become soggy.

INDIAN NAAN

Ingredients:

- ⅔ cup warm water (160ml)
- ¼ cup plain yogurt (60ml)
- 2 tablespoons vegetable oil (30ml)
- 1 large egg
- 2 ¾ cups bread flour (330g)
- 1 teaspoon salt (5g)
- 1 tablespoon sugar (12g)
- 2 ¼ teaspoons active dry yeast (7g)
- 2 tablespoons melted butter or ghee (28g) for brushing

Nutritional Information:
(per naan, assuming 8 naans per batch)

Approx. 210 kcal, 8g fat, 35mg cholesterol, 310mg sodium, 30g carbs, 1g fiber, 3g sugar, 6g protein

Instructions:

Preparation:
Layer Ingredients: Pour the warm water, yogurt, vegetable oil, and beaten egg into the bread machine pan. Add the bread flour, salt, sugar, and yeast on top.

Select Dough Setting: Start your bread machine and select the «Dough» setting. The machine will knead the dough and complete the first rise (which should take about 1.5 hours)

Divide and Shape: Once the cycle is complete, remove it and place it on a lightly floured surface. Knead it for a few minutes, then divide the dough into 8 equal portions shape. Each into a ball.

Roll Out the Naan: Using a rolling pin, flatten each ball into an oval or teardrop shape, about ¼ inch thick.

Cook the Naan: Heat a cast-iron skillet or heavy-bottomed pan over medium-high heat. Place the rolled-out dough on a dry frying pan and cook for 1-2 minutes. Bubbles should form on the surface. Flip and cook the other side for 1-2 minutes until golden brown. Brush the hot naan with ghee.

Serve: Serve warm with your favorite Indian dishes or enjoy as a wrap for sandwiches.

Bill's Tip:

Garlic Naan: Add minced garlic to the melted butter before brushing it onto the naan for a flavorful twist.

Grill It: For a smoky flavor, try grilling the naan over medium heat instead of cooking it in a skillet.

KOREAN SWEET POTATO BREAD

Ingredients:

- 1 cup warm milk (240ml)
- ½ cup mashed sweet potatoes (120g)
- ¼ cup vegetable oil (60ml)
- 1 large egg
- 3 ½ cups bread flour (420g)
- ⅓ cup granulated sugar (67g)
- 1 teaspoon salt (5g)
- 2 teaspoons active dry yeast (6g)
- 1 teaspoon ground cinnamon (2g) (optional for added flavor)
- ¼ cup chopped walnuts or pecans (30g) (optional, for added texture)

Nutritional Information:

(per slice, assuming 12 slices per loaf)

Approx. 220 kcal, 8g fat, 30mg cholesterol, 240mg sodium, 33g carbs, 2g fiber, 12g sugar, 5g protein

Instructions:

Preparation:

Layer Ingredients: Pour the warm milk, mashed sweet potatoes, vegetable oil, and beaten egg into the bread machine pan. Add the bread flour, granulated sugar, salt, and yeast.

Select Dough Setting: Choose the «Dough» setting on your bread machine and start it. The machine will handle the kneading and first rise, which will take about 1.5 hours.

Shape the Bread: After the cycle is complete, remove the dough. Place it on a lightly floured surface. Form it into a loaf or small buns.

Second Rise: Transfer the formed dough to a greased loaf pan or baking sheet. Cover with a clean towel. Let the dough rise for 30-45 minutes.

Bake the Bread: Warm your oven to 350°F (175°C). Bake the bread for 30-35 minutes. It should be golden brown. Check for doneness with a toothpick.

Cool: Allow the bread to cool on a wire rack before slicing.

Bill's Tip:

For smooth sweet potato prep, mash the sweet potatoes well by hand or use a food processor for an extra creamy consistency. Mix chopped nuts or sprinkle cinnamon sugar before baking to add texture and flavor.

THAI COCONUT BREAD

Ingredients:

- 1 cup coconut milk (240ml)
- ¼ cup coconut oil (60ml)
- 2 large eggs
- 3 ½ cups bread flour (420g)
- ½ cup granulated sugar (100g)
- 1 teaspoon salt (5g)
- 2 teaspoons active dry yeast (6g)
- ½ cup shredded coconut (unsweetened) (50g)
- ¼ cup chopped cashews or peanuts (30g) (optional, for added texture)

Nutritional Information:
(per slice, assuming 12 slices per loaf)

Approx. 220 kcal, 10g fat,
30mg cholesterol, 210mg sodium,
29g carbs, 2g fiber, 12g sugar, 5g protein

Instructions:

Preparation:
Layer Ingredients: Pour the coconut milk, coconut oil, and beaten eggs into the bread machine pan. Add the bread flour, granulated sugar, salt, and yeast. Sprinkle the shredded coconut over the ingredients.

Select Dough Setting: Start your bread machine and select the «Dough» setting. The machine will knead the dough and complete the first rise (which should take about 1.5 hours)

Shape the Bread: Once the cycle is complete, remove it and place it on a lightly floured surface. Form it into a loaf or small rolls.

Second Rise: Transfer the formed dough to a greased loaf pan or baking sheet. Cover with a clean towel. Let the dough rise for 30-45 minutes.

Bake the Bread: Warm your oven to 350°F (175°C). Bake the bread for 30-35 minutes. It should be golden brown. Check for doneness with a toothpick.

Cool: After the baking cycle finishes, carefully remove the bread from the pan. Place the bread on a wire rack and let it cool completely before slicing.

Bill's Tip:

Coconut Milk: Use full-fat coconut milk for a richer flavor and softer texture.

Optional Nuts: Adding chopped cashews or peanuts will give the bread a delightful crunch.

VIETNAMESE BAGUETTE

Ingredients:

- 1 ½ cups warm water (360ml)
- 2 teaspoons active dry yeast (6g)
- 1 tablespoon granulated sugar (12g)
- 3 ½ cups bread flour (420g)
- 1 teaspoon salt (5g)
- 1 tablespoon vegetable oil (15ml)

Nutritional Information:

(per slice, assuming 12 slices per baguette)

Approx. 150 kcal, 1g fat, 0mg cholesterol, 300mg sodium, 30g carbs, 1g fiber, 1g sugar, 5g protein

Instructions:

Preparation:

Activate Yeast: In a small bowl, mix the warm water with the sugar and yeast. Let it sit for 5-10 minutes until frothy.

Combine Ingredients: Add the yeast mixture, flour, salt, and vegetable oil to the bread machine pan.

Select Dough Setting: Start your bread machine and select the «Dough» setting. The machine will knead the dough and complete the first rise (which should take about 1.5 hours)

Shape the Baguettes: After the cycle is complete, remove the dough. Place it on a lightly floured surface. Form it into two equal pieces. Shape each piece into a baguette.

Second Rise: Transfer the formed dough to a greased loaf pan or baking sheet. Cover with a clean towel. Let the dough rise for minutes.

Preheat the Oven: Warm up the oven to 450°F (230°C). Place an empty baking pan on the bottom rack of the oven.

Bake the Baguettes: Use a sharp knife to make a few diagonal slashes on top of each baguette. Place the baking sheet with the baguettes in the oven and pour a cup of water into the empty baking pan to create steam. Bake for 20-25 minutes until the golden-brown baguettes sound hollow when tapped on the bottom.

Cool: Allow the baguettes to cool on a wire rack before slicing.

Bill's Tip:

Steam Effect: Adding water to the oven creates steam, which helps the baguettes develop a crisp crust.

Shaping: For an authentic look, shape the baguettes with tapered ends to be long and thin.

85

CHINESE SCALLION PANCAKES

Ingredients:

Dough:
- 2 cups all-purpose flour (240g)
- ¾ cup boiling water (180ml)
- 1 teaspoon salt (5g)
- 2 tablespoons vegetable oil (30ml)

Filling:
- 4 scallions, finely chopped (about 40g)
- 2 tablespoons vegetable oil (30ml)
- 1 teaspoon salt (5g)

Additional:
- 2 tablespoons vegetable oil (30ml), for frying

Nutritional Information:
(per pancake, assuming 4 pancakes)

Approx. 200 kcal, 12g fat, 0mg cholesterol, 500mg sodium, 22g carbs, 1g fiber, 1g sugar, 3g protein

Instructions:

Preparation:

Make the Dough: Mix flour and salt in a bowl. Gradually add boiling water, stirring until the dough begins to stick together. Let it cool slightly. When the dough has cooled enough, knead it on a floured surface for about 5 minutes until smooth. Cover with a damp towel. Let it sit for another 30 minutes.

Prepare the Filling: Mix chopped green onions with 2 tablespoons of vegetable oil in a separate bowl. Add 1 teaspoon of salt. Set aside.

Roll Out the Dough: Divide the rested dough into 4 equal pieces. Sprinkle flour on the surface. Flatten each piece into a thin circle, approximately 8-10 inches in diameter.

Spread the Filling: Brush each dough circle lightly with vegetable oil and sprinkle evenly with the scallion mixture.

Roll and Coil: Roll each circle into a tight log, then coil it into a spiral shape. Gently flatten each spiral with your palm, then roll it out again into a thin pancake about 6-8 inches in diameter.

Cook the Pancakes: Heat 2 tablespoons vegetable oil in a pan over medium heat. Fry each pancake on each side for 2-3 minutes or until golden brown and crispy. Drain pancakes on paper towels.

Serve: Cut the pancakes into wedges and serve warm.

Bill's Tip:

Rolling Technique: Rolling the dough thinly and then coiling it creates the flaky layers in the pancakes.

*Crispy Texture: Ensure the skillet is hot before adding the pancakes to get a crisp, golden **crust**.*

CHINESE BAOZI (STUFFED BUNS)

Ingredients:

Dough:
- ½ cup warm water (120ml)
- ¼ cup milk (60ml)
- 2 tablespoons sugar (25g)
- 2 teaspoons instant yeast (6g)
- 2 ½ cups all-purpose flour (300g)
- 1 teaspoon baking powder (4g)
- ¼ teaspoon salt (1.5g)
- 2 tablespoons vegetable oil (30ml)

Filling:
- 1 cup ground pork (225g)
- 2 tablespoons soy sauce (30ml)
- 1 tablespoon hoisin sauce (15ml)
- 1 tablespoon rice wine (15ml)
- 1 tablespoon sugar (12g)
- 2 cloves garlic, minced (6g)
- 1 tablespoon fresh ginger, minced (10g)
- ¼ cup chopped green onions (30g)
- ¼ cup finely chopped cabbage (25g)
- 1 teaspoon sesame oil (5ml)

Nutritional Information:
(per bun, assuming 12 buns per batch)

Approx. 180 kcal, 8g fat, 30mg cholesterol, 400mg sodium, 18g carbs, 1g fiber, 2g sugar, 7g protein

Instructions:

Preparation:

Prepare the Dough: Take a small bowl. Dissolve sugar in warm water and milk. Sprinkle the instant yeast over the mixture and let it sit for 5 minutes until frothy.

Mix the Dough: In the bread machine pan, combine the flour, baking powder, and salt. Add the yeast mixture and vegetable oil. Select the "Dough" setting. Start.

Prepare the Filling: In a medium bowl, mix the ground pork with soy sauce, hoisin sauce, rice wine, sugar, garlic, ginger, green onions, cabbage, and sesame oil. Mix well until fully combined.

Shape the Buns: Once the cycle is complete, remove the dough and place it on a lightly floured surface. Knead it for a few minutes, then divide it into 12 pieces. Add one tablespoon of filling to the center. Pinch the edges to seal.

Steam the Buns: Place the buns on parchment paper and arrange them in a steamer basket, leaving space between each bun. Steam over boiling water for 15-20 minutes or until the buns are puffed up and cooked.

Serve: Serve the Baozi warm. They are perfect as a main dish or a delicious snack.

Bill's Tip:

Ensure the steamer has enough room for the buns to rise without touching each other. Use parchment paper to prevent sticking.

KOREAN HOTTEOK (SWEET PANCAKES)

Ingredients:

Dough:
- 1 cup warm water (240ml)
- 2 tablespoons sugar (25g)
- 2 teaspoons instant yeast (6g)
- 2 cups all-purpose flour (240g)
- ½ teaspoon salt (3g)
- 1 tablespoon vegetable oil (15ml)

Filling:
- ½ cup brown sugar (100g)
- ¼ cup chopped walnuts or peanuts (30g)
- 1 teaspoon ground cinnamon (2g)
- 1 tablespoon honey (15ml)

For Cooking:
- 2 tablespoons vegetable oil (30ml)

Nutritional Information:
(per Hotteok, assuming 8 Hotteok per batch)
Approx. 220 kcal, 10g fat,
15mg cholesterol, 150mg sodium,
30g carbs, 1g fiber, 15g sugar, 3g protein

Instructions:

Preparation:

Prepare the Dough: Mix the warm water and sugar in a small bowl. Sprinkle the instant yeast over the mixture and let it sit for 5 minutes until frothy.

Mix the Dough: Combine the flour and salt in a large bowl. Add the yeast mixture and vegetable oil. Mix until a soft dough forms. Knead on a floured surface for about 5 minutes until smooth. Cover with a damp towel. Cover with a wet towel. The dough will rise for 1 hour. (Put in a warm place)

Prepare the Filling: In a small bowl, mix the brown sugar, chopped nuts, ground cinnamon, and honey until well combined.

Shape the Hotteok: Punch down the dough and divide it into 8 equal pieces. Flatten each piece into a disk. Place about 1 tablespoon of the filling in the center of each disk. Fold the edges up to seal and form a ball.

Cook the Hotteok: Heat one tablespoon of vegetable oil in a skillet over medium heat. Place the filled dough balls seam-side down and flatten them slightly with a spatula. Cook for about 2 minutes on each side until golden brown and crisp. Press down gently with a spatula to help the pancakes cook evenly.

Serve: Serve the Hotteok warm. They are delicious on their own or with a dusting of powdered sugar.

Bill's Tip:

Filling Tip: Add chocolate chips or dried fruit to the filling mixture for sweetness and texture.

Cooking Tip: Keep the heat at medium to ensure that the Hotteok cooks through without burning on the outside.

THAI ROTI BREAD

Ingredients:

Dough:
- 1 cup warm water (240ml)
- 2 tablespoons sugar (25g)
- 2 teaspoons active dry yeast (7g)
- 3 ½ cups all-purpose flour (420g)
- ½ teaspoon salt (3g)
- 2 tablespoons vegetable oil (30ml)

For Cooking:
- 2 tablespoons melted butter or ghee (30ml)

Nutritional Information:
(per Roti, assuming 8 Roti per batch)

Approx. 150 kcal, 6g fat, 15mg cholesterol, 150mg sodium, 22g carbs, 1g fiber, 2g sugar, 3g protein

Instructions:

Preparation:

Activate the Yeast: Combine the warm water and sugar in a small bowl. Sprinkle the mixture with active dry yeast. Leave for 5 minutes until foam forms.

Make the Dough: In a large bowl, mix the flour and salt. Add the yeast mixture and vegetable oil. Stir until a dough forms. Turn onto a floured surface and knead for about 10 minutes until smooth and elastic.

Let the Dough Rise: Transfer the dough to a greased bowl. Cover it with a wet towel. Let the dough rise for 1 hour. (Place in a warm place)

Shape the Roti: Punch down the dough and divide it into 8 equal pieces. Roll each piece into a thin 8-inch circle. Brush each circle lightly with melted butter or ghee.

Cook the Roti: Heat a non-stick skillet over medium heat. Cook each roti for 1-2 minutes until golden brown and slightly crispy. Brush more melted butter on each side while cooking for extra flavor.

Serve: Serve the Thai Roti Bread warm. It's great on its own or as a side with various dishes.

Bill's Tip:

To make the roti softer, cover the dough with a damp cloth during the resting period to prevent it from drying out.

89

JAPANESE ANKO BREAD

Ingredients:

Dough:
- 1 cup warm milk (240ml)
- 2 large eggs
- ¼ cup unsalted butter, softened (57g)
- ¼ cup granulated sugar (50g)
- 4 cups bread flour (480g)
- 2 teaspoons active dry yeast (7g)
- 1 teaspoon salt (5g)

Filling:
- 1 cup sweet red bean paste (anko) (250g)

Nutritional Information:
(per slice, assuming 12 slices per loaf)

Approx. 220 kcal, 8g fat, 35mg cholesterol, 250mg sodium, 34g carbs, 1g fiber, 14g sugar, 5g protein

Instructions:

Preparation:
Prepare the Dough:
Add warm milk, eggs, and softened butter to the bread machine pan. Sprinkle the sugar, then add the bread flour, creating a well in the center for the yeast.

Add the yeast into the well, and then sprinkle the salt over the top of the flour.

Mix and Knead: Select your bread machine's «Dough» setting and start the cycle. (The program takes 1 hour 30 minutes)

First Rise: Once the dough cycle is complete, remove it from the pan and place it on a lightly floured surface. Shape it into a ball and let it rest for 10 minutes.

Shape and Fill: Roll the dough into a ¼-inch thick rectangle. Spread the sweet red bean paste evenly over the dough. Roll the dough tightly into a log. Pinch the seams.

Second Rise: Place the rolled dough seam-side down in a greased loaf pan. Cover it with a wet towel. Let the dough rise for 45 minutes. (Place in a warm place)

Bake: Warm the oven to 350°F (175°C). Bake the bread for 30 to 35 minutes or until the crust is golden brown. Check that the internal temperature reaches 190°F (88°C) to ensure it is fully cooked.

Cool and Serve: Let the bread cool in the pan for 10 minutes, then transfer it to a wire rack to cool completely before slicing.

Bill's Tip:

The red bean paste should not be too runny. If necessary, drain any excess liquid before spreading it on the dough.

MEDITERRANEAN RECIPES

For most Mediterranean recipes, the bread machine serves as a dough mixer. It allows for more precise control over the kneading process, ensuring the right texture and a good rise. While baking in the oven helps achieve the perfect crust and structure—something that's hard to replicate in a bread machine, especially for traditional loaves like ciabatta, focaccia, or Turkish bread.

Using the bread machine for kneading makes the process less labor-intensive and ensures even mixing, which is especially helpful for those who prefer to avoid kneading dough by hand. The bread machine simplifies the preparation of more complex breads with minimal effort.

ITALIAN CIABATTA BREAD

Ingredients:

- 4 cups bread flour (480g)
- 1 ½ cups warm water (360ml)
- 1 teaspoon salt (5g)
- 1 ½ teaspoons sugar (6g)
- 1 teaspoon olive oil (5ml)
- 1 ¼ teaspoons active dry yeast (4g)

Nutritional Information:
(per slice, assuming 12 slices per loaf)

Approx. 140 kcal, 1g fat, 0mg cholesterol, 290mg sodium, 27g carbs, 1g fiber, 0g sugar, 4g protein.

Instructions:

Mixing the Dough: Combine the warm water and yeast in a large bowl. Let it sit for 5-10 minutes until frothy. Add the flour, salt, sugar, and olive oil. Mix until a sticky dough forms.

First Rise: Seal the bowl with plastic wrap or use a damp cloth. Let the dough rise warmly for 1-2 hours or until it has doubled.

Shaping: Turn the dough out onto a well-floured surface. Stretch and fold the dough into a rectangular shape, careful not to sag it too much. Sprinkle a baking tray with flour. Place the formed dough on it. Cover it with a towel. Let the dough rise for 35-45 minutes.

Bake: Set the bread machine to the 'Dough' cycle. Once the dough is ready, shape it as described above and place it back into the machine. Select the 'Bake' setting and bake according to the machine's instructions.

Baking in Oven: Warm the oven to 425°F (220°C). Bake the ciabatta for 20-25 minutes. It should be golden brown. Check for doneness with a toothpick.

Bill's Tip:

To create steam for an extra-crusty loaf, place a pan of water in the bottom of the oven during the first 10 minutes of baking.

91

TURKISH SIMIT

Ingredients:

- 4 cups all-purpose flour (480g)
- 1 cup warm water (240ml)
- ¼ cup warm milk (60ml)
- 2 ¼ teaspoons active dry yeast (7g)
- 2 tablespoons sugar (25g)
- 1 teaspoon salt (5g)
- ¼ cup olive oil (60ml)
  Topping:
- ½ cup grape molasses (120ml)
- ¼ cup water (60ml)
- 1 ½ cups sesame seeds, toasted (225g)

Nutritional Information:
(per simit, assuming 8 pieces)

Approx. 300 kcal, 13g fat, 0mg cholesterol, 300mg sodium, 40g carbs, 3g fiber,\ 4g sugar, 7g protein.

Instructions:

Preparation:
Mixing the Dough: In a large bowl, combine warm water, warm milk, sugar, and yeast. Let it sit for 5-10 minutes until frothy. Add the flour, salt, and olive oil. Mix until a soft dough forms.

Kneading: Work the dough on a floured surface for 8-10 minutes until it feels smooth and elastic. Place the dough in a lightly greased bowl. Cover the bowl with a cloth. Set it in a warm spot and let it rise for around 1 hour or until it has roughly doubled.

Shaping: Punch down the dough and divide it into 8 equal pieces. Shape each piece into a long rope, approximately 20 inches in length. Fold the rope in half, twist it, and then combine the ends to form a ring.

Coating: Mix the grape molasses with water in a shallow dish. First, dip each ring into the molasses mixture. Next, roll it in the toasted sesame seeds until completely coated.

Bake: Set the bread machine to the 'Dough' cycle. Shape the dough into rings and bake using the 'Bake' setting, according to the machine's instructions.

Baking in Oven: Warm the oven to 375°F (190°C). Line a baking sheet with parchment paper. Place the simit rings on it. Bake for 20–25 minutes or until golden brown and crispy.

Bill's Tip:

Toasting the seeds before coating gives the simit a deeper, nuttier flavor.

GREEK OLIVE BREAD

Ingredients:

- 4 cups bread flour (480g)
- 1 ¼ cups warm water (300ml)
- 2 ¼ teaspoons active dry yeast (7g)
- 1 teaspoon sugar (4g)
- 1 ½ teaspoons salt (8g)
- ¼ cup olive oil (60ml)
- 1 cup Kalamata olives, pitted and chopped (150g)
- 1 tablespoon fresh rosemary, chopped (2g)
- 1 tablespoon fresh oregano, chopped (2g)

Nutritional Information:
(per slice, assuming 12 slices per loaf)

Approx. 210 kcal, 9g fat, 0mg cholesterol, 480mg sodium, 28g carbs, 2g fiber, 1g sugar, 4g protein.

Instructions:

Preparation:
Mixing the Dough: In a large bowl, combine warm water, yeast, and sugar. Let it sit for 5-10 minutes until frothy. Add the flour, salt, and olive oil. Mix until a soft dough forms.

Kneading: Work the dough on a floured surface for 8-10 minutes until it feels smooth and elastic. Place the dough in a lightly greased bowl. Cover the bowl with a cloth. Set it in a warm spot and let it rise for around 1 hour or until it has roughly doubled.

Incorporating Olives and Herbs: Gently punch the dough down once it has risen. Knead the chopped olives, rosemary, and oregano into the dough until evenly distributed.

Shaping: Shape the dough into a round or oval loaf. Place it on a parchment-lined baking sheet. Cover and let it rise for another 30–45 minutes. Cover it with a towel. Let the dough rise for 35-45 minutes.

Bake: Set the bread machine to the 'Dough' cycle. After the first rise, add the olives and herbs. Use the 'Bake' setting to finish.

Baking in Oven: Warm the oven to 375°F (190°C). Bake the loaf for 30-35 minutes until it sounds hollow and is golden brown when tapped.

Bill's Tip:

Fresh herbs add the best flavor, but dried herbs can be substituted if necessary—use half the amount.

MATZO (UNLEAVENED BREAD)

Ingredients:

- 2 cups all-purpose flour (240g)
- ½ teaspoon salt (3g)
- ½ cup water (120ml)
- 2 tablespoons olive oil (30ml), optional

Nutritional Information:
(per piece, assuming 8 pieces per batch)

Approx. 80 kcal, 1g fat, 0mg cholesterol, 120mg sodium, 16g carbs, 1g fiber, 2g protein, 0g sugar

Instructions:

Preparation:
Preheat the Oven: Preheat your oven to 475°F (245°C). Place a baking stone or inverted baking sheet in the oven.

Mix the Dough: Combine the flour and salt in a large bowl. Gradually add the water and mix until a rough dough forms. If using, add the olive oil for a slightly richer flavor.

Kneading: Knead the dough on a lightly floured surface for 3-5 minutes until smooth. The dough should be stiff but pliable.

Divide and Roll: Divide the dough into 8 equal pieces. Roll each piece as thinly as possible into a rough circle or rectangle, about ⅛ inch thick.

Dock the Dough: Prick the dough with a fork to prevent it from puffing up during baking.

Baking: Place the rolled dough directly onto the preheated baking stone or sheet. Bake for 2-4 minutes until the matzo is crisp and lightly browned. Watch carefully, as they can burn quickly.

Cool: Remove the matzo from the oven and let it cool on a wire rack. The matzo will crisp up further as it cools.

Bill's Tip:

Speed is Key: Traditionally, matzo should be made within 18 minutes from start to finish to ensure it remains unleavened.

Flavor Variations: While traditional matzo is plain, you can add flavor with a sprinkle of sea salt, sesame seeds, or herbs before baking.

LEBANESE FLATBREAD (MANAKISH)

Ingredients:

- 3 cups all-purpose flour (360g)
- 1 teaspoon salt (5g)
- 1 tablespoon sugar (12g)
- 2 ¼ teaspoons active dry yeast (7g)
- 1 cup warm water (240ml)
- 2 tablespoons olive oil (30ml)
  For the Topping (Za'atar):
- ¼ cup za'atar spice blend (25g)
- ¼ cup olive oil (60ml)

Nutritional Information:
(per flatbread, assuming 8 flatbreads per batch)
Approx. 200 kcal, 8g fat, 0mg cholesterol, 300mg sodium, 27g carbs, 2g fiber, 0g sugar, 5g protein.

Instructions:

Preparation:

Activate the Yeast: Combine the warm water, sugar, and yeast in a small bowl. Let it sit for 5-10 minutes until it becomes frothy.

Mix the Dough: Combine the flour and salt in a large mixing bowl. Add the yeast mixture and olive oil. Mix until the dough starts to come together.

Kneading: Transfer the dough to a lightly floured surface and knead for 8-10 minutes until smooth and elastic.

First Rise: Place the dough in a greased bowl, cover it with a damp cloth, and let it rise in a warm place for 1-1.5 hours or until doubled in size.

Prepare the Za'atar Topping: Mix the za'atar spice blend with olive oil to form a paste in a small bowl. Set aside.

Shape the Flatbreads: After the dough has risen, punch it down and divide it into 8 equal portions. Roll each portion into a ball and flatten it into a circle about ¼ inches thick.

Topping: Spread a tablespoon of the za'atar mixture over each dough circle, spreading it evenly to the edges.

Final Rise: Let the flatbreads rest for about 15 minutes while you preheat your oven.

Baking: Warm your oven to 475°F (245°C) with a baking stone or an inverted baking sheet inside. Place the flatbreads on the hot stone or sheet and bake for 6-8 minutes or until golden and slightly puffed.

Serve: Remove from the oven and serve warm.

Bill's Tip:

Versatility: You can also top the flatbreads with cheese, minced meat, or vegetables for a different variation.

Freezing: These flatbreads freeze well. Reheat them in the oven before serving.

95

ITALIAN FOCACCIA

Ingredients:

- 4 cups all-purpose flour (480g)
- 1 ½ teaspoons salt (8g)
- 1 ¼ cups warm water (300ml)
- 2 ¼ teaspoons active dry yeast (7g)
- ¼ cup olive oil (60ml)
- 1 teaspoon sugar (4g)
  For the Topping:
- ¼ cup olive oil (60ml)
- 2–3 sprigs fresh rosemary, chopped
- 1 teaspoon coarse sea salt (5g)

Optional: Sliced cherry tomatoes, olives, or thinly sliced red onion for additional toppings

Nutritional Information:

(per serving, assuming 12 servings per loaf)
Approx. 190 kcal, 9g fat, 0mg cholesterol, 330mg sodium, 25g carbs, 1g fiber, 1g sugar, 4g protein.

Instructions:

Preparation:
Activate the Yeast: Combine the warm water, sugar, and yeast in a small bowl. Let it sit for 5-10 minutes until it becomes frothy.

Mix the Dough: Combine the flour and salt in a large mixing bowl. Add the yeast mixture and olive oil. Mix until a sticky dough forms.

Kneading: Turn the dough onto a floured surface and knead for about 5 minutes until smooth and elastic.

First Rise: Place the dough in a greased bowl, cover it with a damp cloth, and let it rise in a warm place for about 1 hour or until doubled in size.

Shape the Dough: After the dough has risen, punch it down and transfer it to a well-oiled baking sheet. Press the dough out to an even thickness, about ½ inch thick.

Second Rise: Cover the dough with a cloth and let it rise for another 20-30 minutes.

Prepare the Topping: Warm your oven to 425°F (220°C). While the dough is rising, mix the olive oil and chopped rosemary in a small bowl.

Dimple the Dough: Using your fingers, press deep dimples all over the surface of the dough. Drizzle the rosemary olive oil mixture over the dough, ensuring it fills the dimples. Sprinkle with coarse sea salt and any additional toppings.

Baking: Bake the focaccia for 20-25 minutes until golden brown and cooked through.

Cool and Serve: Remove from the oven. Let it cool slightly before cutting into squares and serving.

Bill's Tip:

Serving Suggestions: Focaccia is perfect as a side dish, sandwich bread, or dipped in olive oil and balsamic vinegar.

Freezing: Focaccia freezes well. Cut into portions and freeze in airtight bags. Reheat in the oven before serving.

GREEK PITA BREAD

Ingredients:

- 3 cups all-purpose flour (360g)
- 1 teaspoon salt (5g)
- 1 tablespoon sugar (12g)
- 1 tablespoon olive oil (15ml)
- 1 cup warm water (240ml)
- 2 ¼ teaspoons active dry yeast (7g)

Nutritional Information:
(per pita, assuming 8 pitas per batch)

Approx. 180 kcal, 2g fat, 0mg cholesterol, 300mg sodium, 33g carbs, 1g fiber, 1g sugar, 5g protein.

Instructions:

Preparation:
Activate the Yeast: Combine the warm water, sugar, and yeast in a small bowl. Let it sit for 10 minutes until it becomes frothy.

Mix the Dough: Combine the flour and salt in a large mixing bowl. Add the yeast mixture and olive oil. Mix until a dough forms.

Kneading: Turn the dough onto a floured surface and knead for 8-10 minutes until smooth and elastic.

First Rise: Place the dough in a greased bowl, cover it with a damp cloth, and let it rise in a warm place for about 1 hour or until doubled in size.

Divide and Shape: Punch down the dough and divide it into 8 equal pieces. Roll each piece into a ball, then flatten each into a ¼-inch thick round using a rolling pin.

Second Rise: Place the rounds on a floured surface, cover them with a cloth, and let them rise for another 30 minutes.

Cooking: Warm a skillet or griddle over medium-high heat. Cook each round for 1-2 minutes on each side until they puff up and have golden spots.

Cool and Serve: Remove the pitas from the skillet and place them in a towel to keep them soft. Serve warm.

Bill's Tip:

Storage: Store pita bread in an airtight container at room temperature for up to 2 days or freeze for longer storage.

Serving Suggestions: Use pita bread for wraps, dipping in hummus, or as a base for mini pizzas.

TURKISH FLATBREAD (BAZLAMA)

Ingredients:

- 4 cups all-purpose flour (480g)
- 1 teaspoon salt (5g)
- 1 tablespoon sugar (12g)
- 2 tablespoons olive oil (30ml)
- 1 ¼ cups warm water (300ml)
- 2 ¼ teaspoons active dry yeast (7g)
- ½ cup plain yogurt (120g)

Nutritional Information:
(per flatbread, assuming 8 flatbreads per batch)
Approx. 220 kcal, 5g fat, 0mg cholesterol, 290mg sodium, 37g carbs, 1g fiber, 2g sugar, 5g protein.

Instructions:

Preparation:
Activate the Yeast: Combine the warm water, sugar, and yeast in a small bowl. Let it sit for 10 minutes until it becomes frothy.

Mix the Dough: Combine the flour and salt in a large mixing bowl. Add the yeast mixture, yogurt, and olive oil. Mix until a dough forms.

Kneading: Turn the dough onto a floured surface and knead for 8-10 minutes until smooth and elastic.

First Rise: Place the dough in a greased bowl, cover it with a damp cloth, and let it rise in a warm place for about 1 hour or until doubled in size.

Divide and Shape: Punch down the dough and divide it into 8 equal pieces. Roll each piece into a ball, then flatten each into a ¼-inch thick round using a rolling pin.

Cooking: Warm a skillet or griddle over medium heat. Cook each round for 2-3 minutes until golden brown and slightly puffed.

Cool and Serve: Remove the flatbreads from the skillet and place them in a towel to keep them warm. Serve immediately.

Bill's Tip:

These flatbreads are perfect for dipping in olive oil, serving with kebabs, or making sandwiches.

98

SPANISH CIABATTA WITH ANCHOVIES

Ingredients:

- 4 cups bread flour (480g)
- 1 ½ teaspoons salt (8g)
- 1 teaspoon sugar (4g)
- 2 teaspoons active dry yeast (7g)
- 1 ½ cups warm water (360ml)
- ¼ cup olive oil (60ml)
- 8-10 anchovy fillets, drained and chopped (approx. 50g)
- 1 teaspoon dried oregano (1g)
- ½ teaspoon black pepper (1g)

Nutritional Information:
(per slice, assuming 12 slices per loaf)

Approx. 160 kcal, 5g fat, 0mg cholesterol, 350mg sodium, 25g carbs, 1g fiber, 1g sugar, 4g protein.

Instructions:

Preparation:

Activate the Yeast: Combine the warm water, sugar, and yeast in a bowl. Stir and let it sit for 10 minutes until it becomes frothy.

Mix the Dough: In a large mixing bowl, combine the bread flour and salt. Add the yeast mixture and olive oil. Mix until a sticky dough forms.

Kneading: Transfer the dough to a floured surface and knead for 8-10 minutes until smooth and elastic. During the last few minutes of kneading, add the chopped anchovies, oregano, and black pepper to incorporate them evenly.

First Rise: Place the dough in a greased bowl, cover it with a damp cloth, and let it rise in a warm place for about 1 hour or until doubled in size.

Shape the Ciabatta: Punch down the dough and divide it into 2 equal portions. Shape each portion into a long, slightly flattened loaf and place them on a parchment-lined baking sheet.

Second Rise: Cover the loaves with a damp cloth and let them rise for another 30-40 minutes until slightly puffy.

Baking: Warm your oven to 425°F (220°C). Bake the loaves for 20-25 minutes or until golden brown and hollow-sounding when tapped on the bottom.

Cool and Serve: Remove the ciabatta from the oven and let it cool on a wire rack before slicing and serving.

Bill's Tip:

This ciabatta is delicious, served warm with a drizzle of olive oil, or used as a base for bruschetta. The anchovies add a rich, savory flavor.

CHAPTER 9:

SOURDOUGH BREAD

―――――――――――――――――――――――――――――――――――

HOW TO MAKE A SOURDOUGH STARTER

Ingredients:
- 1 cup (120 g) whole wheat flour
- ½ cup (120 ml) water

Equipment:
- A glass jar or non-reactive container
- A cloth or lid to cover the jar (allowing some airflow)

Instructions:

DAY 1:

Mix Ingredients: Combine 1 cup of whole wheat flour and ½ cup of water in a clean glass jar. Stir until you have a thick, paste-like mixture.

Cover and Rest: Loosely cover the jar with a cloth or a lid that allows some airflow. Let it sit at room temperature (70-75°F/21-24°C) for 24 hours.

DAY 2:
Check for Activity: You may see some bubbles forming, which is a good sign that wild yeast is starting to develop. Feed the Starter: Discard half the starter (about ½ cup). Add ½ cups of all-purpose or whole wheat flour and ¼ cups of water. Stir to combine.

Cover and Rest: Loosely cover again and let it sit at room temperature for another 24 hours.

DAY 3–5:
Continue Feeding: Repeat the feeding process every 24 hours. Discard half the starter, then add ½ cup of flour and ¼ cup of water. Stir, cover, and let it rest.

Watch for Activity: You should notice more bubbles over the next few days, and the starter should rise and fall. It should develop a pleasant, tangy aroma.

DAY 6–7:
Increase Feedings: As the starter becomes more active, you may need to feed it twice daily (morning and evening). Continue discarding half and feeding with ½ cup of flour and ¼ cup of water.

Ready to Use:
Mature Starter: After 7 days, your starter should be bubbly, doubled in size between feedings, and have a tangy smell. This indicates it's ready to be used in baking.

Using the Starter in a Bread Machine

Substitution: Use the sourdough starter to replace a portion of the flour and water in your bread recipe. Typically, 1 cup (240g) of starter can replace about ½ cup of flour and ½ cup of water.

Process: Add the starter and the other wet ingredients to the bread machine pan, then add the flour and other dry ingredients. Use the «Basic» or «Whole Wheat» cycle, depending on your recipe. If your bread machine allows custom settings, you may need to adjust the rise time.

HOW TO STORE YOUR STARTER

Short-Term Storage:
If baking regularly, keep your starter on the kitchen counter and continue feeding it daily. This keeps it active and ready for baking.

Long-Term Storage:
If you're not baking often, store the starter in the refrigerator. Once a week, take it out, let it come to room temperature, and feed it with ½ cup of flour and ¼ cup of water.

Allow it to sit at room temperature for a few hours to reactivate the yeast before returning it to the refrigerator. This regular feeding helps maintain a healthy and active starter.

101

Bill's Tips:

Sourdough Discard: Don't throw away the discard! It can be used in recipes such as pancakes, sauces, muffins, and other baked goods. This reduces waste and adds a delightful tangy flavor to your dishes.

Maintaining Your Starter: Watch the consistency and smell of your starter. If it develops a pink or orange tint or a strong, unpleasant odor, it's best to discard it and start over. A healthy starter should have a pleasant, tangy aroma and be bubbly and active.

Rising Time: Let your dough rise longer before baking for a tangier flavor. If you're short on time, using the «rapid» setting will yield good results, though the sourdough taste will be milder. Always watch the dough's consistency during kneading and adjust with a little extra flour or water as needed for a smooth, elastic dough.

These guidelines will help you create a robust sourdough starter and maintain it effectively for your bread machine recipes.

Sourdough Starter Variations:
For variations like rye, gluten-free, and popular starters, follow the same instructions as the basic starter. Just substitute the flour with the type you're using for your variation.

RYE SOURDOUGH STARTER

Ingredients:
- 1 cup (120g) rye flour
- 1 cup (240ml) warm water (70-80°F / 21-27°C)

Bill's Tip:

Rye flour is rich in nutrients that promote fermentation. If you're using this starter for bread, you might need to adjust the water content in your recipe, as rye flour absorbs more water than all-purpose flour.

GLUTEN-FREE SOURDOUGH STARTER

Ingredients:

- ½ cup (60g) gluten-free all-purpose flour
- ½ cup (120ml) warm water (70-80°F / 21-27°C)

Bill's Tip:

Gluten-free starters can be slower to develop than wheat starters. Be patient and use gluten-free flour that contains a blend of different starches and flours to encourage fermentation.

POPULAR SOURDOUGH STARTER

Ingredients:

- 1 cup (120g) all-purpose flour
- 1 cup (240ml) warm water (70-80°F / 21-27°C)

Bill's Tip:

For best results, use filtered or distilled water to avoid chlorine, which can inhibit yeast growth. This starter is versatile and can be used for various sourdough recipes.

REACTIVATING LIEVITO MADRE DISIDRATO STARTER

Lievito Madre Disidrato is a dehydrated version of the traditional Lievito Madre starter. It's designed for convenience and can be reactivated or used directly in recipes. Here's how you can use **Lievito Madre Disidrato** to create a starter or incorporate it directly into your baking:

Ingredients:

- 50 g lievito madre disidrato
- 100 g all-purpose flour
- 50 ml water at room temperature

Instructions:

DAY 1 - INITIAL ACTIVATION:

In a bowl, mix the Lievito Madre Disidrato with the flour and water until a smooth dough forms.

Knead the dough briefly, shape it into a ball, and place it in a jar or a bowl.

Cover the container with a clean cloth or plastic wrap and let it rest at room temperature for 12-24 hours or until the dough has doubled.

DAY 2 TO DAY 3 - FEEDINGS:

After the initial rise, remove half of the dough and discard it.

Feed the remaining dough 100g of flour and 50ml of water.

Knead, cover, and let it rest again at room temperature for another 12-24 hours.

Repeat this process once more on Day 3. By the end of Day 3, your Lievito Madre should be active and ready to use.

Maintenance:

Store the starter in the refrigerator and feed it weekly if you're baking regularly.

For longer storage, feed every 10-14 days, following the same feeding process.

Using Lievito Madre Disidrato Directly in Recipes

You can also use Lievito Madre Disidrato directly in recipes without reactivating it first:

Substitution in Recipes:

Substitute 50g of Lievito Madre Disidrato for about 100g of fresh starter.

Adjust the hydration in your recipe slightly, as the desiderata might absorb more water.

Bill's Tip:

«*Lievito Madre Disidrato is a fantastic time-saver for those who want to enjoy the benefits of a natural starter without lengthy maintenance. Just adjust your hydration levels and give it a few extra hours to rise if you're using it directly in a recipe. It's perfect for traditional Italian breads like Panettone or Focaccia.*»

ORIGINAL SOURDOUGH BREAD

DIFFICULTY: EASY

Ingredients:

- 3 cups bread flour (360g)
- 1 ¼ cups water (300ml)
- ½ cup sourdough starter (120g)
- 1 ½ teaspoons salt (7.5g)
- 1 tablespoon sugar (12g)
- 1 tablespoon olive oil (14g)

Instructions:

Mixing Ingredients: Add the water and sourdough starter to the bread pan. Add the flour, salt, sugar, and olive oil on top.

Kneading and Rising:

Kneading: Knead the dough using the «Dough» or «Manual» setting. This usually takes about 20–30 minutes.

First Rise: After kneading, let the dough rise in the bread machine (still on the «Dough» setting) until it doubles. This may take 2-4 hours, depending on your starter's temperature and strength.

Final Rise and Baking:

Final Rise: If your bread machine has a «Sourdough» or «French» setting, you can use that for the final rise and bake. If not, after the first rise, you can let it rise a second time for about 1-2 hours before manually starting the «Bake» cycle.

Baking: Once the dough has risen, bake the bread using the «Bake» or «Sourdough» setting, depending on your machine.

Cooling: Once baking is complete, take the bread out of the pan. Allow it to cool on a wire rack for at least 30 minutes before slicing.

Nutritional Information:

180 kcal, 4g fat, 0g sat fat, 0mg cholesterol, 320mg sodium, 30g carbs, 1g fiber, 1g sugar, 5g protein.

Bill's Tip:

For a more pronounced sourdough flavor, you can let the dough rise overnight in the refrigerator after the first rise. Just bring it back to room temperature before the final rise and baking. This will enhance the tanginess and depth of flavor in your loaf.

104

In the following recipes, I included active dry yeast as a «safety net» for a couple of reasons, especially when using a bread machine:

Consistency: Bread machines are designed for more controlled, predictable results. Adding a small amount of active dry yeast ensures that the dough rises consistently, even if your sourdough starter is not at its peak activity. This is particularly important in bread machines, which follow strict kneading, growing, and baking cycles.

Time Constraints: To develop the right texture and flavor, traditional sourdough often requires longer rising times, sometimes up to 8-12 hours. However, bread machines typically have shorter rise times. Adding a bit of yeast helps compensate for the shorter rise periods, ensuring the bread achieves a good volume and structure.

Environmental Factors: Factors like room temperature, humidity, and the specific strength of your sourdough starter can vary. Including a small amount of active dry yeast helps mitigate the impact of these variables, leading to more reliable results across different conditions.

Flavor Balance: Even with a small amount of added yeast, the dominant flavor profile will still come from the sourdough starter, especially in longer fermentation recipes. The yeast mainly assists with the rise, not the flavor.

However, you can omit the active dry yeast if you prefer to rely solely on your sourdough starter and have the flexibility to allow longer rising times. Just be prepared for potentially longer rise periods and keep an eye on the dough to ensure it's growing properly.

CLASSIC SOURDOUGH BREAD

DIFFICULTY: BASIC

Ingredients:

- 3 cups (360g) bread flour
- 1 ¼ cups (300ml) water
- 1 cup (240g) sourdough starter (fed and bubbly)
- 2 tablespoons (24g) sugar
- 1 ½ teaspoons (7.5g) salt
- ½ teaspoon (2g) active dry yeast

Nutritional Information:

160 kcal, 2g fat, 0g sat fat, 0mg cholesterol, 300mg sodium, 32g carbs, 1g fiber, 1g sugar, 4g protein.

Instructions:

Add water to the bread pan.

Add flour, sugar, and salt. Mix to combine.

Make a well in the center of the dry ingredients and add the sourdough starter.

Sprinkle yeast over the top of the starter.

Select the «Sourdough» setting on your bread machine.

When the machine signals for additional ingredients, add ¼ cup (40g) mixed seeds (e.g., sunflower, pumpkin, flax).

Allow the bread to bake according to the machine's instructions.

Carefully remove the bread from the pan after the baking cycle finishes. Place the bread on a wire rack and let it cool completely before slicing.

Bill's Tip:

Allow the dough to rise longer before baking for a tangier flavor. If you're in a hurry, using the «rapid» setting will still produce good results but with a milder sourdough taste.

WHOLE WHEAT SOURDOUGH BREAD

DIFFICULTY: BASIC

Ingredients:

- 2 cups (240g) whole wheat flour
- 1 cup (120g) bread flour
- 1 ¼ cups (300ml) water
- 1 cup (240g) sourdough starter (fed and bubbly)
- 2 tablespoons (24g) honey
- 1 ½ teaspoons (7.5g) salt
- ½ teaspoon (2g) active dry yeast

Nutritional Information:

170 kcal, 2g fat, 0g sat fat, 0mg cholesterol, 310mg sodium, 34g carbs, 3g fiber, 5g sugar, 5g protein.

Instructions:

Add water to the bread pan.

Add whole wheat flour, bread flour, honey, and salt. Mix well.

Make a well in the center and add the sourdough starter.

Sprinkle yeast over the starter.

Select the «Whole Wheat» setting on your bread machine.

When the machine signals for additional ingredients, add ¼ cup (40g) of rolled oats or sunflower seeds.

Bake as per the machine's instructions.

Let cool before slicing.

Bill's Tip: *Whole wheat flour can make the dough denser. Adding a small amount of vital wheat gluten can help improve the texture if it is too thick.*

RYE SOURDOUGH BREAD

DIFFICULTY: INTERMEDIATE

Ingredients:

- 1 ½ cups (180g) rye flour
- 1 ½ cups (180g) whole wheat flour
- 1 ¼ cups (300ml) water
- 1 cup (240g) sourdough starter (fed and bubbly)
- 2 tablespoons (24g) molasses
- 1 ½ teaspoons (7.5g) salt
- ½ teaspoon (2g) active dry yeast
- 1 tablespoon (8g) caraway seeds

Nutritional Information:

180 kcal, 1g fat, 0g sat fat, 0mg cholesterol, 290mg sodium, 37g carbs, 4g fiber, 5g sugar, 6g protein.

Instructions:

Add water to the bread pan.

Add rye flour, whole wheat flour, molasses, and salt. Mix thoroughly.

Make a well in the center and add the sourdough starter.

Sprinkle yeast over the starter.

Select the «Rye» or «Whole Wheat» setting on your bread machine.

When the machine signals for additional ingredients, add caraway seeds.

Bake as per the machine's instructions.

Allow to cool on a wire rack.

Bill's Tip: *Rye bread tends to be denser. For a lighter texture, combine rye and whole wheat flour.*

106

SEEDED SOURDOUGH BREAD

DIFFICULTY: INTERMEDIATE

Ingredients:

- 3 cups (360g) bread flour
- 1 ¼ cups (300ml) water
- 1 cup (240g) sourdough starter (fed and bubbly)
- 2 tablespoons (24g) sugar
- 1 ½ teaspoons (7.5g) salt
- ½ teaspoon (2g) active dry yeast
- ¼ cup (40g) mixed seeds (e.g., sunflower, sesame, pumpkin)

Nutritional Information:

190 kcal, 3g fat, 0g sat fat, 0mg cholesterol, 290mg sodium, 38g carbs, 2g fiber, 3g sugar, 6g protein.

Instructions:

Add water to the bread pan.

Add flour, sugar, and salt. Mix well.

Make a well in the center and add the sourdough starter.

Sprinkle yeast over the starter.

Select the «Sourdough» setting on your bread machine.

Add ¼ cup (40g) mixed seeds when the machine signals for additional ingredients.

Proceed with baking as directed by your machine.

Cool on a wire rack.

Bill's Tip:

Experiment with different seed combinations to find your favorite mix. Adding seeds enhances flavor and improves the bread's texture.

HERB SOURDOUGH BREAD

DIFFICULTY: INTERMEDIATE

Ingredients:

- 3 cups (360g) bread flour
- 1 ¼ cups (300ml) water
- 1 cup (240g) sourdough starter (fed and bubbly)
- 2 tablespoons (24g) sugar
- 1 ½ teaspoons (7.5g) salt
- ½ teaspoon (2g) active dry yeast
- 2 tablespoons (6g) dried rosemary or thyme

Nutritional Information:

180 kcal, 1g fat, 0g sat fat, 0mg cholesterol, 290mg sodium, 37g carbs, 1g fiber, 2g sugar, 6g protein.

Instructions:

Add water to the bread pan.

Add flour, sugar, and salt. Mix well.

Make a well in the center and add the sourdough starter.

Sprinkle yeast over the starter.

Select the «Sourdough» setting on your bread machine.

Add dried rosemary or thyme When the machine signals for additional ingredients.

Continue with the baking process.

Cool on a wire rack.

Bill's Tip:

Dried herbs enhance the bread's flavor. For a more intense flavor, try adding fresh herbs and dried ones.

SPELT SOURDOUGH BREAD

DIFFICULTY: INTERMEDIATE

Ingredients:

- 2 cups (240g) spelt flour
- 1 cup (120g) bread flour
- 1 ¼ cups (300ml) water
- 1 cup (240g) sourdough starter (fed and bubbly)
- 2 tablespoons (24g) honey
- 1 ½ teaspoons (7.5g) salt
- ½ teaspoon (2g) active dry yeast

Nutritional Information:

170 kcal, 1g fat, 0g sat fat, 0mg cholesterol, 270mg sodium, 35g carbs, 2g fiber, 3g sugar, 5g protein.

Instructions:

Add water to the bread pan.

Add spelt flour, bread flour, honey, and salt. Mix to combine.

Make a well in the center and add the sourdough starter.

Sprinkle yeast over the starter.

Select the «Whole Wheat» or «Sourdough» setting.

When the machine signals for additional ingredients, you can add a handful of chopped nuts if desired.

Proceed with the baking instructions.

Cool before slicing.

Bill's Tip: *Spelt flour can give the bread a unique flavor and texture. Mix spelt flour with bread flour for a lighter texture to ensure the best results.*

OLIVE SOURDOUGH BREAD

DIFFICULTY: ADVANCED

Ingredients:

- 3 cups (360g) bread flour
- 1 ¼ cups (300ml) water
- 1 cup (240g) sourdough starter (fed and bubbly)
- 2 tablespoons (24g) sugar
- 1 ½ teaspoons (7.5g) salt
- ½ teaspoon (2g) active dry yeast
- ½ cup (80g) chopped olives

Nutritional Information:

180 kcal, 3g fat, 0g sat fat, 0mg cholesterol, 290mg sodium, 33g carbs, 1g fiber, 2g sugar, 5g protein.

Instructions:

Add water to the bread pan.

Add flour, sugar, and salt. Mix thoroughly.

Make a well in the center and add the sourdough starter.

Sprinkle yeast over the starter.

Select the «Sourdough» setting on your bread machine.

When the machine signals for additional ingredients, add chopped olives.

Continue with the baking process.

Let cool on a wire rack.

Bill's Tip:

For extra flavor, try using different types of olives, such as Kalamata or green olives, depending on your preference.

CHEDDAR HERB SOURDOUGH BREAD

Ingredients:

- 3 cups (360g) bread flour
- 1 ¼ cups (300ml) water
- 1 cup (240g) sourdough starter (fed and bubbly)
- 2 tablespoons (24g) sugar
- 1 ½ teaspoons (7.5g) salt
- ½ teaspoon (2g) active dry yeast
- 1 cup (120g) shredded cheddar cheese
- 2 tablespoons (6g) dried mixed herbs (e.g., oregano, basil)

Nutritional Information:

210 kcal, 6g fat, 3g sat fat, 10mg cholesterol, 300mg sodium, 33g carbs, 1g fiber, 2g sugar, 7g protein.

Instructions:

Add water to the bread pan.

Add flour, sugar, and salt. Mix well.

Make a well in the center and add the sourdough starter.

Sprinkle yeast over the starter.

Select the «Sourdough» setting on your bread machine.

add shredded cheddar cheese and dried mixed herbs when the machine signals for additional ingredients.

Continue with the baking process.

Cool on a wire rack.

Bill's Tip:

Adding cheese and herbs enhances the flavor and makes the bread more decadent. For a stronger cheese flavor, try using sharp cheddar.

MULTIGRAIN SOURDOUGH BREAD

Ingredients:

- 2 cups (240g) bread flour
- 1 cup (120g) whole wheat flour
- ½ cup (60g) rolled oats
- ¼ cup (40g) sunflower seeds
- ¼ cup (40g) flax seeds
- 1 ¼ cups (300ml) water
- 1 cup (240g) sourdough starter (fed and bubbly)
- 2 tablespoons (24g) honey
- 1 ½ teaspoons (7.5g) salt
- ½ teaspoon (2g) active dry yeast

Nutritional Information:

180 kcal, 1g fat, 0g sat fat, 0mg cholesterol, 290mg sodium, 37g carbs, 1g fiber, 2g sugar, 6g protein.

Instructions:

Add water to the bread pan.

Add bread, whole wheat, rolled oats, sunflower, and flax seeds. Mix to combine.

Make a well in the center and add the sourdough starter.

Sprinkle yeast over the starter.

Select the «Whole Wheat» or «Multigrain» setting on your bread machine.

When the machine signals for additional ingredients, add extra oats or seeds if desired.

Proceed with the baking instructions.

Cool on a wire rack.

Bill's Tip:

Dried herbs enhance the bread's flavor. For a more intense flavor, try adding fresh herbs and dried ones.

CINNAMON RAISIN SOURDOUGH BREAD

Ingredients:

- 3 cups (360g) bread flour
- 1 ¼ cups (300ml) water
- 1 cup (240g) sourdough starter (fed and bubbly)
- 2 tablespoons (24g) sugar
- 1 ½ teaspoons (7.5g) salt
- ½ teaspoon (2g) active dry yeast
- 1 cup (150g) raisins
- 2 tablespoons (12g) ground cinnamon

Instructions:

Add water to the bread pan.

Add flour, sugar, and salt. Mix thoroughly.

Make a well in the center and add the sourdough starter.

Sprinkle yeast over the starter.

Select the «Sourdough» setting on your bread machine.

Add raisins and ground cinnamon When the machine signals for additional ingredients.

Continue with the baking process.

Let cool on a wire rack.

Nutritional Information:

220 kcal, 2g fat, 0g sat fat, 0mg cholesterol, 320mg sodium, 45g carbs, 3g fiber, 15g sugar, 6g protein.

Bill's Tip:

For an extra touch of sweetness, you can add a cinnamon-sugar swirl by mixing cinnamon and sugar and folding it into the dough during the final kneading phase.

CHAPTER 10:

LIEVITO MADRE DISIDRATO
(Italian Sourdough Bread)

Lievito Madre Disidrato is a dried form of the traditional Italian starter, "lievito madre," used for making bread and other baked goods. This product is based on natural yeast, giving the dough a distinctive flavor, aroma, and texture.

While **Lievito Madre Disidrato** isn't as widely available as regular yeast, you can find it in specialty Italian food stores or online shops that carry European ingredients.

This product is perfect for baking bread with a rich texture and flavor.

Using **Lievito Madre Disidrato** in a bread machine allows you to achieve a more complex taste and aroma that's difficult to replicate with regular yeast. Recipes often require a longer rising time, which helps to develop the full flavor.

TRADITIONAL SOURDOUGH

Ingredients:

- 2 ¾ cups bread flour (330g)
- 60g lievito madre disidrato
- 1 ½ teaspoons salt (7.5g)
- 1 ¼ cups water (300ml)
- 2 tablespoons olive oil (30ml)

Nutritional Information:

160 kcal, 4g fat, 0.5g sat fat, 0mg cholesterol, 320mg sodium, 28g carbs, 2g fiber, 1g sugar, 5g protein.

Instructions:

Mixing Ingredients: Pour the water into the bread pan. Add the olive oil. Next, add the flour and salt. Finally, scatter the Lievito Madre Disidrato on top.

Kneading and Rising: Select the «Whole Wheat» or «French Bread» program, depending on your machine's settings. Choose the «Medium» loaf size and your preferred crust color. The bread machine will handle the kneading, rising, and baking.

Baking: Once baking is complete, take the bread out of the pan. Allow it to cool on a wire rack for at least 30 minutes before slicing.

Bill's Tip:

For an extra-crusty exterior, remove the dough before the last rise, shape it into a round, and bake it on a preheated stone in your oven at 450°F (230°C) for 20-25 minutes.

PAN BRIOCHE

Ingredients:

- 2 ½ cups bread flour (300g)
- 75g lievito madre disidrato
- 3 tablespoons sugar (36g)
- 1 teaspoon salt (5g)
- ¼ cup softened butter (57g)
- 1 large egg + 1 yolk (total approx. 70g)
- ½ cup warm milk (120ml)
- 1 teaspoon vanilla extract (5ml)

Nutritional Information:

190 kcal, 7g fat, 4g sat fat, 50mg cholesterol, 180mg sodium, 28g carbs, 1g fiber, 8g sugar, 5g protein.

Instructions:

Mixing Ingredients: Pour the warm milk (110°F/43°C) into the bread pan. Add the eggs and vanilla extract. Next, add the flour, sugar, and salt. Scatter the Lievito Madre Disidrato over the top. Finally, add the softened butter in small pieces.

Kneading and Rising: Select the «Sweet Bread» program on your bread machine. Choose the «Medium» loaf size setting and your preferred crust color (light, medium, or dark). The machine will knead the dough, allow it to rise, and bake it for about 3-4 hours.

Baking: Once baking is complete, take the bread out of the pan. Allow it to cool on a wire rack for at least 30 minutes before slicing.

Bill's Tip: *To get an even fluffier texture, use the dough setting to let it rise twice before baking. Brushing milk on top before baking will also give your brioche a beautiful golden sheen.*

PANETTONE

Ingredients:

- 50g lievito madre disidrato
- ⅓ cup sugar (67g)
- 1 teaspoon salt (5g)
- ⅓ cup softened butter (75g)
- 2 large eggs (100g)
- ¼ cup warm milk (60ml)
- 1 teaspoon vanilla extract (5ml)
- ½ cup raisins (80g)
- ¼ cup candied orange peel (40g)
- 1 teaspoon lemon zest (2g)

Nutritional Information:

230 kcal, 9g fat, 5g sat fat, 60mg cholesterol, 160mg sodium, 34g carbs, 1g fiber, 12g sugar, 4g protein.

Instructions:

Mixing Ingredients: Pour the warm milk (110°F/43°C) into the bread pan. Add the eggs and vanilla extract. Next, add the flour, sugar, and salt. Scatter the Lievito Madre Disidrato over the top. Finally, add the softened butter in small pieces.

Adding Mix-Ins: Add the raisins, candied orange peel, and lemon zest during the second kneading cycle.

Kneading and Rising: Select the «Sweet Bread» program. Choose the «Medium» loaf size setting and your preferred crust color. The bread machine will take care of kneading, rising, and baking.

Baking: Remove the panettone from the pan and let it cool on a wire rack. Dust with powdered sugar before serving.

Bill's Tip:

To give your panettone that traditional tall shape, use a paper mold inside the bread machine pan or transfer the dough to an oven-safe mold for the final rise and bake.

COLOMBA PASQUALE

Ingredients:

- 2 ½ cups bread flour (300g)
- 75g lievito madre disidrato
- ⅓ cup sugar (67g)
- 1 teaspoon salt (5g)
- ⅓ cup softened butter (75g)
- 2 large eggs (100g)
- ¼ cup warm milk (60ml)
- 1 tablespoon orange zest (6g)
- 1 teaspoon almond extract (5ml)
- ⅓ cup slivered almonds (40g)
- ¼ cup pearl sugar (40g)

Nutritional Information:

240 kcal, 10g fat, 5g sat fat, 55mg cholesterol, 160mg sodium, 33g carbs, 1g fiber, 12g sugar, 5g protein.

Instructions:

Mixing Ingredients: Pour the warm milk into the bread pan. Add the eggs, orange zest, and almond extract. Next, add the flour, sugar, and salt. Scatter the Lievito Madre Disidrato over the top, then add the softened butter in pieces.

Kneading and Rising: Select the «Sweet Bread» program. Choose the «Medium» loaf size setting and crust color. The bread machine will handle kneading, rising, and baking.

Baking: Just before baking, sprinkle the top with slivered almonds and pearl sugar. After the baking cycle finishes, carefully remove the bread from the pan. Place the bread on a wire rack and let it cool completely before slicing.

Bill's Tip:

Shape this dough into a dove for a traditional Colomba look. If your machine allows, you can also bake it in a dove-shaped paper mold.

PANE TOSCANO

Ingredients:

- 2 ¾ cups bread flour (330g)
- 60g lievito madre disidrato
- 1 teaspoon salt (5g)
- 1 ¼ cups water (300ml)
- 1 tablespoon olive oil (15ml)

Nutritional Information:

170 kcal, 3g fat, 0.5g sat fat, 0mg cholesterol, 150mg sodium, 30g carbs, 1g fiber, 0g sugar, 5g protein.

Instructions:

Mixing Ingredients: Pour the water into the bread pan. Add the olive oil. Next, add the flour and salt. Finally, scatter the Lievito Madre Disidrato on top.

Kneading and Rising: Select the «French Bread» or «Basic Bread» program. Choose the «Medium» loaf size and your preferred crust color.

Baking: After the baking cycle finishes, carefully remove the bread from the pan. Place the bread on a wire rack and let it cool completely before slicing.

Bill's Tip:

Pane Toscano is traditionally unsalted, which makes it perfect for pairing with savory dishes. Try it with a drizzle of olive oil and a sprinkle of sea salt.

CIABATTA

Ingredients:

- 2 ½ cups bread flour (300g)
- 50g lievito madre disidrato
- 1 ½ teaspoons salt (7.5g)
- 1 ¼ cups water (300ml)
- 2 tablespoons olive oil (30ml)

Instructions:

Mixing Ingredients: Pour the water into the bread pan. Add the olive oil. Next, add the flour and salt. Scatter the Lievito Madre Disidrato over the top.

Kneading and Rising: Select the «French Bread» program. Choose the «Medium» loaf size setting and your preferred crust color.

Baking: After the baking cycle, remove the ciabatta and cool on a wire rack. Slice and enjoy.

Nutritional Information:

180 kcal, 5g fat, 0.5g sat fat, 0mg cholesterol, 320mg sodium, 28g carbs, 1g fiber, 0g sugar, 5g protein.

Bill's Tip: *For a true ciabatta texture, remove the dough after the last rise, shape it into a flat, oblong loaf, and bake on a preheated stone in your oven.*

FOCACCIA

Ingredients:

- 2 ½ cups bread flour (300g)
- 50g lievito madre disidrato
- 1 ½ teaspoons salt (7.5g)
- 1 ¼ cups water (300ml)
- 3 tablespoons olive oil (45ml)
- 1 tablespoon fresh rosemary (1g)
- 1 teaspoon sea salt (5g)

Instructions:

Mixing Ingredients: Pour the water into the bread pan. Add 2 tablespoons of olive oil. Next, add the flour and salt. Scatter the Lievito Madre Disidrato over the top.

Kneading and Rising: Select the «Dough» program. Once the cycle is complete, transfer the dough to a greased baking sheet. Flatten the dough with your fingers, drizzle with the remaining olive oil, and sprinkle with fresh rosemary and sea salt.

Baking: Bake in a preheated oven at 400°F (200°C) for 20-25 minutes or until golden brown.

Nutritional Information:

190 kcal, 8g fat, 1g sat fat, 0mg cholesterol, 330mg sodium, 28g carbs, 1g fiber, 0g sugar, 5g protein.

Bill's Tip:

For extra flavor, add some sliced cherry tomatoes or olives on top before baking. Serve warm with a side of olive oil and balsamic vinegar for dipping.

CHAPTER 11:

DIET-FRIENDLY RECIPES: GLUTEN-FREE BREAD

INTRODUCTION TO GLUTEN-FREE BREAD

Baking gluten-free bread in a bread machine can be a rewarding experience, but it requires careful attention to detail. Unlike traditional wheat-based breads, gluten-free doughs often lack the elasticity and structure that gluten provides, making them more challenging to work with. However, with the right ingredients, techniques, and patience, you can create delicious gluten-free loaves that rival their gluten-filled counterparts. Whether baking for dietary reasons or exploring new flavors, gluten-free bread can be just as satisfying and enjoyable.

PREVENTING CROSS-CONTAMINATION IN YOUR BREAD MACHINE

When working with gluten-free ingredients, one of the most critical steps is ensuring your bread machine is free from any traces of gluten. Cross-contamination can easily occur if your machine has been used for regular wheat-based breads without proper cleaning. Here's how to avoid it:

Thorough Cleaning: Before using your bread machine for gluten-free bread, thoroughly clean all removable parts, including the pan, kneading blade, and lid. Use warm, soapy water and a clean sponge or cloth to remove flour or dough residues. Pay special attention to the corners and seams where gluten can hide.

Dedicated Equipment: Consider having a separate bread machine or a separate bread pan and kneading blade exclusively for gluten-free baking. This minimizes the risk of cross-contamination and ensures a safe baking environment.

Ingredient Management: Store your gluten-free flours and ingredients separately from regular flours to avoid cross-contamination. Use clearly labeled containers and dedicated measuring tools to keep everything gluten-free. Cycle Check: Some bread machines have special gluten-free cycles that adjust the kneading, rising, and baking times to better suit gluten-free dough. Use this setting if available to help achieve the best results.

First Use Precautions: If you're using a new bread machine or one that has only been used for gluten-free baking, run a cycle with a simple, inexpensive gluten-free dough to ensure there's no residual gluten. Discard the first loaf if needed, and be extra cautious.

You can confidently create safe, delicious gluten-free bread by following these steps, knowing your bread machine is ready. **Happy baking!**

VARIETIES OF GLUTEN-FREE FLOUR

AMARANTH

Amaranth is a grain high in protein and fiber, and its flour is an excellent choice for gluten-free baking. It has a dense texture and a rich, delicate nutty flavor. It is wonderful for making bread, muffins, and pies. Due to its high protein content, amaranth flour helps create lush and juicy baked goods. It's important to remember that amaranth flour has an intense flavor, so it's best to use it with other flour to balance the flavor.

BUCKWHEAT

Buckwheat flour has a natural nutty aroma and a sweet taste. Buckwheat flour contributes to the luxurious texture and deep flavor of baked items because of its high fiber and protein content. However, it is worth noting that buckwheat flour has a distinctive flavor that may differ from everyone's taste. Therefore, for best results, it is recommended to combine buckwheat flour with other gluten-free flour to create a balance in the flavor and texture of your baked goods.

MILLET FLOUR

Millet flour has a light texture that can add fluffiness and lightness to baked goods. Its neutral flavor allows you to use it in various baking recipes.

QUINOA

Quinoa flour has a medium density and unique taste but is slightly nutty. However, it's worth noting that quinoa is best used with other flours to balance flavor. Quinoa also leavens quickly, so using it with different ingredients is recommended.

SORGHUM FLOUR

Sorghum flour is a product made from the seeds of the sorghum plant, also known as sorghum corn. Due to its smooth texture, sorghum flour can be used alone or in combination with other flour to add a richer flavor and texture to baked goods.

TEFF

Teff flour has an intense flavor, light nutty undertones, and a slightly sweet aroma. Its excellent binding properties make it a good ingredient for gluten-free bread, muffins, biscuits, and other baked goods. It is a heavy flour with a strong flavor. Teff flour helps create a lush texture and rich taste in baked goods, but it should be used in small amounts.

CHIA

Chia flour has a delicate flavor and texture. Because of its binding properties, it helps maintain the shape and texture of baked goods and gives them additional nutrients. Because of its neutral flavor, chia flour can easily be incorporated into various gluten-free baking recipes.

PSYLLIUM

Because of its unique binding qualities, psyllium flour can enhance the structure and texture of gluten-free baked products. When using psyllium flour in gluten-free baking recipes, it is essential to follow the proportion guidelines, as psyllium can significantly affect the texture and consistency of the dough. The psyllium husk binds the flour and gives it elasticity and firmness. It is best to use whole psyllium (not powder) in baking.

SOY

Soy flour is usually light yellow or beige. Its texture may be slightly coarse, and its flavor may be neutral or somewhat nutty. Soy flour can be used independently or mixed with other flour for optimal texture.

RICE FLOUR

White Rice has a more neutral flavor and lighter texture, making it ideal for gluten-free baking, especially for those who prefer a more neutral taste. It should be used in small quantities so that the baked goods are not wet.

BROWN RICE

Brown Rice is made from unrefined brown rice that retains its hull and germ. Brown flour has a richer flavor and coarser texture, which adds character and nutrition to baked goods.

You may use rice flour alone or in combination with other flour to get the right flavor and texture. Both are great options for baking without gluten. They are readily available in supermarkets and health food stores. If required, make sure the product is certified gluten-free.

TAPIOCA

Tapioca flour is made from starch derived from the roots of cassava, also known as cassava or tapioca. It has a neutral flavor and light texture and is very good as a thickener. It binds ingredients well and helps create the desired consistency in baked goods and other dishes. However, baked goods will be sticky if you put less in.

BEANS AND BEAN FLOUR

Beans and bean flour have a thicker texture and an intense flavor, which are characteristic of each type of bean. For texture and taste, use them alone or with other flours.

CHICKPEA FLOUR

It is made from ground chickpeas and has a rich taste and texture. Therefore, its use may require experimenting with other flour or blends to achieve the desired taste and texture.

FLAXSEED MEAL

Flaxseed meal is made from ground flax seeds. It is better to grind whole grains at home. Flax flour has a specific texture, which can change the consistency of the batter and add fluffiness to the baking.

COCONUT FLOUR

Coconut flour has a distinctive flavor and aroma of coconut, which can give a unique flavor to biscuits and pastries. It can add more fluffiness and a thicker consistency to biscuits, mainly when used in large quantities.

CORN FLOUR AND CORNSTARCH

Corn flour has a soft, creamy texture similar to traditional wheat flour. It can add fluffiness and lightness to baking. It has a neutral flavor with light, malty notes.

Cornstarch has a beautiful, powdery texture and binds the liquid. It is used to ensure the quality and tenderness of baking. It has a neutral flavor.

Pay attention to the product label and ensure the manufacturer indicates that the product is gluten-free or free from gluten contamination.

NUT FLOUR

Nut flour is made from crushed nuts, such as almonds, peanuts, and walnuts. Its intense, nutty flavor adds character and flavor to your dishes. The texture of nut flour varies depending on the type of nut and how it is processed, but it is often coarse and grainy. The oils in nut flours are excellent binders for various mixtures.

OATS (CERTIFIED)

Certified gluten-free oat flour is made from oat flakes that have been grown, processed, and stored in a way that minimizes the risk of gluten contamination.

Oat flour has a mild and neutral flavor, making it a versatile ingredient for various recipes. The method of production determines its texture.

POTATO

Potato flour has a light texture and neutral flavor. It can add softness and lightness to baked goods and has good binding properties.

Potato starch is like tapioca starch and is also used as a binder to mix different types of flour.

GLUTEN-FREE FLOUR BLENDS FOR BAKING BREAD

These blends can be customized to suit gluten-free baking needs and provide various textures and flavors.

ALL-PURPOSE GLUTEN-FREE MIX 1
Blend: Equal parts rice flour (white or brown), yellow corn flour, and buckwheat flour.

Best For: Versatile use in various baked goods.

ALL-PURPOSE GLUTEN-FREE MIX 2
Blend: 2 parts white rice flour, 1 part tapioca flour, 1 part potato flour.

Best For: Versatile use in various baked goods.

CLASSIC WHITE BREAD MIX
Blend: 2 parts corn white flour, 1 part potato flour, 1 part rice flour.

Best For: Soft and airy white bread.

HEARTY DARK BREAD MIX
Blend: Equal parts corn flour, brown rice flour, millet flour, and optionally amaranth or black bean flour.

Best For: Rich, dense bread with a robust flavor.

RUSTIC CIABATTA MIX

Blend: 2 parts white corn flour, 1-part brown rice flour, 1 part tapioca flour.

Best For: Creating a chewy, rustic ciabatta.

PASTRY FLOUR MIX

Blend: 1-part white rice flour, 1 part potato starch, 1 part tapioca flour.

Best For: Light, tender pastries and pies.

PANCAKE & WAFFLE MIX

Blend: 2 parts brown rice flour, 1 part almond flour, 1 part tapioca starch.

Best For: Fluffy pancakes and crispy waffles.

COOKIE FLOUR MIX

Blend: 1 part sorghum flour, 1 part almond flour, 1 part potato starch.

Best For: Chewy and soft cookies.

PIZZA DOUGH MIX

Blend: 2 parts white rice flour, 1 part tapioca flour, 1 part chickpea flour.

Best For: Crispy and chewy pizza crusts.

MUFFIN & QUICK BREAD MIX

Blend: 2 parts oat flour, 1 part almond flour, 1 part tapioca starch.

Best For: Moist and flavorful muffins and quick breads.

BISCUIT & SCONE MIX

Blend: 1-part white rice flour, 1 part potato starch, 1-part sweet rice flour.

Best For: Flaky biscuits and tender scones.

PASTA FLOUR MIX

Blend: 60% white corn flour, 30% yellow corn flour, 10% brown rice flour.

Best For: Making gluten-free pasta with a good texture and flavor.

119

GLUTEN-FREE BREAD RECIPES

CLASSIC GLUTEN-FREE WHITE BREAD

Ingredients:

- 4 cups gluten-free flour blend (500g) – All-Purpose Gluten-Free Mix 2
- 2 teaspoons xanthan gum
- 2 teaspoons baking powder
- 1 teaspoon salt
- 1 tablespoon sugar (12g)
- ¼ cup olive oil (60ml)
- 1 ½ cups warm water (360ml)
- 1 teaspoon apple cider vinegar
- 3 large eggs, beaten

Instructions:

Preparation: Grease the bread pan with a non-stick spray. Ensure all ingredients are at room temperature.

Mixing: In a large mixing bowl, combine the gluten-free flour blend, xanthan gum, baking powder, salt, and sugar. Add the beaten eggs, olive oil, warm water, and apple cider vinegar. Mix until smooth.

Baking: Transfer the batter to the bread pan. Choose the gluten-free setting on your bread machine and initiate the cycle.

Cooling: Once baking is complete, carefully remove the bread from the machine. Set the bread on a wire rack and allow it to cool fully before cutting.

Nutritional Information:
(Per Slice)

Calories:150, Protein: 5g, Fat: 6g, Carbohydrates: 22g, Fiber: 2g, Sugar: 2g, Sodium: 220mg

Bill's Tip:

Ensure the batter is well-mixed but not overworked for a lighter texture. Add a touch of honey or agave syrup for a hint of sweetness.

GLUTEN-FREE WHOLE GRAIN BREAD WITH SUNFLOWER SEEDS

Ingredients:

- 2 ½ cups bread flour (300g)
- 75g lievito madre disidrato
- ⅓ cup sugar (67g)
- 1 teaspoon salt (5g)
- ⅓ cup softened butter (75g)
- 2 large eggs (100g)
- ¼ cup warm milk (60ml)
- 1 tablespoon orange zest (6g)
- 1 teaspoon almond extract (5ml)
- ⅓ cup slivered almonds (40g)
- ¼ cup pearl sugar (40g)

Nutritional Information:

(Per Slice)

Calories: 180, Protein: 6g, Fat: 7g,
Carbohydrates: 25g, Fiber: 4g,
Sugar: 2g, Sodium: 230mg

Bill's Tip:

Sunflower seeds can be toasted for extra flavor. Ensure the seeds are evenly mixed to avoid clumping.

Instructions:

Preparation: Grease the bread pan with a non-stick spray. Ensure all ingredients are at room temperature.

Mixing: In a large mixing bowl, combine the gluten-free whole grain flour blend, xanthan gum, baking powder, salt, and sugar. Add the beaten eggs, olive oil, warm water, and apple cider vinegar. Mix until smooth.

Additions: Stir in the sunflower seeds until evenly distributed.

Baking: Transfer the batter to the bread pan. Choose the gluten-free setting on your bread machine and initiate the cycle.

Cooling: Once baking is complete, carefully remove the bread from the machine. Set the bread on a wire rack and allow it to cool fully before cutting.

GLUTEN-FREE MILK BREAD

Ingredients:

- 4 cups gluten-free flour blend (500g) (mix of white rice flour, tapioca flour, and potato starch in equal parts)
- 1 ½ cups milk (360ml) (warm, about 110°F or 43°C)
- 2 large eggs (room temperature)
- 4 tablespoons unsalted butter (57g) (melted and slightly cooled)
- 3 tablespoons sugar (38g)
- 1 ½ teaspoons salt (8g)
- 2 ¼ teaspoons dry yeast (7g)

Nutritional Information:

(Per Slice)

Calories: 160, Protein: 3g,
Carbohydrates: 26g, Fat: 5g, Fiber: 2g,
Sugars: 3g

Bill's Tip:

Texture: If you prefer a softer crust, lightly brush the top with melted butter as soon as it comes out of the machine.
Storage: Wrap the bread in a clean kitchen towel and store it in an airtight container at room temperature for up to 3 days. For longer storage, slice and freeze the bread in portions.

Instructions:

Prep the Machine: Set your bread machine to the gluten-free cycle. Use the basic or rapid setting if your machine doesn't have a specific gluten-free setting.

Load the Ingredients: Add warm milk and melted butter to the bread machine pan. Follow with the eggs, sugar, and salt.

Add the Dry Ingredients: Carefully spoon the gluten-free flour blend into the liquid, ensuring it covers it. Make a small well in the center of the flour and add the yeast.

Start the Machine: Close the lid and start the cycle. Do not open the lid during the initial mixing and rising phases.

Monitor and Adjust: During the mixing phase, check the consistency. If the dough appears too dry, add a tablespoon of milk until it forms a soft, slightly sticky dough.

Baking: Allow the machine to complete the cycle. The bread should rise nicely and have a golden-brown crust.

Cool and Serve: Once baking is complete, carefully remove the bread from the machine. Set the bread on a wire rack and allow it to cool fully before cutting.

SUN-DRIED TOMATO & PARMESAN GLUTEN-FREE BREAD

Ingredients:

- 4 cups gluten-free flour blend (500g)
  - 2:1:1 ratio of rice flour, tapioca flour, and almond flour
- 2 teaspoons xanthan gum
- 2 teaspoons baking powder
- 1 ½ teaspoons salt
- 1 tablespoon sugar
- ¼ cup olive oil (60ml)
- 1 ½ cups warm water (360ml)
- 1 teaspoon apple cider vinegar
- 3 large eggs, beaten
- ½ cup sun-dried tomatoes (80g), chopped
- ½ cup Parmesan cheese (60g), grated

Nutritional Information:
(Per Slice)

Calories: 160, Protein: 6g, Fat: 8g, Carbohydrates: 19g, Fiber: 2g, Sugar: 2g, Sodium: 250mg

Instructions:

Preparation: Grease the bread pan with a non-stick spray. Ensure all ingredients are at room temperature.

Mixing: In a large mixing bowl, combine the gluten-free flour blend, xanthan gum, baking powder, salt, and sugar. Add the beaten eggs, olive oil, warm water, and apple cider vinegar. Mix until a smooth batter forms.

Additions: Gently fold the chopped sun-dried tomatoes and grated Parmesan cheese.

Baking: Transfer the batter to the bread pan. Choose the gluten-free setting on your bread machine and initiate the cycle.

Cooling: Once baking is complete, carefully remove the bread from the machine. Set the bread on a wire rack and allow it to cool fully before cutting.

Bill's Tip:

If you prefer a stronger flavor, increase the amount of sun-dried tomatoes and Parmesan. Make sure to squeeze excess oil from the sun-dried tomatoes to avoid adding too much moisture to the dough.

HERBED GLUTEN-FREE BREAD

Ingredients:

- 4 cups gluten-free flour blend (500g) - 2:1:1 ratio of rice flour, tapioca flour, and almond flour
- 2 teaspoons xanthan gum
- 2 teaspoons baking powder
- 1 ½ teaspoons salt
- 1 tablespoon sugar
- ¼ cup olive oil (60ml)
- 1 ½ cups warm water (360ml)
- 1 teaspoon apple cider vinegar
- 3 large eggs, beaten
- 2 tablespoons mixed dried herbs (e.g., rosemary, thyme, oregano)

Nutritional Information:

(Per Slice)

Calories:150, Protein: 5g, Fat: 6g,
Carbohydrates: 21g, Fiber: 3g,
Sugar: 2g, Sodium: 220mg

Instructions:

Preparation: Grease the bread pan with a non-stick spray. Ensure all ingredients are at room temperature.

Mixing: In a large mixing bowl, combine the gluten-free flour blend, xanthan gum, baking powder, salt, and sugar. Add the beaten eggs, olive oil, warm water, and apple cider vinegar. Mix until a smooth batter forms.

Additions: Stir in the mixed dried herbs until evenly distributed. Baking: Transfer the batter to the bread pan. Choose the gluten-free setting on your bread machine and initiate the cycle.

Cooling: Once baking is complete, carefully remove the bread from the machine. Set the bread on a wire rack and allow it to cool fully before cutting.

Bill's Tip:

Experiment with different herb combinations to match your taste preferences. Increase the amount of dried herbs for a stronger herb flavor.

PUMPKIN SPICE GLUTEN-FREE BREAD

Ingredients:

- 4 cups gluten-free flour blend (500g) - 2:1:1 ratio of rice flour, tapioca flour, and almond flour
- 2 teaspoons xanthan gum
- 2 teaspoons baking powder
- 1 teaspoon salt
- ½ cup sugar (100g)
- 1 teaspoon ground cinnamon
- ½ teaspoon ground nutmeg
- 1 cup pumpkin puree (240g)
- ¼ cup olive oil (60ml)
- 1 cup warm water (240ml)
- 1 teaspoon apple cider vinegar
- 3 large eggs, beaten

Nutritional Information:

(Per Slice)

Calories: 170, Protein: 5g, Fat: 6g,
Carbohydrates: 26g, Fiber: 3g,
Sugar: 10g, Sodium: 220mg

Instructions:

Preparation: Grease the bread pan with a non-stick spray. Ensure all ingredients are at room temperature.

Mixing: In a large mixing bowl, combine the gluten-free flour blend, xanthan gum, baking powder, salt, sugar, cinnamon, and nutmeg. Add the beaten eggs, pumpkin puree, olive oil, warm water, and apple cider vinegar. Mix until well combined.

Baking: Transfer the batter to the bread pan. Choose the gluten-free setting on your bread machine and initiate the cycle.

Cooling: Once baking is complete, carefully remove the bread from the machine. Set the bread on a wire rack and allow it to cool fully before cutting.

Bill's Tip:

Consider mixing chopped nuts or raisins for added texture and flavor. Ensure the pumpkin puree is well-drained to avoid excess moisture in the batter.

CINNAMON RAISIN GLUTEN-FREE BREAD

Ingredients:

- 4 cups gluten-free flour blend (500g) - 2:1:1 ratio of rice flour, tapioca flour, and almond flour
- 2 teaspoons xanthan gum
- 2 teaspoons baking powder
- 1 teaspoon salt
- ½ cup sugar (100g)
- 2 teaspoons ground cinnamon
- ½ cup raisins (80g)
- ¼ cup olive oil (60ml)
- 1 ½ cups warm water (360ml)
- 1 teaspoon apple cider vinegar
- 3 large eggs, beaten

Nutritional Information:
(Per Slice)

Calories: 160, Protein: 5g, Fat: 6g, Carbohydrates: 23g, Fiber: 2g, Sugar: 10g, Sodium: 220mg

Instructions:

Preparation: Grease the bread pan with a non-stick spray. Ensure all ingredients are at room temperature.

Mixing: In a large mixing bowl, combine the gluten-free flour blend, xanthan gum, baking powder, salt, sugar, and cinnamon. Add the beaten eggs, olive oil, warm water, and apple cider vinegar. Mix until smooth.

Additions: Fold in the raisins until evenly distributed.

Baking: Transfer the batter to the bread pan. Choose the gluten-free setting on your bread machine and initiate the cycle.

Cooling: Once baking is complete, carefully remove the bread from the machine. Set the bread on a wire rack and allow it to cool fully before cutting.

Bill's Tip: *To create a swirled cinnamon effect, sprinkle cinnamon sugar between the layers of batter. Ensure raisins are evenly distributed to avoid clumping.*

ALMOND FLOUR GLUTEN-FREE BREAD

Ingredients:
- 4 cups almond flour (500g)
- 2 teaspoons xanthan gum
- 2 teaspoons baking powder
- 1 ½ teaspoons salt
- 4 large eggs, beaten
- ¼ cup olive oil (60ml)
- 1 cup warm water (240ml)
- 1 teaspoon apple cider vinegar

Nutritional Information:
(Per Slice)

Calories: 180, Protein: 7g, Fat: 14g, Carbohydrates: 10g, Fiber: 2g, Sugar: 1g, Sodium: 230mg

Instructions:

Preparation: Grease the bread pan with a non-stick spray. Ensure all ingredients are at room temperature.

Mixing: In a large mixing bowl, combine the almond flour, xanthan gum, baking powder, and salt. Add the beaten eggs, olive oil, warm water, and apple cider vinegar. Mix until smooth.

Baking: Transfer the batter to the bread pan. Choose the gluten-free setting on your bread machine and initiate the cycle.

Cooling: Once baking is complete, carefully remove the bread from the machine. Set the bread on a wire rack and allow it to cool fully before cutting.

Bill's Tip: *Almond flour gives a denser texture; do not overmix. Add herbs or spices for added flavor.*

124

CHIA SEED GLUTEN-FREE BREAD

Ingredients:

- 4 cups gluten-free flour blend (500g) - 2:1:1 ratio of rice flour, tapioca flour, and almond flour
- 2 teaspoons xanthan gum
- 2 teaspoons baking powder
- 1 teaspoon salt
- 2 tablespoons sugar (25g)
- ¼ cup chia seeds (40g)
- ¼ cup olive oil (60ml)
- 1 ½ cups warm water (360ml)
- 1 teaspoon apple cider vinegar
- 3 large eggs, beaten

Nutritional Information:
(Per Slice)
Calories: 160, Protein: 6g, Fat: 7g, Carbohydrates: 20g, Fiber: 4g, Sugar: 2g, Sodium: 230mg

Instructions:

Preparation: Grease the bread pan with a non-stick spray. Ensure all ingredients are at room temperature.

Mixing: In a large mixing bowl, combine the gluten-free flour blend, xanthan gum, baking powder, salt, and sugar. Add the beaten eggs, olive oil, warm water, and apple cider vinegar. Mix until smooth.

Additions: Stir in the chia seeds until evenly distributed.

Baking: Transfer the batter to the bread pan. Choose the gluten-free setting on your bread machine and initiate the cycle.

Cooling: Once baking is complete, carefully remove the bread from the machine. Set the bread on a wire rack and allow it to cool fully before cutting.

Bill's Tip:
Chia seeds add a nice crunch; ensure they are evenly mixed. If you prefer a softer bread, reduce the chia seeds.

ZUCCHINI & HERB GLUTEN-FREE BREAD

Ingredients:

- 4 cups gluten-free flour blend (500g) - 2:1:1 ratio of rice flour, tapioca flour, and almond flour
- 2 teaspoons xanthan gum
- 2 teaspoons baking powder
- 1 teaspoon salt
- 2 tablespoons sugar (25g)
- ¼ cup olive oil (60ml)
- 1 ½ cups warm water (360ml)
- 1 teaspoon apple cider vinegar
- 3 large eggs, beaten
- 1 cup grated and squeezed dry zucchini (120g)
- 2 tablespoons chopped fresh herbs (e.g., basil, parsley)

Nutritional Information:
(Per Slice)
Calories: 150, Protein: 5g, Fat: 6g, Carbohydrates: 22g, Fiber: 3g, Sugar: 3g, Sodium: 220mg

Instructions:

Preparation: Grease the bread pan with a non-stick spray. Ensure all ingredients are at room temperature.

Mixing: In a large mixing bowl, combine the gluten-free flour blend, xanthan gum, baking powder, salt, and sugar. Add the beaten eggs, olive oil, warm water, and apple cider vinegar. Mix until smooth.

Additions: Fold in the grated zucchini and fresh herbs.

Baking: Transfer the batter to the bread pan. Choose the gluten-free setting on your bread machine and initiate the cycle.

Cooling: Once baking is complete, carefully remove the bread from the machine. Set the bread on a wire rack and allow it to cool fully before cutting.

Bill's Tip:
Ensure zucchini is well-drained to prevent excess moisture. Adjust the amount of fresh herbs to taste.

SWEET POTATO GLUTEN-FREE BREAD

Ingredients:

- 4 cups gluten-free flour blend (500g) - 2:1:1 ratio of rice flour, tapioca flour, and almond flour
- 2 teaspoons xanthan gum
- 2 teaspoons baking powder
- 1 teaspoon salt
- ½ cup sugar (100g)
- 1 cup sweet potato puree (240g)
- ¼ cup olive oil (60ml)
- 1 cup warm water (240ml)
- 1 teaspoon apple cider vinegar
- 3 large eggs, beaten

Nutritional Information:
(Per Slice)

Calories: 170, Protein: 5g, Fat: 6g, Carbohydrates: 28g, Fiber: 3g, Sugar: 10g, Sodium: 220mg

Instructions:

Preparation: Grease the bread pan with a non-stick spray. Ensure all ingredients are at room temperature.

Mixing: In a large mixing bowl, combine the gluten-free flour blend, xanthan gum, baking powder, salt, and sugar. Add the beaten eggs, sweet potato puree, olive oil, warm water, and apple cider vinegar. Mix until smooth.

Baking: Transfer the batter to the bread pan. Choose the gluten-free setting on your bread machine and initiate the cycle.

Cooling: Once baking is complete, carefully remove the bread from the machine. Set the bread on a wire rack and allow it to cool fully before cutting.

Bill's Tip: *Use well-drained sweet potato puree to avoid excess moisture. Add a bit more sugar or a sprinkle of cinnamon for extra sweetness.*

POPPY SEED GLUTEN-FREE BREAD

Ingredients:

- 4 cups gluten-free flour blend (500g) - 2:1:1 ratio of rice flour, tapioca flour, and almond flour
- 2 teaspoons xanthan gum
- 2 teaspoons baking powder
- 1 teaspoon salt
- 2 tablespoons sugar (25g)
- ¼ cup poppy seeds (30g)
- ¼ cup olive oil (60ml)
- 1 ½ cups warm water (360ml)
- 1 teaspoon apple cider vinegar
- 3 large eggs, beaten

Nutritional Information:
(Per Slice)

Calories: 160, Protein: 5g, Fat: 7g, Carbohydrates: 21g, Fiber: 3g, Sugar: 2g, Sodium: 230mg

Instructions:

Preparation: Grease the bread pan with a non-stick spray. Ensure all ingredients are at room temperature.

Mixing: In a large mixing bowl, combine the gluten-free flour blend, xanthan gum, baking powder, salt, and sugar. Add the beaten eggs, olive oil, warm water, and apple cider vinegar. Mix until smooth.

Additions: Stir in the poppy seeds until evenly distributed. Baking: Transfer the batter to the bread pan. Choose the gluten-free setting on your bread machine and initiate the cycle.

Cooling: Once baking is complete, carefully remove the bread from the machine. Set the bread on a wire rack and allow it to cool fully before cutting.

Bill's Tip: *Adjust the amount of poppy seeds based on your preference. Ensure the seeds are well-mixed to avoid clumping.*

GLUTEN-FREE BREAD WITH RAISINS AND WALNUTS

Ingredients:

- 4 cups gluten-free flour blend (500g) - All-Purpose Gluten-Free Mix 2
- 2 teaspoons xanthan gum
- 2 teaspoons baking powder
- 1 teaspoon salt
- 2 tablespoons sugar (25g)
- ½ cup raisins (80g)
- ½ cup walnuts, chopped (60g)
- ¼ cup olive oil (60ml)
- 1 ½ cups warm water (360ml)
- 1 teaspoon apple cider vinegar
- 3 large eggs, beaten

Nutritional Information:
(Per Slice)

Calories: 200, Protein: 6g, Fat: 8g, Carbohydrates: 28g, Fiber: 3g, Sugar: 10g, Sodium: 230mg

Instructions:

Preparation: Grease the bread pan with a non-stick spray. Ensure all ingredients are at room temperature.

Mixing: In a large mixing bowl, combine the gluten-free flour blend, xanthan gum, baking powder, salt, and sugar. Add the beaten eggs, olive oil, warm water, and apple cider vinegar. Mix until smooth.

Additions: Gently fold in the raisins and walnuts.

Baking: Transfer the batter to the bread pan. Choose the gluten-free setting on your bread machine and initiate the cycle.

Cooling: Once baking is complete, carefully remove the bread from the machine. Set the bread on a wire rack and allow it to cool fully before cutting.

Bill's Tip:

Toast the walnuts lightly for enhanced flavor. Ensure raisins are evenly distributed to prevent clumping.

GLUTEN-FREE OLIVE AND ROSEMARY BREAD

Ingredients:

- 4 cups gluten-free flour blend (500g) - 2 parts brown rice flour, 1 part sorghum flour, 1 part millet flour
- 2 teaspoons xanthan gum
- 2 teaspoons baking powder
- 1 ½ teaspoons salt
- ½ cup chopped olives (80g)
- 1 tablespoon rosemary, finely chopped
- ¼ cup olive oil (60ml)
- 1 ½ cups warm water (360ml)
- 1 teaspoon apple cider vinegar
- 3 large eggs, beaten

Nutritional Information:
(Per Slice)

Calories: 190, Protein: 5g, Fat: 8g, Carbohydrates: 26g, Fiber: 3g, Sugar: 1g, Sodium: 260mg

Instructions:

Preparation: Grease the bread pan with a non-stick spray. Ensure all ingredients are at room temperature.

Mixing: In a large mixing bowl, combine the gluten-free flour blend, xanthan gum, baking powder, salt, and chopped rosemary. Add the beaten eggs, olive oil, warm water, and apple cider vinegar. Mix until smooth.

Additions: Gently fold in the chopped olives.

Baking: Transfer the batter to the bread pan. Choose the gluten-free setting on your bread machine and initiate the cycle.

Cooling: Once baking is complete, carefully remove the bread from the machine. Set the bread on a wire rack and allow it to cool fully before cutting.

Bill's Tip:

Use kalamata or green olives for a stronger flavor. Sprinkle additional rosemary on top before baking for extra aroma.

GLUTEN-FREE HERB AND PARMESAN BREAD

Ingredients:
- 4 cups gluten-free flour blend (500g) - All-Purpose Gluten-Free Mix 2
- 2 teaspoons xanthan gum
- 2 teaspoons baking powder
- 1 teaspoon salt
- ½ cup grated Parmesan cheese (50g)
- 1 tablespoon mixed herbs (thyme, basil, oregano)
- ¼ cup olive oil (60ml)
- 1 ½ cups warm water (360ml)
- 1 teaspoon apple cider vinegar
- 3 large eggs, beaten

Nutritional Information:
(Per Slice)

Calories: 210, Protein: 7g, Fat: 9g, Carbohydrates: 27g, Fiber: 2g, Sugar: 1g, Sodium: 290mg

Instructions:

Preparation: Grease the bread pan with a non-stick spray. Ensure all ingredients are at room temperature.

Mixing: In a large mixing bowl, combine the gluten-free flour blend, xanthan gum, baking powder, salt, and mixed herbs. Add the beaten eggs, olive oil, warm water, and apple cider vinegar. Mix until smooth.

Additions: Fold in the grated Parmesan cheese.

Baking: Transfer the batter to the bread pan. Choose the gluten-free setting on your bread machine and initiate the cycle.

Cooling: Once baking is complete, carefully remove the bread from the machine. Set the bread on a wire rack and allow it to cool fully before cutting.

Bill's Tip:

Add more Parmesan to the dough before baking for a crispier crust. Experiment with different herbs for varied flavors.

GLUTEN-FREE BREAD WITH SUN-DRIED TOMATOES AND BASIL

Ingredients:

- 4 cups gluten-free flour blend (500g) - 2 parts brown rice flour, 1 part sorghum flour, 1 part millet flour
- 2 teaspoons xanthan gum
- 2 teaspoons baking powder
- 1 ½ teaspoons salt
- ½ cup sun-dried tomatoes (60g), chopped
- 1 tablespoon basil, finely chopped
- ¼ cup olive oil (60ml)
- 1 ½ cups warm water (360ml)
- 1 teaspoon apple cider vinegar
- 3 large eggs, beaten

Nutritional Information:
(Per Slice)

Calories: 190, Protein: 5g, Fat: 8g, Carbohydrates: 27g, Fiber: 3g, Sugar: 3g, Sodium: 240mg

Bill's Tip:

Soak the sun-dried tomatoes in water before adding them to the dough for extra flavor. If desired, garnish with additional basil before baking.

Instructions:

Preparation: Grease the bread pan with a non-stick spray. Ensure all ingredients are at room temperature.

Mixing: In a large mixing bowl, combine the gluten-free flour blend, xanthan gum, baking powder, salt, and chopped basil. Add the beaten eggs, olive oil, warm water, and apple cider vinegar. Mix until smooth.

Additions: Gently fold in the chopped sun-dried tomatoes.

Baking: Transfer the batter to the bread pan. Choose the gluten-free setting on your bread machine and initiate the cycle.

Cooling: Once baking is complete, carefully remove the bread from the machine. Set the bread on a wire rack and allow it to cool fully before cutting.

GLUTEN-FREE OATMEAL BREAD

Ingredients:

- 4 cups gluten-free flour blend (500g) - All-Purpose Gluten-Free Mix 2
- 2 teaspoons xanthan gum
- 2 teaspoons baking powder
- 1 teaspoon salt
- ½ cup gluten-free oats (50g)
- ¼ cup olive oil (60ml)
- 1 ½ cups warm water (360ml)
- 1 teaspoon apple cider vinegar
- 3 large eggs, beaten

Nutritional Information:
(Per Slice)

Calories: 200, Protein: 6g, Fat: 7g, Carbohydrates: 29g, Fiber: 4g, Sugar: 2g, Sodium: 220mg

Instructions:

Preparation: Grease the bread pan with a non-stick spray. Ensure all ingredients are at room temperature.

Mixing: In a large mixing bowl, combine the gluten-free flour blend, xanthan gum, baking powder, salt, and gluten-free oats. Add the beaten eggs, olive oil, warm water, and apple cider vinegar. Mix until smooth.

Baking: Transfer the batter to the bread pan. Choose the gluten-free setting on your bread machine and initiate the cycle.

Cooling: Once baking is complete, carefully remove the bread from the machine. Set the bread on a wire rack and allow it to cool fully before cutting.

Bill's Tip:

Ensure oats are certified gluten-free to avoid cross-contamination. Sprinkle some oats on the dough before baking for a rustic look.

GLUTEN-FREE HONEY OAT BREAD

Ingredients:

- 4 cups gluten-free flour blend (500g) - 2 parts brown rice flour, 1 part sorghum flour, 1 part millet flour
- 2 teaspoons xanthan gum
- 2 teaspoons baking powder
- 1 teaspoon salt
- ½ cup gluten-free oats (50g)
- 3 tablespoons honey
- ¼ cup olive oil (60ml)
- 1 ½ cups warm water (360ml)
- 1 teaspoon apple cider vinegar
- 3 large eggs, beaten

Nutritional Information:
(Per Slice)

Calories: 210, Protein: 6g, Fat: 7g, Carbohydrates: 31g, Fiber: 4g, Sugar: 5g, Sodium: 220mg

Instructions:

Preparation: Grease the bread pan with a non-stick spray. Ensure all ingredients are at room temperature.

Mixing: In a large mixing bowl, combine the gluten-free flour blend, xanthan gum, baking powder, salt, and gluten-free oats. Add the beaten eggs, olive oil, warm water, apple cider vinegar, and honey. Mix until smooth.

Baking: Transfer the batter to the bread pan. Choose the gluten-free setting on your bread machine and initiate the cycle.

Cooling: Once baking is complete, carefully remove the bread from the machine. Set the bread on a wire rack and allow it to cool fully before cutting.

Bill's Tip:
Use raw honey for a more natural sweetness. Add a bit more oats on top for added texture.

GLUTEN-FREE BREAD WITH FLAXSEEDS

Ingredients:
- 4 cups gluten-free flour blend (500g) - All-Purpose Gluten-Free Mix 2
- 2 teaspoons xanthan gum
- 2 teaspoons baking powder
- 1 teaspoon salt
- ¼ cup ground flaxseeds (30g)
- ¼ cup olive oil (60ml)
- 1 ½ cups warm water (360ml)
- 1 teaspoon apple cider vinegar
- 3 large eggs, beaten

Nutritional Information:
(Per Slice)

Calories: 190, Protein: 6g, Fat: 8g, Carbohydrates: 25g, Fiber: 5g, Sugar: 1g, Sodium: 220mg

Instructions:

Preparation: Grease the bread pan with a non-stick spray. Ensure all ingredients are at room temperature.

Mixing: In a large mixing bowl, combine the gluten-free flour blend, xanthan gum, baking powder, salt, and ground flaxseeds. Add the beaten eggs, olive oil, warm water, and apple cider vinegar. Mix until smooth.

Baking: Transfer the batter to the bread pan. Choose the gluten-free setting on your bread machine and initiate the cycle.

Cooling: Once baking is complete, carefully remove the bread from the machine. Set the bread on a wire rack and allow it to cool fully before cutting.

Bill's Tip:
Flaxseeds can be toasted lightly for a richer flavor. Ensure flaxseeds are ground for better texture and absorption.

GLUTEN-FREE SOURDOUGH BREAD

Ingredients:

- 1 cup gluten-free sourdough starter (240g)
- 3 cups gluten-free flour blend (375g) - 2 parts white rice flour, 1 part tapioca flour
- 2 teaspoons xanthan gum
- 1 teaspoon salt
- 1 ¼ cups warm water (300ml)
- 2 tablespoons olive oil (30ml)
- 1 teaspoon apple cider vinegar

Nutritional Information:

(Per Slice)

Calories: 180, Protein: 5g, Fat: 6g, Carbohydrates: 26g, Fiber: 3g, Sugar: 2g, Sodium: 230mg

Instructions:

Preparation: Grease the bread pan with a non-stick spray. Ensure all ingredients are at room temperature.

Mixing: In a large mixing bowl, combine the gluten-free flour blend, xanthan gum, and salt. Add the sourdough starter, warm water, olive oil, and apple cider vinegar. Mix until smooth.

Baking: Transfer the batter to the bread pan. Choose the gluten-free setting on your bread machine and initiate the cycle.

Cooling: Once baking is complete, carefully remove the bread from the machine. Set the bread on a wire rack and allow it to cool fully before cutting.

Bill's Tip:

Allow the dough to rise for a few hours before baking for a tangier flavor. After removing the bread from the machine, bake in a preheated oven for a thicker crust.

GLUTEN-FREE CHEESE BREAD

Ingredients:

- 4 cups gluten-free flour blend (500g) - All-Purpose Gluten-Free Mix 2
- 2 teaspoons xanthan gum
- 2 teaspoons baking powder
- 1 teaspoon salt
- ½ cup cheddar cheese (50g), shredded
- ¼ cup olive oil (60ml)
- 1 ½ cups warm water (360ml)
- 1 teaspoon apple cider vinegar
- 3 large eggs, beaten

Nutritional Information:

(Per Slice)

Calories: 220, Protein: 8g, Fat: 10g, Carbohydrates: 26g, Fiber: 2g, Sugar: 1g, Sodium: 290mg

Instructions:

Preparation: Grease the bread pan with a non-stick spray. Ensure all ingredients are at room temperature.

Mixing: In a large mixing bowl, combine the gluten-free flour blend, xanthan gum, baking powder, and salt. Add the beaten eggs, olive oil, warm water, and apple cider vinegar. Mix until smooth.

Additions: Gently fold in the shredded cheddar cheese.

Baking: Transfer the batter to the bread pan. Choose the gluten-free setting on your bread machine and initiate the cycle.

Cooling: Once baking is complete, carefully remove the bread from the machine. Set the bread on a wire rack and allow it to cool fully before cutting.

Bill's Tip:

Use a mix of cheeses for a more complex flavor. Sprinkle additional cheese on top before baking for a crispy crust.

GLUTEN-FREE BREAD WITH SESAME AND POPPY SEEDS

Ingredients:

- 4 cups gluten-free flour blend (500g) - All-Purpose Gluten-Free Mix 2
- 2 teaspoons xanthan gum
- 2 teaspoons baking powder
- 1 teaspoon salt
- 2 tablespoons sesame seeds (20g)
- 2 tablespoons poppy seeds (20g)
- ¼ cup olive oil (60ml)
- 1 ½ cups warm water (360ml)
- 1 teaspoon apple cider vinegar
- 3 large eggs, beaten

Nutritional Information:
(Per Slice)

Calories: 200, Protein: 6g, Fat: 9g, Carbohydrates: 26g, Fiber: 3g, Sugar: 1g, Sodium: 220mg

Instructions:

Preparation: Grease the bread pan with a non-stick spray. Ensure all ingredients are at room temperature.

Mixing: In a large mixing bowl, combine the gluten-free flour blend, xanthan gum, baking powder, and salt. Add the beaten eggs, olive oil, warm water, and apple cider vinegar. Mix until smooth.

Additions: Gently fold in the sesame and poppy seeds.

Baking: Transfer the batter to the bread pan. Choose the gluten-free setting on your bread machine and initiate the cycle.

Cooling: Once baking is complete, carefully remove the bread from the machine. Set the bread on a wire rack and allow it to cool fully before cutting.

Bill's Tip:

Lightly toast the sesame and poppy seeds for enhanced flavor. Sprinkle additional seeds on top of the dough before baking.

GLUTEN-FREE QUINOA BREAD

Ingredients:

- 4 cups gluten-free flour blend (500g) - 2 parts brown rice flour, 1 part sorghum flour, 1 part millet flour
- 2 teaspoons xanthan gum
- 2 teaspoons baking powder
- 1 teaspoon salt
- ½ cup quinoa (80g), cooked and cooled
- ¼ cup olive oil (60ml)
- 1 ½ cups warm water (360ml)
- 1 teaspoon apple cider vinegar
- 3 large eggs, beaten

Nutritional Information:
(Per Slice)

Calories: 210, Protein: 7g, Fat: 7g, Carbohydrates: 30g, Fiber: 4g, Sugar: 2g, Sodium: 230mg

Instructions:

Preparation: Grease the bread pan with a non-stick spray. Ensure all ingredients are at room temperature.

Mixing: In a large mixing bowl, combine the gluten-free flour blend, xanthan gum, baking powder, and salt. Add the cooked quinoa, beaten eggs, olive oil, warm water, and apple cider vinegar. Mix until smooth.

Baking: Transfer the batter to the bread pan. Choose the gluten-free setting on your bread machine and initiate the cycle.

Cooling: Once baking is complete, carefully remove the bread from the machine. Set the bread on a wire rack and allow it to cool fully before cutting.

Bill's Tip:

This recipe uses leftover quinoa for convenience. To enhance the flavor, quinoa can be slightly toasted before adding it.

GLUTEN-FREE BREAD WITH DRIED FIGS AND ALMONDS

Ingredients:

- 4 cups gluten-free flour blend (500g) - 2 parts brown rice flour, 1 part sorghum flour, 1 part millet flour
- 2 teaspoons xanthan gum
- 2 teaspoons baking powder
- 1 teaspoon salt
- ½ cup dried figs (60g), chopped
- ½ cup almonds (50g), sliced
- ¼ cup olive oil (60ml)
- 1 ½ cups warm water (360ml)
- 1 teaspoon apple cider vinegar
- 3 large eggs, beaten

Nutritional Information:

(Per Slice)

Calories: 220, Protein: 6g, Fat: 8g, Carbohydrates: 30g, Fiber: 4g, Sugar: 12g, Sodium: 230mg

Instructions:

Preparation: Grease the bread pan with a non-stick spray. Ensure all ingredients are at room temperature.

Mixing: In a large mixing bowl, combine the gluten-free flour blend, xanthan gum, baking powder, and salt. Add the beaten eggs, olive oil, warm water, and apple cider vinegar. Mix until smooth.

Additions: Gently fold the chopped dried figs and sliced almonds.

Baking: Transfer the batter to the bread pan. Choose the gluten-free setting on your bread machine and initiate the cycle.

Cooling: Once baking is complete, carefully remove the bread from the machine. Set the bread on a wire rack and allow it to cool fully before cutting.

Bill's Tip:

For a softer texture, soak dried figs in warm water for 10 minutes before using them. Lightly toast almonds before adding them to enhance their flavor.

GLUTEN-FREE WALNUT AND CRANBERRY BREAD

Ingredients:

- 4 cups gluten-free flour blend (500g) - All-Purpose Gluten-Free Mix 2
- 2 teaspoons xanthan gum
- 2 teaspoons baking powder
- 1 teaspoon salt
- ½ cup walnuts (60g), chopped
- ½ cup cranberries (60g), dried
- ¼ cup olive oil (60ml)
- 1 ½ cups warm water (360ml)
- 1 teaspoon apple cider vinegar
- 3 large eggs, beaten

Nutritional Information:

(Per Slice)

Calories: 220, Protein: 6g, Fat: 8g, Carbohydrates: 31g, Fiber: 3g, Sugar: 10g, Sodium: 230mg

Instructions:

Preparation: Grease the bread pan with a non-stick spray. Ensure all ingredients are at room temperature.

Mixing: In a large mixing bowl, combine the gluten-free flour blend, xanthan gum, baking powder, and salt. Add the beaten eggs, olive oil, warm water, and apple cider vinegar. Mix until smooth.

Additions: Gently fold in the chopped walnuts and dried cranberries.

Baking: Transfer the batter to the bread pan. Choose the gluten-free setting on your bread machine and initiate the cycle.

Cooling: Once baking is complete, carefully remove the bread from the machine. Set the bread on a wire rack and allow it to cool fully before cutting.

Bill's Tip:

Use unsweetened dried cranberries to control sugar levels, and toast walnuts slightly for a more robust flavor.

GLUTEN-FREE BREAD WITH BLACK OLIVES AND THYME

Ingredients:

- 4 cups gluten-free flour blend (500g) - All-Purpose Gluten-Free Mix 2
- 2 teaspoons xanthan gum
- 2 teaspoons baking powder
- 1 teaspoon salt
- ½ cup black olives (60g), pitted and chopped
- 1 tablespoon dried thyme (5g)
- ¼ cup olive oil (60ml)
- 1 ½ cups warm water (360ml)
- 1 teaspoon apple cider vinegar
- 3 large eggs, beaten

Nutritional Information:
(Per Slice)

Calories: 210, Protein: 6g, Fat: 8g, Carbohydrates: 30g, Fiber: 3g, Sugar: 1g, Sodium: 250mg

Instructions:

Preparation: Grease the bread pan with a non-stick spray. Ensure all ingredients are at room temperature.

Mixing: In a large mixing bowl, combine the gluten-free flour blend, xanthan gum, baking powder, and salt. Add the chopped olives, dried thyme, beaten eggs, olive oil, warm water, and apple cider vinegar. Mix until smooth.

Baking: Transfer the batter to the bread pan. Choose the gluten-free setting on your bread machine and initiate the cycle.

Cooling: Once baking is complete, carefully remove the bread from the machine. Set the bread on a wire rack and allow it to cool fully before cutting.

Bill's Tip:

For the best flavor, use high-quality black olives. Adjust the amount of thyme based on your preference.

GLUTEN-FREE RUSTIC CIABATTA

Ingredients:

- 4 cups gluten-free flour blend (500g) - All-Purpose Gluten-Free Mix 2
- 2 teaspoons xanthan gum
- 2 teaspoons baking powder
- 1 teaspoon salt
- ¼ cup olive oil (60ml)
- 1 ¼ cups warm water (300ml)
- 1 teaspoon apple cider vinegar
- 2 large eggs, beaten
- 2 teaspoons active dry yeast

Nutritional Information:
(Per Slice)

Calories: 210, Protein: 6g, Fat: 7g, Carbohydrates: 30g, Fiber: 3g, Sugar: 2g, Sodium: 220mg

Instructions:

Preparation: Grease the bread pan with a non-stick spray. Ensure all ingredients are at room temperature.

Mixing: In a large mixing bowl, combine the gluten-free flour blend, xanthan gum, baking powder, and salt. Dissolve the yeast in warm water and let it sit for 5 minutes. Add the yeast mixture, beaten eggs, olive oil, and apple cider vinegar to the flour mixture. Mix until smooth.

Baking: Transfer the batter to the bread pan. Choose the gluten-free setting on your bread machine and initiate the cycle. Use a higher water-to-flour ratio and a longer baking time for a more rustic texture.

Cooling: Once baking is complete, carefully remove the bread from the machine. Set the bread on a wire rack and allow it to cool fully before cutting.

Bill's Tip:

For a more authentic ciabatta feel, try baking the dough in a preheated oven after removing it from the bread machine. Keep the dough slightly sticky for a better texture.

GLUTEN-FREE BREAD WITH PARMESAN AND GARLIC

Ingredients:

- 4 cups gluten-free flour blend (500g) - All-Purpose Gluten-Free Mix 2
- 2 teaspoons xanthan gum
- 2 teaspoons baking powder
- 1 teaspoon salt
- ½ cup Parmesan cheese (50g), grated
- 1 teaspoon garlic powder
- ¼ cup olive oil (60ml)
- 1 ½ cups warm water (360ml)
- 1 teaspoon apple cider vinegar
- 3 large eggs, beaten

Nutritional Information:
(Per Slice)

Calories: 220, Protein: 7g, Fat: 8g, Carbohydrates: 31g, Fiber: 2g, Sugar: 1g, Sodium: 300mg

Instructions:

Preparation: Grease the bread pan with a non-stick spray. Ensure all ingredients are at room temperature.

Mixing: In a large mixing bowl, combine the gluten-free flour blend, xanthan gum, baking powder, and salt. Add the grated Parmesan cheese, garlic powder, beaten eggs, olive oil, warm water, and apple cider vinegar. Mix until smooth.

Baking: Transfer the batter to the bread pan. Choose the gluten-free setting on your bread machine and initiate the cycle.

Cooling: Once baking is complete, carefully remove the bread from the machine. Set the bread on a wire rack and allow it to cool fully before cutting.

Bill's Tip:

Increase the garlic powder or add fresh minced garlic for a more intense flavor. Use freshly grated Parmesan for better melting and flavor.

GLUTEN-FREE SUNFLOWER AND PUMPKIN SEED BREAD

Ingredients:

- 4 cups gluten-free flour blend (500g) - All-Purpose Gluten-Free Mix 2
- 2 teaspoons xanthan gum
- 2 teaspoons baking powder
- 1 teaspoon salt
- ¼ cup sunflower seeds (30g)
- ¼ cup pumpkin seeds (30g)
- ¼ cup olive oil (60ml)
- 1 ½ cups warm water (360ml)
- 1 teaspoon apple cider vinegar
- 3 large eggs, beaten

Nutritional Information:
(Per Slice)

Calories: 210, Protein: 6g, Fat: 9g, Carbohydrates: 27g, Fiber: 4g, Sugar: 1g, Sodium: 230mg

Instructions:

Preparation: Grease the bread pan with a non-stick spray. Ensure all ingredients are at room temperature.

Mixing: In a large mixing bowl, combine the gluten-free flour blend, xanthan gum, baking powder, and salt. Add the sunflower and pumpkin seeds, beaten eggs, olive oil, warm water, and apple cider vinegar. Mix until smooth.

Baking: Transfer the batter to the bread pan. Choose the gluten-free setting on your bread machine and initiate the cycle.

Cooling: Once baking is complete, carefully remove the bread from the machine. Set the bread on a wire rack and allow it to cool fully before cutting.

Bill's Tip:

Lightly toast the seeds before adding to the dough for enhanced flavor. Reserve some seeds to sprinkle on top of the dough before baking.

GLUTEN-FREE BREAD WITH DRIED APRICOTS AND PECANS

Ingredients:

- 4 cups gluten-free flour blend (500g) - 2 parts brown rice flour, 1 part sorghum flour, 1 part millet flour
- 2 teaspoons xanthan gum
- 2 teaspoons baking powder
- 1 teaspoon salt
- ½ cup dried apricots (60g), chopped
- ½ cup pecans (60g), chopped
- ¼ cup olive oil (60ml)
- 1 ½ cups warm water (360ml)
- 1 teaspoon apple cider vinegar
- 3 large eggs, beaten

Nutritional Information:
(Per Slice)

Calories: 230, Protein: 6g, Fat: 9g, Carbohydrates: 32g, Fiber: 3g, Sugar: 12g, Sodium: 230mg

Instructions:

Preparation: Grease the bread pan with a non-stick spray. Ensure all ingredients are at room temperature.

Mixing: In a large mixing bowl, combine the gluten-free flour blend, xanthan gum, baking powder, and salt. Add the chopped dried apricots and chopped pecans, beaten eggs, olive oil, warm water, and apple cider vinegar. Mix until smooth.

Baking: Transfer the batter to the bread pan. Choose the gluten-free setting on your bread machine and initiate the cycle.

Cooling: Once baking is complete, carefully remove the bread from the machine. Set the bread on a wire rack and allow it to cool fully before cutting.

Bill's Tip:

Chop dried apricots into smaller pieces to distribute them evenly throughout the bread. Toast pecans slightly before adding to enhance their flavor.

GLUTEN-FREE BANANA BREAD

Ingredients:

- 4 cups gluten-free flour blend (500g) - All-Purpose Gluten-Free Mix 2
- 2 teaspoons xanthan gum
- 2 teaspoons baking powder
- 1 teaspoon salt
- 1 ½ cups ripe bananas (300g), mashed (about 4 medium bananas)
- ¼ cup olive oil (60ml)
- 1 ½ cups warm water (360ml)
- 1 teaspoon apple cider vinegar
- 3 large eggs, beaten
- ¼ cup brown sugar (50g), optional

Nutritional Information:
(Per Slice)

Calories: 220, Protein: 4g, Fat: 7g, Carbohydrates: 35g, Fiber: 3g, Sugar: 14g, Sodium: 210mg

Instructions:

Preparation: Grease the bread pan with a non-stick spray. Ensure all ingredients are at room temperature.

Mixing: In a large mixing bowl, combine the gluten-free flour blend, xanthan gum, baking powder, and salt. Add the mashed bananas, beaten eggs, olive oil, warm water, apple cider vinegar, and brown sugar (if using). Mix until smooth.

Baking: Transfer the batter to the bread pan. Choose the gluten-free setting on your bread machine and initiate the cycle.

Cooling: Once baking is complete, carefully remove the bread from the machine. Set the bread on a wire rack and allow it to cool fully before cutting.

Bill's Tip:

Use ripe bananas for the best flavor and sweetness. For extra flavor, add a teaspoon of cinnamon to the dry ingredients.

GLUTEN-FREE BREAD WITH CARAWAY SEEDS

Ingredients:

- 4 cups gluten-free flour blend (500g) - All-Purpose Gluten-Free Mix 2
- 2 teaspoons xanthan gum
- 2 teaspoons baking powder
- 1 teaspoon salt
- 2 tablespoons caraway seeds (10g)
- ¼ cup olive oil (60ml)
- 1 ½ cups warm water (360ml)
- 1 teaspoon apple cider vinegar
- 3 large eggs, beaten

Nutritional Information:
(Per Slice)

Calories: 200, Protein: 6g, Fat: 8g, Carbohydrates: 28g, Fiber: 3g, Sugar: 1g, Sodium: 220mg

Instructions:

Preparation: Grease the bread pan with a non-stick spray. Ensure all ingredients are at room temperature.

Mixing: In a large mixing bowl, combine the gluten-free flour blend, xanthan gum, baking powder, salt, and caraway seeds. Add the beaten eggs, olive oil, warm water, and apple cider vinegar. Mix until smooth.

Baking: Transfer the batter to the bread pan. Choose the gluten-free setting on your bread machine and initiate the cycle.

Cooling: Once baking is complete, carefully remove the bread from the machine. Set the bread on a wire rack and allow it to cool fully before cutting.

Bill's Tip:

Toast the caraway seeds lightly to enhance their flavor. Adjust the amount of seeds based on your taste preference.

GLUTEN-FREE SEEDED LOAF

Ingredients:

- 4 cups gluten-free flour blend (500g) - All-Purpose Gluten-Free Mix 2
- 2 teaspoons xanthan gum
- 2 teaspoons baking powder
- 1 teaspoon salt
- ¼ cup mixed seeds (30g) - sunflower seeds, pumpkin seeds, chia seeds
- ¼ cup olive oil (60ml)
- 1 ½ cups warm water (360ml)
- 1 teaspoon apple cider vinegar
- 3 large eggs, beaten

Nutritional Information:
(Per Slice)

Calories: 210, Protein: 7g, Fat: 9g, Carbohydrates: 27g, Fiber: 4g, Sugar: 1g, Sodium: 230mg

Instructions:

Preparation: Grease the bread pan with a non-stick spray. Ensure all ingredients are at room temperature.

Mixing: In a large mixing bowl, combine the gluten-free flour blend, xanthan gum, baking powder, salt, and mixed seeds. Add the beaten eggs, olive oil, warm water, and apple cider vinegar. Mix until smooth.

Baking: Transfer the batter to the bread pan. Choose the gluten-free setting on your bread machine and initiate the cycle.

Cooling: Once baking is complete, carefully remove the bread from the machine. Set the bread on a wire rack and allow it to cool fully before cutting.

Bill's Tip:

Experiment with different combinations of seeds for varied flavor and texture. Sprinkle additional seeds on the loaf before baking for a decorative finish.

GLUTEN-FREE FOCACCIA WITH ROSEMARY AND SEA SALT

Ingredients:

- 4 cups gluten-free flour blend (500g) - All-Purpose Gluten-Free Mix 2
- 2 teaspoons xanthan gum
- 2 teaspoons baking powder
- 1 teaspoon salt
- 2 tablespoons fresh rosemary (10g), chopped
- 1 teaspoon sea salt
- ¼ cup olive oil (60ml)
- 1 ½ cups warm water (360ml)
- 1 teaspoon apple cider vinegar
- 3 large eggs, beaten

Nutritional Information:
(Per Slice)

Calories: 220, Protein: 6g, Fat: 9g, Carbohydrates: 30g, Fiber: 2g, Sugar: 1g, Sodium: 250mg

Instructions:

Preparation: Grease the bread pan with a non-stick spray. Ensure all ingredients are at room temperature.

Mixing: In a large mixing bowl, combine the gluten-free flour blend, xanthan gum, baking powder, and salt. Add the chopped rosemary, beaten eggs, olive oil, warm water, and apple cider vinegar. Mix until smooth.

Baking: Transfer the batter to the bread pan. Drizzle additional olive oil on top and sprinkle with sea salt. Choose the gluten-free setting on your bread machine and initiate the cycle.

Cooling: Once baking is complete, carefully remove the bread from the machine. Set the bread on a wire rack and allow it to cool fully before cutting.

Bill's Tip:

Use fresh rosemary for the best flavor; dried rosemary can be used, but adjust the quantity. For extra flavor, you can add garlic powder or additional herbs.

GLUTEN-FREE DOUGH

GLUTEN-FREE PIZZA DOUGH

Ingredients:

- 2 cups gluten-free all-purpose flour blend (240g)
- 1 cup warm water (240ml) - 110°F/43°C
- 2 tablespoons olive oil (30ml)
- 1 tablespoon honey (21g)
- 1 tablespoon active dry yeast (9g)
- 1 teaspoon salt (5g)
- ½ teaspoon garlic powder (optional) (1g)

Nutritional Information:
(per 1 slice, assuming 8 slices per pizza)

150 calories, 6g fat, 18g carbs, 3g protein

Instructions:

Add warm water, honey, and yeast to the bread machine pan. Let it sit for 5 minutes to activate the yeast.

Add flour blend, salt, olive oil, and garlic powder (if using) to the pan.

Select the "Dough" setting and start the machine.

Once the dough cycle is complete, roll out on a floured surface and transfer to a pizza stone or baking sheet.

Warm up the oven to 425°F (220°C)). Bake for 10-15 minutes until the crust is golden brown.

GLUTEN-FREE PASTA DOUGH

Ingredients:

- 2 cups gluten-free all-purpose flour blend (240g)
- 2 large eggs
- ¼ cup water (60ml)
- 1 tablespoon olive oil (15ml)
- ½ teaspoon salt (3g)

Nutritional Information:
(per 1 serving, assuming 4 servings)

220 calories, 9g fat, 25g carbs, 6g protein

Instructions:

Combine flour and salt in the bread machine pan.

Add eggs, water, and olive oil.

Select the "Dough" setting and start the machine.

Once the dough cycle is complete, remove and roll it out on a floured surface.

Cut into desired pasta shapes and cook in boiling salted water for 2-4 minutes until tender.

GLUTEN-FREE CINNAMON ROLLS

Ingredients:

- 2 ½ cups gluten-free all-purpose flour blend (300g)
- 1 cup warm milk (240ml) (110°F/43°C)
- ¼ cup melted butter (60ml)
- ¼ cup granulated sugar (50g)
- 1 packet active dry yeast (2 ¼ tsp)
- ½ teaspoon salt (3g)
- 1 teaspoon ground cinnamon (2g)
- ½ cup brown sugar (100g)

Nutritional Information:
(per roll, assuming 8 rolls)

280 calories, 12g fat, 40g carbs, 4g protein

Instructions:

Add warm milk, yeast, and sugar to the bread machine pan. Let it sit for 5 minutes to activate the yeast.

Add flour blend, melted butter, salt, and cinnamon.

Select the "Dough" setting and start the machine.

Once the dough cycle is complete, roll out the dough, spread it with butter, and sprinkle it with brown sugar and cinnamon.

Roll up, slice into rolls, and place in a greased baking dish.

Bake at 350°F (175°C) for 20-25 minutes until golden brown.

GLUTEN-FREE FOCACCIA

Ingredients:

- 2 ½ cups gluten-free all-purpose flour blend (300g)
- 1 cup warm water (240ml, 110°F/43°C)
- ¼ cup olive oil (60ml)
- 2 tablespoons fresh rosemary, chopped
- 1 packet active dry yeast (2 ¼ tsp)
- 1 teaspoon salt (5g)
- 1 tablespoon honey (21g)

Nutritional Information:
(per 1 slice, assuming 8 slices)

250 calories, 11g fat, 32g carbs, 4g protein

Instructions:

Add warm water, honey, and yeast to the bread machine pan. Let it sit for 5 minutes to activate the yeast.

Add flour blend, salt, and olive oil.

Select the "Dough" setting and start the machine.

Once the dough cycle is complete, spread the dough in a greased baking pan and sprinkle with rosemary.

Bake at 400°F (200°C) for 25-30 minutes until golden brown.

GLUTEN-FREE BREADSTICKS

Ingredients:

- 2 cups gluten-free all-purpose flour blend (240g)
- 1 cup warm water (240ml, 110°F/43°C)
- ¼ cup olive oil (60ml)
- 2 tablespoons grated Parmesan cheese (10g)
- 1 packet active dry yeast (2 ¼ tsp)
- 1 teaspoon salt (5g)
- 1 teaspoon dried oregano (1g)

Nutritional Information:
(per 1 stick, assuming 12 sticks)

120 calories, 6g fat, 14g carbs, 5g protein

Instructions:

Add warm water, yeast, and salt to the bread machine pan. Let it sit for 5 minutes.

Add flour blend, olive oil, and Parmesan cheese.

Select the "Dough" setting and start the machine.

Once the dough cycle is complete, roll it out and cut it into sticks. Place on a baking sheet.

Bake at 375°F (190°C) for 15-20 minutes until golden brown.

GLUTEN-FREE PRETZELS

Ingredients:

- 2 ½ cups gluten-free all-purpose flour blend (300g)
- 1 cup warm water (240ml, 110°F/43°C)
- ¼ cup melted butter (60ml)
- 1 packet active dry yeast (2 ¼ teaspoon)
- 1 teaspoon salt (5g)
- 1 tablespoon baking soda (15g)
- Coarse salt for topping

Nutritional Information:
(per 1 pretzel, assuming 8 pretzels)

220 calories, 8g fat, 30g carbs, 6g protein

Instructions:

Add warm water, yeast, and salt to the bread machine pan. Let it sit for 5 minutes.

Add flour blend and melted butter.

Select the "Dough" setting and start the machine.

Once the dough cycle is complete, shape it into pretzels and place it on a baking sheet.

Boil water with baking soda, briefly dip pretzels, and sprinkle with coarse salt.

Bake at 425°F (220°C) for 12-15 minutes until golden brown.

GLUTEN-FREE NAAN

Ingredients:

- 2 cups gluten-free all-purpose flour blend (240g)
- ½ cup plain yogurt (120ml)
- ½ cup warm water (120ml, 110°F/43°C)
- 1 packet active dry yeast (2 ¼ tsp)
- 1 tablespoon olive oil (15ml)
- 1 teaspoon salt (5g)
- 1 tablespoon honey (21g)

Nutritional Information:

(per 1 naan, assuming 6 naans)

200 calories, 8g fat, 25g carbs, 5g protein

Instructions:

Add warm water, honey, and yeast to the bread machine pan. Let it sit for 5 minutes.

Add flour blend, yogurt, olive oil, and salt.

Select the "Dough" setting and start the machine.

Once the dough cycle is complete, roll out the dough and cook on a hot skillet for 2-3 minutes on each side.

GLUTEN-FREE BAGELS

Ingredients:

- 2 ½ cups gluten-free all-purpose flour blend (300g)
- 1 cup warm water (240ml, 110°F/43°C)
- ¼ cup honey (60ml)
- 1 packet active dry yeast (2 ¼ tsp)
- 1 teaspoon salt (5g)
- 1 tablespoon baking soda (15g)
- Sesame seeds for topping

Nutritional Information:

(per 1 bagel, assuming 6 bagels)

240 calories, 7g fat, 36g carbs, 8g protein

Instructions:

Add warm water, honey, and yeast to the bread machine pan. Let it sit for 5 minutes.

Add flour blend and salt.

Select the "Dough" setting and start the machine.

Once the dough cycle is complete, shape into bagels, boil briefly in water with baking soda, and bake at 375°F (190°C) for 20-25 minutes.

GLUTEN-FREE CIABATTA

Ingredients:

- 2 ½ cups gluten-free all-purpose flour blend (300g)
- 1 ½ cups warm water (360ml, 110°F/43°C)
- 1 packet active dry yeast (2 ¼ teaspoons)
- ¼ cup olive oil (60ml)
- 1 teaspoon salt (5g)

Nutritional Information:
(per 1 slice, assuming 8 slices)

230 calories, 8g fat, 30g carbs, 5g protein

Instructions:

Add warm water and yeast to the bread machine pan. Let it sit for 5 minutes.

Add flour blend, olive oil, and salt.

Select the "Dough" setting and start the machine.

Once the dough cycle is complete, shape the dough into a loaf on a baking sheet and bake at 425°F (220°C) for 30-35 minutes until golden brown.

GLUTEN-FREE SOFT ROLLS

Ingredients:

- 2 ½ cups gluten-free all-purpose flour blend (300g)
- 1 cup warm milk (240ml, 110°F/43°C)
- ¼ cup melted butter (60ml)
- 2 tablespoons sugar (25g)
- 1 packet active dry yeast (2 ¼ teaspoons)
- ½ teaspoon salt (3g)

Nutritional Information:
(per roll, assuming 12 rolls)

180 calories, 8g fat, 22g carbs, 4g protein

Instructions:

Add warm milk, sugar, and yeast to the bread machine pan. Let it sit for 5 minutes.

Add flour blend, melted butter, and salt.

Select the "Dough" setting and start the machine.

Once the dough cycle is complete, divide it into rolls and place them on a baking sheet.

Bake at 375°F (190°C) for 15-20 minutes until golden brown.

143

GLUTEN-FREE FLATBREAD DOUGH

Ingredients:

- 2 cups gluten-free all-purpose flour (240g)
- 1 cup brown rice flour (120g)
- ½ cup tapioca flour (60g)
- ¼ cup olive oil (60ml)
- ½ cup warm water (120ml)
- 1 tablespoon sugar (12g)
- 2 teaspoons baking powder (10g)
- ½ teaspoon salt (3g)

Nutritional Information:
(per serving, 1 flatbread)

Calories: 160, Fat: 7g, Carbs: 22g, Protein: 3g

Instructions:

Combine gluten-free brown rice, tapioca, baking powder, and salt in a large bowl.

Mix warm water, olive oil, and sugar separately.

Add wet ingredients to dry ingredients and mix until smooth.

Roll out dough to the desired thickness on a floured surface.

Warm up the oven to 375°F (190°C). Bake for 12-15 minutes or until the top is golden brown.

GLUTEN-FREE TORTILLA DOUGH

Ingredients:

- 2 cups gluten-free all-purpose flour (240g)
- 1 cup corn flour (120g)
- ¼ cup olive oil (60ml)
- ½ cup warm water (120ml)
- ½ teaspoon salt (3g)
- ½ teaspoon baking powder (2g)

Nutritional Information:
(per serving, 1 tortilla)

Calories: 120, Fat: 5g, Carbs: 15g, Protein: 2g

Instructions:

Combine gluten-free flour, corn flour, baking powder, and salt in a large bowl.

Add olive oil and warm water to the dry ingredients. Mix until smooth.

Divide dough into small balls and roll each on a floured surface.

Heat a skillet over medium heat and cook each tortilla for 1-2 minutes on each side.

GLUTEN-FREE PITA BREAD DOUGH

Ingredients:

- 2 cups gluten-free all-purpose flour (240g)
- 1 cup rice flour (120g)
- ¼ cup olive oil (60ml)
- ½ cup warm water (120ml)
- 1 tablespoon sugar (12g)
- 2 teaspoons active dry yeast (6g)
- ½ teaspoon salt (3g)

Nutritional Information:
(per serving, 1 pita)

Calories: 140, Fat: 6g, Carbs: 18g, Protein: 3g

Instructions:

Dissolve sugar in warm water and add yeast. Let it sit for 5-10 minutes.

Mix gluten-free flour, rice flour, and salt in a large bowl.

Add yeast mixture and olive oil to the dry ingredients. Mix until dough forms.

Divide dough into small balls and roll each into a flat circle.

Warm the oven to 450°F (230°C) and bake pita bread for 5-7 minutes or until puffed up.

GLUTEN-FREE STROMBOLI DOUGH

Ingredients:

- 2 cups gluten-free all-purpose flour (240g)
- 1 cup rice flour (120g)
- ¼ cup olive oil (60ml)
- ½ cup warm water (120ml)
- 1 tablespoon sugar (12g)
- 2 teaspoons active dry yeast (6g)
- ½ teaspoon salt (3g)

Nutritional Information:
(per serving, ⅛ of stromboli)

Calories: 220, Fat: 10g, Carbs: 28g, Protein: 5g

Instructions:

Dissolve sugar in warm water and add yeast. Let it sit for 5-10 minutes.

Mix gluten-free flour, rice flour, and salt in a large bowl.

Add yeast mixture and olive oil to the dry ingredients. Mix until smooth.

Roll out dough into a rectangle and fill with desired ingredients.

Roll up the dough and place seam-side down on a greased baking sheet. Bake at 375°F (190°C) for 25–30 minutes.

GLUTEN-FREE CALZONE DOUGH

Ingredients:

- 2 cups gluten-free all-purpose flour (240g)
- 1 cup tapioca flour (120g)
- ¼ cup olive oil (60ml)
- ½ cup warm water (120ml)
- 1 tablespoon sugar (12g)
- 2 teaspoons active dry yeast (6g)
- ½ teaspoon salt (3g)

Nutritional Information:
(per serving, 1 calzone)

*Calories: 250, Fat: 12g, Carbs: 30g,
Protein:6g*

Instructions:

Dissolve sugar in warm water and add yeast. Let it sit for 5-10 minutes.

Mix gluten-free flour, tapioca flour, and salt in a large bowl.

Add yeast mixture and olive oil to the dry ingredients. Mix until smooth.

Roll out dough into circles, fill with desired ingredients, and fold in half.

Warm up the oven to 375°F (190°C). Bake for 20-25 minutes until the top is golden brown.

CLASSIC GLUTEN-FREE PASTA

Ingredients:

- 1 ½ cups gluten-free flour (180g) - 60% white corn flour, 30% yellow corn flour, 10% brown rice flour
- 2 large eggs
- ½ teaspoon salt (3g)
- Additional corn flour for dusting (if needed)

Nutritional Information:
(per serving)

*Calories: 250, Carbohydrates: 50 g,
Fiber: 3 g, Sodium: 200 mg, Protein: 8 g,
Fat: 2 g*

Instructions:

In a large bowl, mix gluten-free flour and salt.
Make a well in the center of the flour mixture and crack the eggs into it.

Gradually mix the eggs into the flour, continuously incorporating more flour from the sides of the well.

Mix until the dough becomes homogeneous and you can form a soft ball.

Dust your hands with corn flour and roll the dough onto a flat surface.

Divide the dough into several portions and roll each into a thin sheet using a pasta machine or a rolling pin.

Cut the pasta into desired shapes, such as strips for spaghetti or circles for ravioli.

Let the pasta dry slightly while you prepare boiling water.
Heat a big saucepan of salted water until boiling.

Add the pasta to the boiling water and cook until al dente, about 8–10 minutes, depending on its thickness.
Drain the pasta and add the sauce or filling of your choice.

GLUTEN-FREE DESSERT AND BAKING RECIPES

GLUTEN-FREE BANANA WALNUT MUFFINS

FLOUR BLEND: MUFFIN & QUICK BREAD MIX

Ingredients:

- 2 cups Muffin & Quick Bread Mix (240g)
- 1 teaspoon baking soda (5g)
- ½ teaspoon salt (3g)
- 3 ripe bananas, mashed (about 1 ½ cups or 360g)
- ½ cup unsalted butter, melted (115g)
- ¾ cup brown sugar (150g)
- 1 large egg, beaten
- 1 teaspoon vanilla extract (5ml)
- ½ cup chopped walnuts (60g)

Nutritional Information:
(per muffin)

Calories 220, Protein 4g, Carbs 28g, Fat 11g

Instructions:

Mix the flour blend, baking soda, and salt in the bread machine pan.

Mix mashed bananas, melted butter, brown sugar, egg, and vanilla in a separate bowl.

Mix the wet ingredients into the bread machine pan until combined. Stir in chopped walnuts.

Set the machine to the «Cake» or «Quick Bread» setting and start.

Bake until the top turns golden brown. Check for doneness by inserting a toothpick into the center of the muffins; it should come out clean when fully baked.

GLUTEN-FREE CINNAMON ROLLS

FLOUR BLEND: BISCUIT & SCONE MIX

Ingredients:

- 3 cups Biscuit & Scone Mix (360g)
- 2 teaspoons baking powder (10g)
- ½ teaspoon baking soda (3g)
- ½ teaspoon salt (3g)
- ¼ cup sugar (50g)
- 1 cup buttermilk (240ml)
- ½ cup unsalted butter, melted (115g)
- ¼ cup brown sugar (50g)
- 1 tablespoon cinnamon (8g)
- ½ cup raisins (optional) (80g)
- ½ cup chopped pecans (optional) (60g)

Nutritional Information:
(per roll)

Calories 250, Protein 3g, Carbs 30g, Fat 13g

Instructions:

Mix the flour blend, baking powder, baking soda, salt, and sugar in the bread machine pan.

Add buttermilk and melted butter. Mix until a dough forms.

Roll out the dough on a floured surface, brush with melted butter, and sprinkle with brown sugar, cinnamon, raisins, and pecans.

Roll up the dough and slice it into rolls.

Place the rolls in the bread machine pan and set to the «Cake» or «Quick Bread» setting.

Bake until golden brown and cooked through.

147

GLUTEN-FREE CHOCOLATE CHIP CAKE

FLOUR BLEND: ALL-PURPOSE GLUTEN-FREE MIX 1

Ingredients:

- 2 cups All-Purpose Gluten-Free Mix 1 (240g)
- 1 teaspoon baking powder (5g)
- ½ teaspoon baking soda (3g)
- ¼ teaspoon salt (1.5g)
- ½ cup unsalted butter, softened (115g)
- ¾ cup granulated sugar (150g)
- 2 large eggs
- 1 teaspoon vanilla extract (5ml)
- ½ cup milk (120ml)
- 1 cup chocolate chips (175g)

Nutritional Information:
(per slice)

Calories 280, Protein 4g, Carbs 35g, Fat 14g

Instructions:

In the bread machine pan, cream together butter and sugar.

Add eggs one at a time, then vanilla extract.

Mix the flour blend, baking powder, baking soda, and salt.

Gradually add milk, mixing until smooth.

Fold in chocolate chips.

Set the machine to the «Cake» setting and bake until a toothpick comes out clean.

GLUTEN-FREE LEMON POPPY SEED LOAF

FLOUR BLEND: MUFFIN & QUICK BREAD MIX

Ingredients:

- 2 cups Muffin & Quick Bread Mix (240g)
- ½ teaspoon baking powder (2g)
- ¼ teaspoon baking soda (1.5g)
- ¼ teaspoon salt (1.5g)
- ½ cup unsalted butter, softened (115g)
- ¾ cup sugar (150g)
- 2 large eggs
- ¼ cup lemon juice (60ml)
- 1 tablespoon lemon zest (6g)
- ½ cup milk (120ml)
- 2 tablespoons poppy seeds (15g)

Nutritional Information:
(per slice)

Calories 260, Protein 4g, Carbs 32g, Fat 13g

Instructions:

Cream together butter and sugar in the bread machine pan.

Add eggs one at a time, then lemon juice and zest.

Mix the flour blend, baking powder, baking soda, and salt.

Gradually add milk, mixing until smooth.

Stir in poppy seeds.

Set the bread machine to the «Cake» setting and allow the mixture to bake until the top turns golden brown. Check for doneness by inserting a toothpick into the center; it should come out clean when fully baked.

GLUTEN-FREE PUMPKIN SPICE CAKE

FLOUR BLEND: ALL-PURPOSE GLUTEN-FREE MIX 2

Ingredients:

- 2 cups All-Purpose Gluten-Free Mix 2 (240g)
- 1 teaspoon baking powder (4g)
- ½ teaspoon baking soda (3g)
- ¼ teaspoon salt (1.5g)
- ½ teaspoon cinnamon (1g)
- ½ teaspoon nutmeg (1g)
- ¼ teaspoon ground ginger (0.5g)
- ¼ teaspoon ground cloves (0.5g)
- 1 cup canned pumpkin puree (240g)
- ½ cup unsalted butter, softened (115g)
- ¾ cup sugar (150g)
- 2 large eggs
- ¼ cup milk (60ml)

Nutritional Information:
(per slice)

Calories 240, Protein 4g, Carbs 32g, Fat 0g

Instructions:

In the bread machine pan, cream together butter and sugar.

Incorporate the eggs one at a time, then add the pumpkin puree.

Mix the flour blend, baking powder, baking soda, salt, and spices.

Gradually add milk, mixing until smooth.

Set the bread machine to the «Cake» setting and allow the mixture to bake until the top turns golden brown. Check for doneness by inserting a toothpick into the center of the loaf; it should come out clean when fully baked.

GLUTEN-FREE BLUEBERRY SCONES

FLOUR BLEND: BISCUIT & SCONE MIX

Ingredients:

- 2 cups Biscuit & Scone Mix (240g)
- ¼ cup sugar (50g)
- ½ teaspoon baking powder (2g)
- ¼ teaspoon baking soda (1.5g)
- ½ cup unsalted butter, cold and cubed (115g)
- ½ cup buttermilk (120ml)
- 1 large egg
- 1 teaspoon vanilla extract (5ml)
- 1 cup fresh blueberries (150g)

Nutritional Information:
(per scone)

Calories 210, Protein 3g, Carbs 28g, Fat 10g

Instructions:

Mix the flour blend, sugar, baking powder, and baking soda in the bread machine pan.

Cut in cold butter until the mixture resembles coarse crumbs.

Whisk together buttermilk, egg, and vanilla in a separate bowl.

Mix the wet ingredients in the bread machine pan until combined.

Gently fold in blueberries.

Set the machine to the «Cake» or «Quick Bread» setting and bake until golden brown.

GLUTEN-FREE CHOCOLATE BROWNIES

FLOUR BLEND: COOKIE FLOUR MIX

Ingredients:

- 1 cup Cookie Flour Mix (120g)
- ½ cup unsalted butter, melted (115g)
- 1 cup sugar (200g)
- 2 large eggs
- 1 teaspoon vanilla extract (5ml)
- ⅓ cup cocoa powder (30g)
- ¼ teaspoon salt (1.5g)
- ½ cup chocolate chips (optional) (90g)
- ½ cup chopped walnuts (optional) (60g)

Nutritional Information:

(per brownie)

Calories 250, Protein 3g, Carbs 35g, Fat 12g

Instructions:

Whisk together melted butter and sugar in the bread machine pan.

Add eggs one at a time, then vanilla extract.

Mix cocoa powder, flour blend, and salt until smooth.

Fold in chocolate chips and walnuts if using.

Set the machine to the «Cake» setting and bake until set.

GLUTEN-FREE APPLE CINNAMON BREAD PUDDING

FLOUR BLEND: USE ANY GLUTEN-FREE BREAD

Ingredients:

- 6 cups cubed gluten-free bread from a previously baked loaf (450g)
- 2 large apples, peeled and diced
- ½ cup raisins (75g)
- 2 teaspoons cinnamon (8g)
- ¼ teaspoon nutmeg (1g)
- 4 large eggs
- 2 cups milk (480ml)
- ½ cup sugar (100g)
- 1 teaspoon vanilla extract (5ml)

Nutritional Information:
(per serving)

Calories 220, Protein 6g, Carbs 35g, Fat 7g

Instructions:

Combine bread cubes, apples, raisins, cinnamon, and nutmeg in the bread machine pan.

Whisk together eggs, milk, sugar, and vanilla in a separate bowl.

Pour the mixture over the bread and stir to combine.

Set the machine to the «Cake» or «Quick Bread» setting and bake until set and golden brown.

GLUTEN-FREE RASPBERRY ALMOND COFFEE CAKE

FLOUR BLEND: PASTRY FLOUR MIX

Ingredients:

- 2 cups Pastry Flour Mix (240g)
- 1 tsp baking powder (4g)
- ¼ tsp baking soda (1.5g)
- ¼ tsp salt (1.5g)
- ½ cup unsalted butter, softened (115g)
- ¾ cup sugar (150g)
- 2 large eggs
- ½ cup sour cream (120ml)
- 1 tsp almond extract (5ml)
- 1 cup fresh raspberries (150g)
- ½ cup sliced almonds (60g)

Nutritional Information:

(per slice)

Calories 250, Protein 5g, Carbs 30g, Fat 12g

Instructions:

In the bread machine pan, cream together butter and sugar.

Add eggs one at a time, then sour cream and almond extract.

Mix in the flour blend, baking powder, baking soda, and salt until smooth.

Gently fold in raspberries and almonds.

Set the bread machine to the «Cake» setting and allow the mixture to bake until the top turns golden brown. Check for doneness by inserting a toothpick into the center; it should come out clean when fully baked.

GLUTEN-FREE CARROT CAKE WITH CREAM CHEESE FROSTING

FLOUR BLEND: ALL-PURPOSE GLUTEN-FREE MIX 1

Ingredients:

- 2 cups All-Purpose Gluten-Free Mix 1 (240g)
- 1 teaspoon baking powder (4g)
- ½ teaspoon baking soda (3g)
- ¼ teaspoon salt (1.5g)
- 1 teaspoon cinnamon (2g)
- ¼ teaspoon ground ginger (0.5g)
- ¼ teaspoon nutmeg (0.5g)
- ½ cup unsalted butter, melted (115g)
- ¾ cup brown sugar (150g)
- 2 large eggs
- 1 teaspoon vanilla extract (5ml)
- ½ cup crushed pineapple, drained (120g)
- 1 ½ cups grated carrots (150g)
- ½ cup chopped walnuts (60g)
  Cream Cheese Frosting:
  ½ cup cream cheese, softened (120g)
  ¼ cup unsalted butter, softened (60g)
  1 cup powdered sugar (120g)
  1 teaspoon vanilla extract (5ml)

Nutritional Information:

(per slice)   *Calories 320, Protein 5g, Carbs 42g, Fat 16g*

Instructions:

Mix the flour blend, baking powder, baking soda, salt, cinnamon, ginger, and nutmeg in the bread machine pan.

Mix melted butter, brown sugar, eggs, and vanilla in a separate bowl.

Mix the wet ingredients into the bread machine pan until combined.

Stir in pineapple, grated carrots, and walnuts.

Set the bread machine to the «Cake» setting and allow the mixture to bake until the top turns golden brown. Check for doneness by inserting a toothpick into the center of the loaf; it should come out clean when fully baked.

For the frosting, beat cream cheese, butter, powdered sugar, and vanilla until smooth. Spread over the cooled cake.

151

GLUTEN-FREE LEMON DRIZZLE CAKE

FLOUR BLEND: ALL-PURPOSE GLUTEN-FREE MIX 2

Ingredients:

- 2 cups All-Purpose Gluten-Free Mix 2 (240g)
- 1 teaspoon baking powder (4g)
- ¼ teaspoon baking soda (1.5g)
- ¼ teaspoon salt (1.5g)
- ½ cup unsalted butter, softened (115g)
- ¾ cup granulated sugar (150g)
- 2 large eggs
- ¼ cup lemon juice (60ml)
- 1 tablespoon lemon zest (6g)
- ½ cup milk (120ml)
  Lemon Glaze:
- ¼ cup lemon juice (60ml)
- ½ cup powdered sugar (60g)

Nutritional Information:
(per slice)

Calories 240, Protein 4g, Carbs 32g, Fat 10g

Instructions:

In the bread machine pan, cream together butter and sugar.

Add eggs one at a time, then lemon juice and zest.

Mix the flour blend, baking powder, baking soda, and salt.

Gradually add milk, mixing until smooth.

Set the bread machine to the «Cake» setting and allow the mixture to bake until the top turns golden brown. Check for doneness by inserting a toothpick into the center of the loaf; it should come out clean when fully baked.

Mix lemon juice and powdered sugar to glaze while the cake is still warm. Drizzle over the cake.

GLUTEN-FREE CRANBERRY ORANGE MUFFINS

FLOUR BLEND: MUFFIN & QUICK BREAD MIX

Ingredients:

- 2 cups Muffin & Quick Bread Mix (240g)
- 1 teaspoon baking powder (4g)
- ¼ teaspoon baking soda (1.5g)
- ¼ teaspoon salt (1.5g)
- ½ cup unsalted butter, softened (115g)
- ¾ cup sugar (150g)
- 2 large eggs
- ½ cup orange juice (120ml)
- 1 tablespoon orange zest (6g)
- ½ cup dried cranberries (60g)
- ½ cup chopped walnuts (optional) (60g)

Nutritional Information:
(per muffin)

Calories 210, Protein 4g, Carbs 28g, Fat 10g

Instructions:

In the bread machine pan, cream together butter and sugar.

Add eggs one at a time, then orange juice and zest.

Mix the flour blend, baking powder, baking soda, and salt.

Stir in dried cranberries and walnuts if using.

Set the machine to the «Cake» or «Quick Bread» setting and bake until a toothpick comes out clean.

GLUTEN-FREE DOUBLE CHOCOLATE LOAF

FLOUR BLEND: ALL-PURPOSE GLUTEN-FREE MIX 1

Ingredients:

- 2 cups All-Purpose Gluten-Free Mix 1 (240g)
- ½ cup cocoa powder (50g)
- 1 teaspoon baking powder (4g)
- ½ teaspoon baking soda (3g)
- ¼ teaspoon salt (1.5g)
- ½ cup unsalted butter, softened (115g)
- ¾ cup sugar (150g)
- 2 large eggs
- 1 teaspoon vanilla extract (5ml)
- ½ cup milk (120ml)
- 1 cup chocolate chips (175g)

Nutritional Information:
(per slice)

Calories 270, Protein 4g, Carbs 35g, Fat 14g

Instructions:

In the bread machine pan, cream together butter and sugar.

Incorporate the eggs one at a time, then add the vanilla extract.

Mix cocoa powder, flour blend, baking powder, baking soda, and salt.

Gradually add milk, mixing until smooth.

Stir in chocolate chips.

Set the bread machine to the «Cake» setting and allow the mixture to bake until the top turns golden brown. Check for doneness by inserting a toothpick into the center of the loaf; it should come out clean when fully baked.

GLUTEN-FREE ALMOND FLOUR POUND CAKE

FLOUR BLEND: ALMOND FLOUR MIX

Ingredients:

- 2 cups Almond Flour Mix (240g)
- 1 teaspoon baking powder (4g)
- ¼ teaspoon salt (1.5g)
- ½ cup unsalted butter, softened (115g)
- ¾ cup sugar (150g)
- 3 large eggs
- 1 teaspoon vanilla extract (5ml)
- ¼ cup almond milk (60ml)

Nutritional Information:
(per slice)

Calories 290, Protein 6g, Carbs 18g, Fat 22g

Instructions:

In the bread machine pan, cream together butter and sugar.

Incorporate the eggs one at a time, then add the vanilla extract.

Mix the almond flour blend, baking powder, and salt.

Gradually add almond milk, mixing until smooth.

Set the bread machine to the «Cake» setting and allow the mixture to bake until the top turns golden brown. Check for doneness by inserting a toothpick into the center of the loaf; it should come out clean when fully baked.

GLUTEN-FREE VANILLA CUPCAKES

FLOUR BLEND: CAKE FLOUR MIX

Ingredients:

- 2 cups Cake Flour Mix (240g)
- 1 teaspoon baking powder (4g)
- ¼ teaspoon baking soda (1.5g)
- ¼ teaspoon salt (1.5g)
- ½ cup unsalted butter, softened (115g)
- ¾ cup sugar (150g)
- 2 large eggs
- 1 teaspoon vanilla extract (5ml)
- ½ cup milk (120ml)

Nutritional Information:

(per cupcake)

Calories 210, Protein 4g, Carbs 28g, Fat 10g

Instructions:

In the bread machine pan, cream together butter and sugar.

Incorporate the eggs one at a time, then add the vanilla extract.

Mix the flour blend, baking powder, baking soda, and salt.

Gradually add milk, mixing until smooth.

Set the bread machine to the «Cake» setting and allow the mixture to bake until the top turns golden brown. Check for doneness by inserting a toothpick into the center of the loaf; it should come out clean when fully baked.

GLUTEN-FREE CHOCOLATE CHIP BANANA BREAD

FLOUR BLEND: MUFFIN & QUICK BREAD MIX

Ingredients:

- 2 cups Muffin & Quick Bread Mix (240g)
- ½ teaspoon baking soda (2g)
- ¼ teaspoon salt (1.5g)
- 3 ripe bananas, mashed (about 300g)
- ½ cup unsalted butter, melted (115g)
- ¾ cup brown sugar (150g)
- 1 large egg
- 1 teaspoon vanilla extract (5ml)
- ½ cup chocolate chips (90g)

Nutritional Information:

(per slice)

Calories 250, Protein 4g, Carbs 35g, Fat 11g

Instructions:

Mix the flour blend, baking soda, and salt in the bread machine pan.

Mix mashed bananas, melted butter, brown sugar, egg, and vanilla in a separate bowl.

Mix the wet ingredients into the bread machine pan until combined.

Stir in chocolate chips.

Set the machine to the «Cake» or «Quick Bread» setting and bake until a toothpick comes out clean.

154

GLUTEN-FREE CHOCOLATE HAZELNUT BREAD

FLOUR BLEND: ALL-PURPOSE GLUTEN-FREE MIX 1

Ingredients:

- 2 cups All-Purpose Gluten-Free Mix 1 (240g)
- ½ cup cocoa powder (50g)
- 1 teaspoon baking powder (4g)
- ½ teaspoon baking soda (3g)
- ¼ teaspoon salt (1.5g)
- ½ cup unsalted butter, softened (115g)
- ¾ cup sugar (150g)
- 2 large eggs
- 1 teaspoon vanilla extract (5ml)
- ½ cup milk (120ml)
- ½ cup chopped hazelnuts (60g)
- ½ cup chocolate chips (optional) (90g)

Nutritional Information:

(per slice)

Calories 270, Protein 5g, Carbs 32g, Fat 14g

Instructions:

In the bread machine pan, cream together butter and sugar.

Incorporate the eggs one at a time, then add the vanilla extract.

Mix cocoa powder, flour blend, baking powder, baking soda, and salt.

Gradually add milk, mixing until smooth.

Stir in chopped hazelnuts and chocolate chips if using.

Set the bread machine to the «Cake» setting and allow the mixture to bake until the top turns golden brown. Check for doneness by inserting a toothpick into the center of the loaf; it should come out clean when fully baked.

GLUTEN-FREE PEACH COBBLER CAKE

FLOUR BLEND: BISCUIT & SCONE MIX

Ingredients:

- 2 cups Almond Flour Mix (240g)
- 2 cups Biscuit & Scone Mix (240g)
- ¼ cup sugar (50g)
- 1 teaspoon baking powder (4g)
- ¼ teaspoon baking soda (1.5g)
- ½ teaspoon salt (2.5g)
- ½ cup unsalted butter, cold and cubed (115g)
- ½ cup buttermilk (120ml)
- 1 large egg
- 1 teaspoon vanilla extract (5ml)
- 2 cups sliced peaches (fresh or canned) (300g)
- ¼ cup brown sugar (50g)
- ½ teaspoon cinnamon (1g)

Nutritional Information:

(per serving)

Calories 260, Protein 4g, Carbs 38g, Fat 10g

Instructions:

Mix the flour blend, sugar, baking powder, baking soda, and salt in the bread machine pan.

Cut in cold butter until the mixture resembles coarse crumbs.

Whisk together buttermilk, egg, and vanilla in a separate bowl.

Mix the wet ingredients in the bread machine pan until combined.

Layer sliced peaches on the batter and sprinkle with brown sugar and cinnamon.

Set the machine to the «Cake» or «Quick Bread» setting and bake until the cake is golden brown.

GLUTEN-FREE MOCHA COFFEE CAKE

FLOUR BLEND: CAKE FLOUR MIX

Ingredients:

- 2 cups Cake Flour Mix (240g)
- ¼ cup cocoa powder (25g)
- 1 teaspoon baking powder (4g)
- ¼ teaspoon baking soda (1.5g)
- ¼ teaspoon salt (1.5g)
- ½ cup unsalted butter, softened (115g)
- ¾ cup sugar (150g)
- 2 large eggs
- 1 teaspoon vanilla extract (5ml)
- ½ cup brewed coffee, cooled (120ml)
- ½ cup sour cream (120ml)
- ½ cup chocolate chips (optional) (90g)

Nutritional Information:
(per slice)

Calories 280, Protein 5g, Carbs 38g, Fat 12g

Instructions:

In the bread machine pan, cream together butter and sugar.

Incorporate the eggs one at a time, then add the vanilla extract.

Mix cocoa powder, flour blend, baking powder, baking soda, and salt.

Gradually add coffee and sour cream, mixing until smooth.

Stir in chocolate chips if using.

Set the bread machine to the «Cake» setting and allow the mixture to bake until the top turns golden brown. Check for doneness by inserting a toothpick into the center of the loaf; it should come out clean when fully baked.

GLUTEN-FREE HONEY BUTTER BISCUITS

FLOUR BLEND: BISCUIT & SCONE MIX

Ingredients:

- 2 cups Biscuit & Scone Mix (240g)
- 1 tablespoon baking powder (12g)
- ½ teaspoon baking soda (3g)
- ¼ teaspoon salt (1.5g)
- ¼ cup unsalted butter, cold and cubed (57g)
- ¾ cup buttermilk (180ml)
- ¼ cup honey (85g)
- 1 large egg, beaten

Nutritional Information:
(per biscuit)

Calories 220, Protein 4g, Carbs 30g, Fat 9g

Instructions:

Mix the flour blend, baking powder, baking soda, and salt in the bread machine pan.

Cut in cold butter until the mixture resembles coarse crumbs.

Whisk together buttermilk, honey, and beaten egg separately.

Mix the wet ingredients in the bread machine pan until combined.

Set the machine to the «Dough» setting, then shape the dough into biscuits and bake in a preheated oven at 375°F (190°C) until golden brown.

CHAPTER 12:

DIET-FRIENDLY RECIPES: WHOLE GRAIN BREAD

WHOLE GRAIN BREAD FOR BREAD MACHINES: BILL'S TIPS

Whole-grain bread is beneficial in various diets due to its high fiber content, which aids digestion and helps maintain stable blood sugar levels. It's a key component of the Mediterranean diet and weight management plans, supports heart health, and can be useful for people with diabetes because of its low glycemic index. Whole-grain bread also boosts metabolism and can fit into low-carb diets, depending on the specific type.

WHOLE GRAIN BREAD FOR BREAD MACHINES:

When making whole-grain bread in a bread machine, it's crucial to recognize the distinct qualities of whole-grain flour. Whole-grain bread is an excellent choice for those looking for a healthier option, but it does require some specific considerations.

1. Choosing the Flour

Whole grain flour includes the entire grain—bran, germ, and endosperm—adding rich flavor and nutritional value to the bread. However, it's heavier and takes longer to rise. Bill recommends using freshly ground flour, which retains the most nutrients and flavor.

2. Kneading and Mixing

Due to its higher fiber content, whole-grain dough requires more water than white flour dough. Bill advises monitoring the dough's consistency during mixing. It should be soft but not too sticky. If the dough is too dense, add a tablespoon of water. If it's too sticky, add a little more flour.

3. Rising and Baking Time

Whole-grain dough rises more slowly than white flour dough. If your bread machine has a whole-grain setting, use it. This setting typically allows longer rising and baking times for the right texture.

4. Adding Sweeteners and Fats

Bill suggests adding a small amount of natural sweetener (such as honey) and oil to enhance flavor and help the dough rise better. Additionally, incorporating seeds, nuts, or oats can enrich the taste and texture of your bread.

5. Storing the Bread

Due to its lower fat content, whole-grain bread tends to stale faster. Bill recommends storing it in an airtight container at room temperature for 2-3 days. For longer storage, slice and freeze the bread.

6. Bill's Tips

Check the dough 10 minutes after starting the kneading cycle. It should be elastic and pull away from the sides of the pan. This is a key indicator that the dough is the right consistency.

Don't be afraid to experiment with add-ins. Flax seeds, sunflower seeds, or even dried berries can make your bread unique and more nutritious.

157

Remember to be patient. Whole grain bread may take longer to rise, but the result is worth the wait.

CLASSIC WHOLE WHEAT BREAD

Ingredients:

- 3 cups whole wheat flour (360g)
- 1 ½ cups warm water (360ml)
- 2 tablespoons honey (30ml)
- 2 teaspoons active dry yeast (7g)
- ¼ cup olive oil (60ml)
- 1 teaspoon salt (5g)

Nutritional Information:
(on one slice, assuming 12 slices)

140 calories, 3g fat, 24g carbs, 6g protein

Instructions:

Activate Yeast: In a small bowl, dissolve the yeast in warm water and stir in the honey. Let the mixture sit for 5-10 minutes until it becomes foamy.

Load Ingredients: Add the yeast mixture, whole wheat flour, olive oil, and salt to the bread machine pan in the order recommended by the manufacturer.

Select Settings: On your bread machine, select the whole wheat cycle. Then, set the crust color and loaf size according to your preference.

Start: Close the lid and press start. The bread machine will handle the kneading, rising, and baking process.

Bill's Tip:
Cover the bread with foil during the last 10 minutes of baking for a softer crust.

WHOLE WHEAT OAT BREAD

Ingredients:

- 2 cups whole wheat flour (240g)
- 1 cup oat flour (120g)
- 1 ½ cups warm water (360ml)
- 2 tablespoons maple syrup (30ml)
- 2 teaspoons active dry yeast (7g)
- ¼ cup melted butter (60g)
- 1 teaspoon salt (5g)

Nutritional Information:
(on one slice, assuming 12 slices)

160 calories, 5g fat, 22g carbs, 5g protein

Instructions:

Activate Yeast: Combine warm water and maple syrup in a small bowl, then sprinkle the yeast. Let it sit for 5–10 minutes until it becomes foamy.

Load Ingredients: Add the yeast mixture, whole wheat flour, oat flour, melted butter, and salt into the bread machine pan in the order recommended by the manufacturer.

Select Settings: On your bread machine, select the whole wheat cycle. Then, set the crust color and loaf size according to your preference.

Start: Close the lid and press start. The machine will handle the kneading, rising, and baking process.

Bill's Tip:
For added texture, sprinkle a handful of oats on top of the dough before the final rise.

WHOLE WHEAT & FLAXSEED BREAD

Ingredients:

- 2 cups whole wheat flour (240g)
- ½ cup ground flaxseed (50g)
- 1 ½ cups warm water (360ml)
- 2 tablespoons honey (30ml)
- 2 teaspoons active dry yeast (7g)
- ¼ cup vegetable oil (60ml)
- 1 teaspoon salt (5g)

Nutritional Information:
(on one slice, assuming 12 slices)
150 calories, 6g fat, 22g carbs, 5g protein

Instructions:

Activate Yeast: Mix the yeast with warm water and honey in a small bowl. Allow it to sit until it becomes bubbly, about 5-10 minutes.

Load Ingredients: Add the yeast mixture, whole wheat flour, ground flaxseed, vegetable oil, and salt to the bread machine pan in the order the manufacturer recommends.

Select Settings: Select the whole wheat cycle on your bread machine, then select your preferred crust color and loaf size.

Start: Close the lid and press start. The machine will handle the kneading, rising, and baking for you.

Bill's Tip:

For added texture, sprinkle a handful of oats on top of the dough before the final rise.

WHOLE WHEAT & SUNFLOWER SEED BREAD

Ingredients:

- 2 cups whole wheat flour (240g)
- ½ cup sunflower seeds (70g)
- 1 ½ cups warm water (360ml)
- 2 tablespoons brown sugar (28g)
- 2 teaspoons active dry yeast (7g)
- ¼ cup olive oil (60ml)
- 1 teaspoon salt (5g)

Instructions:

Activate Yeast: In a small bowl, dissolve the yeast in warm water with brown sugar. Let it sit until foamy, about 5–10 minutes.

Load Ingredients: Add the yeast mixture, whole wheat flour, sunflower seeds, olive oil, and salt to the bread machine pan in the manufacturer's recommended order.

Select Settings: Select the whole wheat cycle on your bread machine, then select your preferred crust color and loaf size.

Start: Close the lid and press start. The machine will take care of the kneading, rising, and baking.

Nutritional Information:
(on one slice, assuming 12 slices)

160 calories, 7g fat, 21g carbs, 5g protein

Bill's Tip:

Lightly toast the sunflower seeds before adding them to the dough for a flavor boost.

WHOLE WHEAT RYE BREAD

Ingredients:

- 1 ½ cups whole wheat flour (180g)
- 1 ½ cups rye flour (180g)
- 1 ½ cups warm water (360ml)
- 2 tablespoons molasses (30ml)
- 2 teaspoons active dry yeast (7g)
- ¼ cup vegetable oil (60ml)
- 1 teaspoon salt (5g)

Instructions:

Activate Yeast: Mix the yeast with warm water and molasses in a small bowl. Let it sit until foamy, about 5–10 minutes.

Load Ingredients: Add the yeast mixture, whole wheat flour, rye flour, vegetable oil, and salt to the bread machine pan in the order recommended by the manufacturer.

Select Settings: On your bread machine, select the whole wheat or rye cycle, your preferred crust color, and loaf size.

Start: Close the lid and press start. The machine will handle the kneading, rising, and baking.

Nutritional Information:
(on one slice, assuming 12 slices)

140 calories, 3g fat, 24g carbs, 6g protein

Bill's Tip:

Rye flour can be dense, so allow the machine to knead thoroughly to achieve a light, airy texture.

WHOLE WHEAT HONEY BREAD

Ingredients:

- 2 cups whole wheat flour (240g)
- ½ cup honey (120ml)
- 1 ½ cups warm water (360ml)
- 2 teaspoons active dry yeast (7g)
- ¼ cup melted butter (60ml)
- 1 teaspoon salt (5g)

Instructions:

Activate Yeast: Combine the yeast with warm water and honey in a small bowl. Let sit until it becomes bubbly, about 5–10 minutes.

Load Ingredients: Pour the yeast mixture into the bread machine pan, followed by the whole wheat flour, melted butter, and salt.

Select Settings: Choose the whole wheat cycle on your bread machine, adjusting for your desired crust color and loaf size.

Start: Close the lid and press start. The machine will take care of the kneading, rising, and baking.

Nutritional Information:
(on one slice, assuming 12 slices)

180 calories, 7g fat, 26g carbs, 5g protein

Bill's Tip:

For an extra sweet touch, brush the loaf's top with honey before baking.

WHOLE WHEAT & ALMOND BREAD

Ingredients:

- 2 cups whole wheat flour (240g)
- ½ cup almond flour (60g)
- 1 ½ cups warm water (360ml)
- 2 tablespoons maple syrup (30ml)
- 2 teaspoons active dry yeast (7g)
- ¼ cup olive oil (60ml)
- 1 teaspoon salt (5g)

Instructions:

Activate Yeast: In a small bowl, mix the yeast with warm water and maple syrup. Let sit for 5–10 minutes until foamy.

Load Ingredients: Pour the yeast mixture into the bread machine pan. Add the whole wheat flour, almond flour, olive oil, and salt.

Select Settings: Choose the whole wheat cycle on your bread machine, adjusting for crust color and loaf size.

Start: Close the lid and press start. The machine will take care of the kneading, rising, and baking.

Nutritional Information:

(on one slice, assuming 12 slices)

190 calories, 8g fat, 21g carbs, 6g protein

Bill's Tip:

To enhance the flavor of the dough, lightly toast the almond flour before adding it.

WHOLE WHEAT & CHIA BREAD

Ingredients:

- 2 cups whole wheat flour (240g)
- ¼ cup chia seeds (40g)
- 1 ½ cups warm water (360ml)
- 2 tablespoons honey (30ml)
- 2 teaspoons active dry yeast (7g)
- ¼ cup vegetable oil (60ml)
- 1 teaspoon salt (5g)

Instructions:

Activate Yeast: Combine the yeast with warm water and honey in a small bowl. Let it sit for 5–10 minutes until foamy.

Load Ingredients: Add the yeast mixture into the bread machine pan. Then, add the whole wheat flour, chia seeds, vegetable oil, and salt.

Select Settings: Choose the whole wheat cycle on your bread machine, adjusting for crust color and loaf size if needed.

Start: Close the lid and press start. The machine will handle the kneading, rising, and baking.

Nutritional Information:

(on one slice, assuming 12 slices)

170 calories, 6g fat, 22g carbs, 6g protein

Bill's Tip:

For added crunch, sprinkle chia seeds on the loaf before baking.

WHOLE WHEAT & CARAMELIZED ONION BREAD

Ingredients:

- 2 cups whole wheat flour (240g)
- 1 cup caramelized onions, cooled (150g)
- 1 ½ cups warm water (360ml)
- 2 tablespoons honey (30ml)
- 2 teaspoons active dry yeast (7g)
- ¼ cup olive oil (60ml)
- 1 teaspoon salt (5g)

Instructions:

Activate Yeast: In a small bowl, mix the yeast with warm water and honey. Let it sit for 5–10 minutes until it becomes foamy.

Load Ingredients: Add the yeast mixture into the bread machine pan. Then, add the whole wheat flour, caramelized onions, olive oil, and salt.

Select Settings: Select the whole wheat cycle on your bread machine. If necessary, adjust the crust color and loaf size settings.

Start: Close the lid and press start. The machine will handle the kneading, rising, and baking.

Nutritional Information:

(on one slice, assuming 12 slices)

180 calories, 7g fat, 25g carbs, 5g protein

Bill's Tip:

Caramelized onions should be cool before adding to the dough to prevent killing the yeast.

WHOLE WHEAT & PUMPKIN BREAD

Ingredients:

- 2 cups whole wheat flour (240g)
- 1 cup pumpkin puree (240g)
- 1 ½ cups warm water (360ml)
- 2 tablespoons honey (30ml)
- 2 teaspoons active dry yeast (7g)
- ¼ cup vegetable oil (60ml)
- 1 teaspoon salt (5g)
- 1 teaspoon cinnamon (optional, 2g)

Instructions:

Activate Yeast: Combine yeast with warm water and honey in a small bowl. Let it sit for 5–10 minutes until bubbly.

Load Ingredients: Add the yeast mixture to the bread machine pan. Then add the whole wheat flour, pumpkin puree, vegetable oil, salt, and cinnamon (if using).

Select Settings: Select the whole wheat cycle on your bread machine. If necessary, adjust the crust color and loaf size settings.

Start: Close the lid and press start. The machine will handle the kneading, rising, and baking.

Nutritional Information:

(on one slice, assuming 12 slices)

160 calories, 6g fat, 24g carbs, 5g protein

Bill's Tip:

For a more intense pumpkin flavor, add a pinch of nutmeg or cloves.

HOW TO BAKE PUMPKIN BREAD IN A BREAD MACHINE: BILL'S TIPS

Pumpkin bread dough can be quite moist, making it challenging to work with in some bread machines. If you encounter issues with your pumpkin bread dough, here are a few tips to improve the results:

Reduce Moisture: If the dough is too wet, try reducing the amount of liquid or adding a bit more flour. Pumpkin puree contains a lot of moisture, so a slight increase in flour can help make the dough more manageable.

Use Parchment Paper: If the dough sticks to the bread machine pan, use parchment paper to make it easier to remove the bread.

Adjust Baking Time: Since pumpkin bread can be denser, check for doneness with a toothpick. If it comes out clean, the bread is done, even if it needs extra time in the machine.

Choose the Right Flour: Sometimes, using a flour blend with less moisture can help. For instance, high-protein flour, such as whole wheat flour, can improve the texture of the dough.

Check Puree Moisture: If you make the pumpkin puree yourself, ensure it is smooth enough. Avoid adding extra liquid.

CHAPTER 13:

DIET-FRIENDLY RECIPES: VEGAN BREAD

VEGAN BREAD FOR BREAD MACHINES: BILL'S TIPS

Vegan bread is crafted without animal products, meaning no dairy, eggs, or honey. This type of bread often relies on plant-based ingredients to achieve the desired texture, flavor, and nutrition. Here are some key considerations for making vegan bread:

SUBSTITUTES FOR TRADITIONAL INGREDIENTS:

Dairy Alternatives: Plant-based milk (almond, soy, or oat) is used instead of cow's milk. Vegan butter or oils like coconut or olive oil can replace traditional butter.

Egg Replacements: Depending on the recipe's needs, eggs are often substituted with flaxseed or chia seed «eggs» (made by mixing ground seeds with water), applesauce, mashed bananas, or commercial egg replacers.

Sweeteners: Instead of honey, which is not vegan, maple syrup, agave nectar, or other plant-based sweeteners are used.

NUTRITIONAL FOCUS:

Healthy Fats: These breads often include healthy fats from nuts, seeds, or avocados, providing essential fatty acids.

Whole Grains: Many vegan breads incorporate whole grains, such as entire wheat, spelt, or oats, which are higher in fiber and nutrients.

Protein: Since vegans don't consume animal products, adding protein-rich ingredients like quinoa, amaranth, or seeds (chia, flax, hemp) can boost the bread's protein content.

FLAVOR AND TEXTURE:

Flavors: Herbs, spices, and other natural flavorings, such as garlic, rosemary, or sun-dried tomatoes, are often used to enhance the flavor.

Texture: Vegan bread may have a slightly different texture due to the absence of eggs and dairy. Techniques like properly balancing liquids, fat, and leavening agents help achieve a satisfying crumb and crust.

HEALTH BENEFITS:

Cholesterol-Free: Since there are no animal products, vegan bread is naturally cholesterol-free.

Dietary Restrictions: Vegan bread suits those with lactose intolerance, egg allergies, and anyone following a vegan diet.

BAKING CONSIDERATIONS:

Rise and Structure: Vegan bread sometimes needs more time to rise or different rising techniques since eggs and dairy traditionally help with structure. Ensuring the correct balance of moisture and flour is key.

Binding Agents: Since eggs are a common binder in traditional bread, alternatives like flaxseed or chia seed «eggs» or xanthan gum can help maintain the bread's structure.

Incorporating these elements ensures that vegan bread is not just a substitute but a delicious and nutritious option.

VEGAN WHOLE WHEAT BREAD

Ingredients:

- 3 cups whole wheat flour (360g)
- 1 ½ cups warm water (360ml)
- 2 tablespoons olive oil (30ml)
- 2 tablespoons maple syrup (30ml)
- 2 ¼ teaspoons active dry yeast (7g)
- 1 teaspoon salt (5g)

Nutritional Information:
(per slice, assuming 12 slices)

150 calories, 6g protein, 3g fat, 27g carbs

Instructions:

Prepare Ingredients: Add warm water, olive oil, and maple syrup to your bread machine pan.

Activate Yeast: Sprinkle yeast over the liquid and let it sit for 5 minutes until it becomes frothy.

Add Dry Ingredients: Add the whole wheat flour and salt to the activated yeast mixture.

Select Settings: Choose your bread machine's «Whole Wheat» setting.

Bake: Close the lid and press start. The machine will handle the kneading, rising, and baking.

Bill's Tip:

Add ¼ cup sunflower seeds to the dough for a nutty flavor.

VEGAN ROSEMARY OLIVE BREAD

Ingredients:

- 3 cups bread flour (360g)
- 1 ½ cups warm water (360ml)
- ¼ cup olive oil (60ml)
- 1 tablespoon maple syrup (15ml)
- 2 teaspoons active dry yeast (6g)
- 1 teaspoon salt (5g)
- ½ cup chopped black olives (75g)
- 2 tablespoons fresh rosemary, chopped (6g)

Nutritional Information:
(per slice, assuming 12 slices)

170 calories, 4g protein, 7g fat, 23g carbs

Instructions:

Prepare Ingredients: Pour warm water, olive oil, and maple syrup into the bread machine pan.

Activate Yeast: Sprinkle the yeast over the liquid mixture. Allow it to sit for 5 minutes until it becomes foamy.

Add Dry Ingredients: Add bread flour, salt, chopped olives, and rosemary to the activated yeast mixture.

Select Settings: Choose the «Basic» or «French» setting on your bread machine.

Bake: Close the lid and press start. The machine will handle the mixing, rising, and baking.

Bill's Tip:

Use high-quality olive oil for the best flavor!

VEGAN CINNAMON RAISIN BREAD

Ingredients:

- 3 cups bread flour (360g)
- 1 ¼ cups warm water (300ml)
- 2 tablespoons coconut oil, melted (30ml)
- 3 tablespoons maple syrup (45ml)
- 2 teaspoons active dry yeast (6g)
- 1 teaspoon salt (5g)
- 1 tablespoon ground cinnamon (8g)
- ½ cup raisins (75g)

Nutritional Information:
(per slice, assuming 12 slices)

180 calories, 4g protein, 4g fat, 35g carbs

Instructions:

Prepare Ingredients: Add warm water, melted coconut oil, and maple syrup to the bread machine pan.

Activate Yeast: Sprinkle the yeast over the liquid mixture and activate it for 5 minutes.

Add Dry Ingredients: Add bread flour, salt, and ground cinnamon to the activated yeast mixture.

Add Raisins: Sprinkle raisins on top of the dough ingredients.

Select Settings: Choose the «Sweet» or «Basic» setting on your bread machine.

Bake: Let the machine complete its cycle.

Bill's Tip:

For extra sweetness, top the loaf with a cinnamon sugar glaze after baking.

VEGAN GARLIC HERB BREAD

Ingredients:

- 3 cups all-purpose flour (360g)
- 1 ¼ cups warm water (300ml)
- 3 tablespoons olive oil (45ml)
- 1 tablespoon maple syrup (15ml)
- 2 teaspoons active dry yeast (6g)
- 1 teaspoon salt (5g)
- 1 tablespoon minced garlic (8g)
- 1 teaspoon dried oregano (1g)
- 1 teaspoon dried thyme (1g)

Nutritional Information:
(per slice, assuming 12 slices)

160 calories, 4g protein, 5g fat, 26g carbs

Instructions:

Prepare Ingredients: Pour warm water, olive oil, and maple syrup into the bread machine pan.

Activate Yeast: Add the yeast to the liquid mixture and let it sit for 5 minutes.

Add Dry Ingredients: Add all-purpose flour, salt, minced garlic, oregano, and thyme to the pan.

Select Settings: Choose your bread machine's «Basic» setting.

Bake: Let the machine complete its cycle.

Bill's Tip:

Just before baking, brush the top of the loaf with additional olive oil and sprinkle with sea salt to enhance the flavor.

VEGAN BANANA NUT BREAD

Ingredients:

- 2 ½ cups all-purpose flour (300g)
- 1 cup mashed ripe bananas (240g)
- ½ cup coconut oil, melted (120ml)
- ½ cup maple syrup (120ml)
- 1 teaspoon vanilla extract (5ml)
- 2 teaspoons baking powder (8g)
- ½ teaspoon baking soda (2g)
- ½ teaspoon salt (2.5g)
- ½ cup chopped walnuts (60g)

Nutritional Information:

(per slice, assuming 12 slices)

220 calories, 3g protein, 10g fat, 32g carbs

Instructions:

Prepare Ingredients: Add mashed bananas, melted coconut oil, maple syrup, and vanilla extract to the bread machine pan.

Add Dry Ingredients: Add all-purpose flour, baking powder, baking soda, and salt.

Add Nuts: Stir in the chopped walnuts.

Select Settings: Select your bread machine's «Quick Bread» or «Cake» settings.

Bake: Allow the machine to complete its cycle.

Bill's Tip:

Use extra ripe bananas for the richest flavor and sweetest result.

VEGAN OATMEAL BREAD

Ingredients:

- 2 cups whole wheat flour (240g)
- 1 cup rolled oats (90g)
- 1 ¼ cups warm water (300ml)
- 2 tablespoons olive oil (30ml)
- 2 tablespoons maple syrup (30ml)
- 2 teaspoons active dry yeast (6g)
- 1 teaspoon salt (5g)

Instructions:

Prepare Ingredients: Pour warm water, olive oil, and maple syrup into the bread machine pan.

Add Yeast: Sprinkle in the yeast and let it activate for about 5 minutes.

Add Dry Ingredients: Add whole wheat flour, rolled oats, and salt.

Select Settings: Choose your bread machine's «Whole Wheat» setting.

Bake: Allow the machine to complete its cycle.

Nutritional Information:

(per slice, assuming 12 slices)

180 calories, 5g protein, 6g fat, 28g carbs

Bill's Tip:

Add a handful of chopped nuts for extra texture and flavor.

VEGAN CHOCOLATE CHIP BREAD

Ingredients:

- 2 ½ cups bread flour (300g)
- 1 cup almond milk (240ml)
- ½ cup coconut oil, melted (120ml)
- ½ cup maple syrup (120ml)
- 1 teaspoon vanilla extract (5ml)
- 2 teaspoons active dry yeast (6g)
- 1 teaspoon salt (5g)
- ½ cup vegan chocolate chips (90g)

Nutritional Information:
(per slice, assuming 12 slices)

220 calories, 4g protein, 9g fat, 34g carbs

Instructions:

Prepare Ingredients: Add almond milk, melted coconut oil, maple syrup, and vanilla extract to the bread machine pan.

Add Dry Ingredients: Bread flour, yeast, and salt.

Add Chocolate Chips: Add vegan chocolate chips last.

Select Settings: Choose the «Sweet» or «Basic» setting on your bread machine.

Bake: Allow the machine to complete its cycle.

Bill's Tip:

Serve warm for gooey chocolate goodness!

VEGAN PUMPKIN SPICE BREAD

Ingredients:

- 2 ½ cups all-purpose flour (300g)
- 1 cup canned pumpkin puree (240g)
- ½ cup coconut oil, melted (120ml)
- ½ cup maple syrup (120ml)
- 1 teaspoon vanilla extract (5ml)
- 2 teaspoons pumpkin pie spice (6g)
- 2 teaspoons baking powder (8g)
- ½ teaspoon baking soda (2g)
- ½ teaspoon salt (3g)

Nutritional Information:
(per slice, assuming 12 slices)

200 calories, 3g protein, 9g fat, 30g carbs

Instructions:

Prepare Ingredients: Combine the pumpkin puree, melted coconut oil, maple syrup, and vanilla extract in the bread machine pan.

Add Dry Ingredients: Flour, pumpkin pie spice, baking powder, baking soda, and salt.

Select Settings: Select your bread machine's «Quick Bread» or «Cake» settings.

Bake: Allow the machine to complete its cycle.

Bill's Tip:

Add a handful of chopped pecans for a crunchy topping.

VEGAN ZUCCHINI BREAD

Ingredients:

- 2 ½ cups all-purpose flour (300g)
- 1 cup grated zucchini (120g)
- ½ cup coconut oil, melted (120ml)
- ½ cup maple syrup (120ml)
- 1 teaspoon vanilla extract (5ml)
- 2 teaspoons ground cinnamon (4g)
- 2 teaspoons baking powder (8g)
- ½ teaspoon baking soda (2g)
- ½ teaspoon salt (3g)

Instructions:

Prepare Ingredients: Add grated zucchini, melted coconut oil, maple syrup, and vanilla extract to the bread machine pan.

Add Dry Ingredients: Flour, cinnamon, baking powder, baking soda, and salt.

Select Settings: Select your bread machine's «Quick Bread» or «Cake» settings.

Bake: Allow the machine to complete its cycle.

Nutritional Information:

(per slice, assuming 12 slices)

190 calories, 3g protein, 9g fat, 28g carbs

Bill's Tip:

Squeeze out excess moisture from the zucchini to avoid soggy bread.

VEGAN SUNFLOWER SEED BREAD

Ingredients:

- 3 cups bread flour (360g)
- 1 ¼ cups warm water (300ml)
- 2 tablespoons olive oil (30ml)
- 2 tablespoons maple syrup (30ml)
- 2 teaspoons active dry yeast (6g)
- 1 teaspoon salt (6g)
- ½ cup sunflower seeds (70g)

Instructions:

Prepare Ingredients: Pour warm water, olive oil, and maple syrup into the bread machine pan.

Activate Yeast: Sprinkle in the yeast and let it sit for 5 minutes to activate.

Combine Ingredients: Add flour, salt, and sunflower seeds to the pan.

Select Settings: Choose the «Basic» or «Whole Wheat» setting on your bread machine.

Bake: Allow the machine to complete its cycle.

Nutritional Information:

(per slice, assuming 12 slices)

170 calories, 5g protein, 7g fat, 24g carbs

Bill's Tip:

Toast the sunflower seeds before adding them to the dough for a nutty flavor.

169

SUN-DRIED TOMATO & OLIVE BREAD

Ingredients:

- 2 cups all-purpose gluten-free flour mix (240g)
- ½ cup sun-dried tomatoes, chopped (60g)
- ½ cup pitted black olives, chopped (75g)
- 1 teaspoon dried oregano (1g)
- 1 teaspoon dried basil (1g)
- 1 teaspoon sea salt (6g)
- 1 tablespoon olive oil (15ml)
- 1 ½ cups warm water (360ml)
- 1 teaspoon sugar (4g)
- 2 teaspoons instant yeast (6g)

Nutritional Information:
(per slice, assuming 12 slices)

120 calories, 3g protein, 4g fat, 18g carbs

Instructions:

Prepare Yeast: Dissolve sugar in warm water and sprinkle yeast on top. Let sit until bubbly.

Mix Dry Ingredients: Combine flour, oregano, basil, and sea salt in a bowl.

Combine Ingredients: Combine the yeast mixture and olive oil with the dry ingredients, stirring until a dough forms.

Add Mix-Ins: Fold in sun-dried tomatoes and olives.

Bake: Transfer dough to the bread machine and select the «Basic» or «French» setting.

Bill's Tip:

Add a touch of garlic powder to the dough for extra flavor. If your olives are salty, consider reducing the salt in the recipe.

CARROT & WALNUT BREAD

Ingredients:

- 2 cups whole wheat flour (240g)
- ½ cup grated carrots (60g)
- ½ cup chopped walnuts (60g)
- ¼ cup maple syrup (60ml)
- ¼ cup olive oil (60ml)
- 1 teaspoon cinnamon (2g)
- ½ teaspoon nutmeg (1g)
- ½ teaspoon sea salt (3g)
- 1 ¼ cups warm water (300ml)
- 2 teaspoons instant yeast (6g)

Nutritional Information:
(per slice, assuming 12 slices)

130 calories, 4g protein, 5g fat, 20g carbs

Instructions:

Prepare Yeast: Dissolve yeast in warm water and sit for 5 minutes.

Mix Dry Ingredients: Combine flour, cinnamon, nutmeg, and sea salt in a bowl.

Add Mix-Ins: Stir in grated carrots and chopped walnuts.

Combine Ingredients: Add yeast mixture, olive oil, and maple syrup. Mix until combined.

Bake: Place dough in the bread machine and select the «Sweet Bread» setting.

Bill's Tip:

For a more pronounced carrot flavor, add a bit of freshly grated ginger. It pairs beautifully with the sweetness of the carrots.

MEDITERRANEAN HERB & OLIVE BREAD

Ingredients:

- 2 cups all-purpose flour (240g)
- ½ cup chopped kalamata olives (60g)
- 1 tablespoon dried rosemary (1g)
- 1 tablespoon dried thyme (1g)
- 1 teaspoon sea salt (3g)
- ¼ cup olive oil (60ml)
- 1 ¼ cups warm water (300ml)
- 2 teaspoons instant yeast (6g)

Instructions:

Activate Yeast: Dissolve yeast in warm water, and it sits until it is frothy.

Mix Dry Ingredients: Combine flour, rosemary, thyme, and sea salt in a bowl.

Combine Ingredients: Add olive oil and yeast mixture to the dry ingredients, stirring to form dough.

Add Olives: Fold in chopped olives.

Bake: Transfer dough to the bread machine and select the «Basic» or «French» setting.

Nutritional Information:
(per slice, assuming 12 slices)

125 calories, 3g protein, 5g fat, 19g carbs

Bill's Tip:

If available, try using fresh herbs. They add a vibrant, fresh flavor that dried herbs can't match. Also, ensure the olives are well-drained to avoid excess moisture in the dough.

ZUCCHINI & ROSEMARY BREAD

Ingredients:

- 2 cups whole wheat flour (240g)
- ½ cup grated zucchini (60g)
- 1 tablespoon dried rosemary (1g)
- 1 teaspoon sea salt (3g)
- 2 tablespoons olive oil (30ml)
- 1 ¼ cups warm water (300ml)
- 2 teaspoons instant yeast (6g)

Instructions:

Activate Yeast: Dissolve yeast in warm water.

Mix Dry Ingredients: Combine flour, rosemary, and sea salt in a bowl.

Combine Ingredients: Stir in grated zucchini, olive oil, and yeast mixture.

Bake: Transfer dough to the bread machine and select the «Quick Bread» setting.

Nutritional Information:
(per slice, assuming 12 slices)

115 calories, 3g protein, 4g fat, 17g carbs

Bill's Tip:

To prevent excess moisture, squeeze out extra water from the zucchini before adding it to the dough. This will keep your bread from becoming too dense.

171

SPINACH & GARLIC BREAD

Ingredients:

- 2 cups all-purpose gluten-free flour mix (240g)
- ½ cup cooked spinach, drained and chopped (60g)
- 2 cloves garlic, minced (6g)
- 1 teaspoon sea salt (3g)
- ¼ cup olive oil (60ml)
- 1 ¼ cups warm water (300ml)
- 2 teaspoons instant yeast (6g)

Instructions:

Activate Yeast: Dissolve yeast in warm water.

Mix Dry Ingredients: Combine flour, sea salt, and minced garlic in a bowl.

Combine Ingredients: Stir in chopped spinach, olive oil, and yeast mixture.

Bake: Transfer dough to the bread machine and select the «Basic» setting.

Nutritional Information:

(per slice, assuming 12 slices)

110 calories, 3g protein, 3.5g fat, 16g carbs

Bill's Tip:

Roast the garlic before adding it to the dough for a deeper flavor. It will mellow out and become sweeter.

SUNFLOWER SEED & FLAX BREAD

Whole Wheat Seed Bread (Bread Machine)

Ingredients:

- 2 cups whole wheat flour (240g)
- ¼ cup sunflower seeds (30g)
- ¼ cup flaxseeds (30g)
- 1 teaspoon sea salt (3g)
- 2 tablespoons olive oil (30ml)
- 1 ¼ cups warm water (300ml)
- 2 teaspoons instant yeast (6g)

Instructions:

Activate Yeast: Dissolve yeast in warm water.

Mix Dry Ingredients: Combine flour, sunflower seeds, flaxseeds, and sea salt.

Combine Ingredients: Stir in olive oil and yeast mixture.

Bake: Transfer dough to the bread machine and select the «Whole Wheat» setting.

Nutritional Information:

(per slice, assuming 12 slices)

140 calories, 5g protein, 6g fat, 18g carbs

Bill's Tip:

Toasting the sunflower seeds and flaxseeds before adding them to the dough can enhance their nutty flavor. Just be careful not to burn them!

TOMATO & BASIL BREAD

Ingredients:

- 2 cups all-purpose gluten-free flour mix (240g)
- ½ cup chopped sun-dried tomatoes (60g)
- 2 tablespoons fresh basil, chopped (6g)
- 1 teaspoon sea salt (3g)
- 2 tablespoons olive oil (30ml)
- 1 ¼ cups warm water (300ml)
- 2 teaspoons instant yeast (6g)

Instructions:

Activate Yeast: Dissolve yeast in warm water.

Mix Dry Ingredients: Combine flour, basil, and sea salt.

Combine Ingredients: Stir in chopped sun-dried tomatoes, olive oil, and yeast mixture.

Bake: Place dough in the bread machine and select the «French Bread» setting.

Nutritional Information:
(per slice, assuming 12 slices)
125 calories, 3g protein, 4g fat, 19g carbs

Bill's Tip:

Fresh basil gives a burst of flavor, but if you're using dried basil, you might need to adjust the quantity as it's more concentrated.

OLIVE & ROSEMARY FOCACCIA

Ingredients:

- 2 cups all-purpose flour (240g)
- ½ cup pitted green olives, sliced (60g)
- 1 tablespoon dried rosemary (3g)
- 1 teaspoon sea salt (3g)
- ¼ cup olive oil (60ml)
- 1¼ cups warm water (300ml)
- 2 teaspoons instant yeast (6g)

Instructions:

Activate Yeast: Dissolve yeast in warm water.

Mix Dry Ingredients: Combine flour, rosemary, and sea salt.

Combine Ingredients: Stir in sliced olives, olive oil, and yeast mixture.

Prepare Dough: Transfer to the bread machine and select the «Dough» setting.

Shape & Bake: Press dough into a baking pan and bake at 375°F (190°C) for 25-30 minutes.

Nutritional Information:
(per slice, assuming 12 slices)

135 calories, 3g protein, 5g fat, 20g carbs

Bill's Tip:

Focaccia benefits from being dimpled with your fingers before baking. This helps the olive oil soak into the dough and adds to the crispy texture.

SWEET POTATO & SAGE BREAD

Ingredients:

- 2 cups whole wheat flour (240g)
- ½ cup mashed sweet potatoes (120g)
- 1 tablespoon dried sage (3g)
- 1 teaspoon sea salt (3g)
- 2 tablespoons olive oil (30ml)
- 1¼ cups warm water (300ml)
- 2 teaspoons instant yeast (6g)

Instructions:

Activate Yeast: Dissolve yeast in warm water.

Mix Dry Ingredients: Combine flour, sage, and sea salt.

Combine Ingredients: Stir in mashed sweet potatoes, olive oil, and yeast mixture.

Prepare Dough: Transfer to the bread machine and select the «Whole Wheat» setting.

Nutritional Information:

(per slice, assuming 12 slices)

120 calories, 3g protein, 4g fat, 18g carbs

Bill's Tip:

Sweet potatoes add moisture and sweetness, so ensure they are well-mashed and not too watery. This helps achieve a perfect texture.

PUMPKIN SEED & CARROT BREAD

Whole Wheat Seed Bread (Bread Machine)

Ingredients:

- 2 cups all-purpose gluten-free flour mix (240g)
- ½ cup grated carrots (60g)
- ¼ cup pumpkin seeds (30g)
- 1 teaspoon ground cinnamon (2g)
- ½ teaspoon nutmeg (1g)
- 1 teaspoon sea salt (3g)
- 2 tablespoons olive oil (30ml)
- 1¼ cups warm water (300ml)
- 2 teaspoons instant yeast (6g)

Instructions:

Activate Yeast: Dissolve yeast in warm water.

Mix Dry Ingredients: Combine flour, cinnamon, nutmeg, and sea salt.

Combine Ingredients: Stir in grated carrots, pumpkin seeds, olive oil, and yeast mixture.

Prepare Dough: Place in the bread machine and select the «Quick Bread» setting.

Nutritional Information:

(per slice, assuming 12 slices)

135 calories, 4g protein, 5g fat, 19g carbs

Bill's Tip:

For an extra crunch, lightly toast the pumpkin seeds before adding them. They'll add a wonderful texture to the bread.

CHAPTER 14:

DIET-FRIENDLY RECIPES: DIABETIC-FRIENDLY BREAD (With Low-Sodium Bread)

DIABETIC-FRIENDLY BREAD FOR BREAD MACHINES: BILL'S TIPS

PROHIBITIONS AND RECOMMENDATIONS:

Sugar: Reduce or eliminate sugar and sweet additives. Use substitutes such as stevia or erythritol instead of sugar.

Carbohydrates: Focus on breads that contain complex carbohydrates and fiber. Whole-grain flour and legume flour can be good options.

Ingredients: Avoid high-carbohydrate ingredients such as white flour. Use gluten-free flour blends that include whole-grain ingredients.

Glycemic Index: Use ingredients with a low glycemic index to minimize sudden fluctuations in blood sugar levels.

WHOLE GRAIN BREAD WITH FLAXSEEDS AND NUTS

Ingredients:

- 1½ cups warm water (110°F / 275ml)
- 2¼ teaspoons active dry yeast (7g)
- 2 tablespoons honey (or stevia) (30g)
- 2 tablespoons olive oil (30ml)
- 1 teaspoon salt (6g)
- 2 cups whole grain flour (240g)
- ¼ cup ground flaxseeds (30g)
- ¼ cup chopped walnuts (30g)

Nutritional Information:
(per slice, assuming 12 slices)

120 calories, 3g protein, 4g fat, 18g carbs

Instructions:

Activate Yeast: Mix warm water and yeast in a bowl. Allow it to sit for 5 minutes until it becomes frothy.

Combine Wet Ingredients: Stir in honey (or stevia), olive oil, and salt.

Mix Dry Ingredients: In another bowl, mix whole grain flour, flaxseeds, and walnuts.

Combine Ingredients: Mix the wet ingredients first, then introduce the dry ingredients gradually. Stir slowly after each addition to blend them well. Keep mixing until the batter reaches a smooth, consistent texture.

Prepare Dough: Pour into the bread pan of your bread machine.
Select the «Whole Grain» or «Gluten-Free» setting.
Bake: Start the machine. Cool on a wire rack before slicing.

Bill's Tip:

Lightly toast the walnuts before mixing for added texture.

CHICKPEA AND OAT FLOUR BREAD

Ingredients:

- 1½ cups warm water (110°F / 275ml)
- 2¼ teaspoons active dry yeast (7g)
- 2 tablespoons honey (or stevia) (30g)
- 2 tablespoons olive oil (30ml)
- 1 teaspoon salt (6g)
- 1½ cups chickpea flour (180g)
- 1 cup oat flour (120g)
- ¼ cup ground flaxseeds (30g)

Nutritional Information:
(per slice, assuming 12 slices)

130 calories, 4g protein, 5g fat, 19g carbs

Instructions:

Activate Yeast: Mix warm water and yeast in a bowl. Allow it to sit for 5 minutes until it becomes frothy.

Combine Wet Ingredients: Stir in honey (or stevia), olive oil, and salt.

Mix Dry Ingredients: In another bowl, mix chickpea flour, oat flour, and flaxseeds.

Combine Ingredients: Mix the wet ingredients first, then introduce the dry ingredients gradually. Stir slowly after each addition to blend them well. Keep mixing until the batter reaches a smooth, consistent texture.

Prepare Dough: Pour into the bread pan of your bread machine.

Select Setting: Choose the «Gluten-Free» setting.

Bake: Start the machine. Cool on a wire rack before slicing.

Bill's Tip:

Adjust flour amounts slightly if the dough appears too wet or dry.

RYE BREAD WITH CHIA SEEDS

Ingredients:

- 1½ cups warm water (110°F / 275ml)
- 2¼ teaspoons active dry yeast (7g)
- 2 tablespoons honey (or stevia) (30g)
- 2 tablespoons olive oil (30ml)
- 1 teaspoon salt (6g)
- 1 cup rye flour (120g)
- 1 cup whole wheat flour (120g)
- ¼ cup chia seeds (30g)

Nutritional Information:
(per slice, assuming 12 slices)

125 calories, 4g protein, 6g fat, 20g carbs

Instructions:

Activate Yeast: Mix warm water and yeast in a bowl. Allow it to sit for 5 minutes until it becomes frothy.

Combine Wet Ingredients: Stir in honey (or stevia), olive oil, and salt.

Mix Dry Ingredients: In another bowl, mix rye flour, whole wheat flour, and chia seeds.

Combine Ingredients: Mix the wet ingredients first, then introduce the dry ingredients gradually. Stir slowly after each addition to blend them well. Keep mixing until the batter reaches a smooth, consistent texture.

Prepare Dough: Pour into the bread pan of your bread machine.

Select Setting: Choose the «Whole Grain» setting.

Bake: Start the machine. Cool on a wire rack before slicing.

Bill's Tip:

Use more rye flour for a stronger rye flavor.

LOW-SODIUM SPELT BREAD

Ingredients:

- 1½ cups warm water (110°F / 275ml)
- 2¼ teaspoons active dry yeast (7g)
- 2 tablespoons honey (or stevia) (30g)
- 2 tablespoons olive oil (30ml)
- ½ teaspoon salt (3g)
- 2 cups spelt flour (240g)
- ¼ cup sunflower seeds (30g)

Instructions:

Activate Yeast: Combine warm water and yeast in a bowl. Let sit for 5 minutes until frothy.

Combine Wet Ingredients: Stir in honey (or stevia), olive oil, and salt.

Mix Dry Ingredients: Mix spelt flour and sunflower seeds in another bowl.

Combine Ingredients: Mix the wet ingredients first, then introduce the dry ingredients gradually. Stir slowly after each addition to blend them well. Keep mixing until the batter reaches a smooth, consistent texture.

Prepare Dough: Pour into the bread pan of your bread machine.

Select Setting: Choose the «Whole Grain» setting.

Bake: Start the machine. Cool on a wire rack before slicing.

Nutritional Information:
(per slice, assuming 12 slices)
120 calories, 4g protein, 5g fat, 19g carbs

Bill's Tip:
Add herbs for extra flavor without increasing sodium.

QUINOA AND FLAXSEED BREAD

Ingredients:

- 1½ cups warm water (110°F / 275ml)
- 2¼ teaspoons active dry yeast (7g)
- 2 tablespoons honey (or stevia) (30g)
- 2 tablespoons olive oil (30ml)
- 1 teaspoon salt (5g)
- 1 cup quinoa flour (120g)
- 1 cup whole grain flour (120g)
- ¼ cup ground flaxseeds (30g)

Instructions:

Activate Yeast: Mix warm water and yeast in a bowl. Allow it to sit for 5 minutes until it becomes frothy.

Combine Wet Ingredients: Stir in honey (or stevia), olive oil, and salt.

Mix Dry Ingredients: In another bowl, mix quinoa flour, whole grain flour, and flaxseeds.

Combine Ingredients: Mix the wet ingredients first, then introduce the dry ingredients gradually. Stir slowly after each addition to blend them well. Keep mixing until the batter reaches a smooth, consistent texture.

Prepare Dough: Pour into the bread pan of your bread machine.

Select Setting: Choose the «Gluten-Free» setting.

Bake: Start the machine. Cool on a wire rack before slicing.

Nutritional Information:
(per slice, assuming 12 slices)

130 calories, 5g protein, 5g fat, 21g carbs

Bill's Tip:
Adding a small amount of apple cider vinegar can help improve the texture.

177

ALMOND FLOUR AND CHIA SEED BREAD

Ingredients:

- 1½ cups warm water (110°F / 275ml)
- 2¼ teaspoons active dry yeast (7g)
- 2 tablespoons honey (or stevia) (30g)
- 2 tablespoons olive oil (30ml)
- 1 teaspoon salt (5g)
- 1 cup almond flour (96g)
- 1 cup gluten-free flour blend (120g)
- ¼ cup chia seeds (30g)

Nutritional Information:
(per slice, assuming 12 slices)

140 calories, 6g protein, 8g fat, 15g carbs

Instructions:

Activate Yeast: Mix warm water and yeast in a bowl. Allow it to sit for 5 minutes until it becomes frothy.

Combine Wet Ingredients: Stir in honey (or stevia), olive oil, and salt.

Mix Dry Ingredients: In another bowl, mix almond flour, gluten-free flour blend, and chia seeds.

Combine Ingredients: Mix the wet ingredients first, then introduce the dry ingredients gradually. Stir slowly after each addition to blend them well. Keep mixing until the batter reaches a smooth, consistent texture.

Prepare Dough: Pour into the bread pan of your bread machine.

Select Setting: Choose the «Gluten-Free» setting.

Bake: Start the machine. Cool on a wire rack before slicing.

Bill's Tip:

Almond flour can be dense, so thoroughly mix the dough.

SWEET POTATO AND CINNAMON BREAD

Ingredients:

- 1½ cups warm water (110°F / 275ml)
- 2¼ teaspoons active dry yeast (7g)
- 2 tablespoons honey (or stevia) (30g)
- 2 tablespoons olive oil (30ml)
- 1 teaspoon salt (5g)
- 1 cup sweet potato puree (245g)
- 1½ cups gluten-free flour blend (180g)
- 1 teaspoon cinnamon (2g)

Nutritional Information:
(per slice, assuming 12 slices)

130 calories, 3g protein, 4g fat, 24g carbs

Instructions:

Activate Yeast: Mix warm water and yeast in a bowl. Allow it to sit for 5 minutes until it becomes frothy.

Combine Wet Ingredients: Stir in honey (or stevia), olive oil, and salt.

Mix Dry Ingredients: Mix gluten-free flour blend and cinnamon in another bowl.

Combine Ingredients: Mix the wet ingredients first, then introduce the dry ingredients gradually. Stir slowly after each addition to blend them well. Keep mixing until the batter reaches a smooth, consistent texture.

Add Sweet Potato: Stir in sweet potato puree.

Prepare Dough: Pour into the bread pan of your bread machine.

Select Setting: Choose the «Gluten-Free» setting.

Bake: Start the machine. Cool on a wire rack before slicing.

Bill's Tip:

Sweet potato adds moisture; add more flour if the dough is too wet.

BUCKWHEAT AND ALMOND BREAD

Ingredients:

- 1½ cups warm water (110°F / 275ml)
- 2¼ teaspoons active dry yeast (7g)
- 2 tablespoons honey (or stevia) (30g)
- 2 tablespoons olive oil (30ml)
- 1 teaspoon salt (5g)
- 1 cup buckwheat flour (120g)
- 1 cup almond flour (96g)
- ¼ cup sunflower seeds (30g)

Nutritional Information:

(per slice, assuming 12 slices)

140 calories, 5g protein, 6g fat, 18g carbs

Instructions:

Activate Yeast: Mix warm water and yeast in a bowl. Allow it to sit for 5 minutes until it becomes frothy.

Combine Wet Ingredients: Stir in honey (or stevia), olive oil, and salt.

Mix Dry Ingredients: In another bowl, mix buckwheat flour, almond flour, and sunflower seeds.

Combine Ingredients: Mix the wet ingredients first, then introduce the dry ingredients gradually. Stir slowly after each addition to blend them well. Keep mixing until the batter reaches a smooth, consistent texture.

Prepare Dough: Pour into the bread pan of your bread machine.

Select Setting: Choose the «Gluten-Free» setting.

Bake: Start the machine. Cool on a wire rack before slicing.

Bill's Tip:

Buckwheat flour has a strong flavor, so balance it with almond flour for a milder taste.

CARROT AND ZUCCHINI BREAD

Ingredients:

- 1½ cups warm water (110°F / 275ml)
- 2¼ teaspoons active dry yeast (7g)
- 2 tablespoons honey (or stevia) (30g)
- 2 tablespoons olive oil (30ml)
- 1 teaspoon salt (5g)
- 1 cup grated carrot (130g)
- 1 cup grated zucchini (120g)
- 1½ cups gluten-free flour blend (180g)

Nutritional Information:

(per slice, assuming 12 slices)

125 calories, 3g protein, 4g fat, 22g carbs

Instructions:

Activate Yeast: Mix warm water and yeast in a bowl. Allow it to sit for 5 minutes until it becomes frothy.

Combine Wet Ingredients: Stir in honey (or stevia), olive oil, and salt.

Mix Dry Ingredients: In another bowl, mix grated carrot, grated zucchini, and gluten-free flour blend.

Combine Ingredients: Mix the wet ingredients first, then introduce the dry ingredients gradually. Stir slowly after each addition to blend them well. Keep mixing until the batter reaches a smooth, consistent texture.

Prepare Dough: Pour into the bread pan of your bread machine.

Select Setting: Choose the «Gluten-Free» setting.

Bake: Start the machine. Cool on a wire rack before slicing.

Bill's Tip:

Squeeze excess moisture from the zucchini to avoid a soggy loaf.

PUMPKIN AND SUNFLOWER SEED BREAD

Ingredients:

- 1½ cups warm water (110°F / 275ml)
- 2¼ teaspoons active dry yeast (7g)
- 2 tablespoons honey (or stevia) (30g)
- 2 tablespoons olive oil (30ml)
- 1 teaspoon salt (5g)
- 1 cup pumpkin puree (245g)
- 1½ cups gluten-free flour blend (180g)
- ¼ cup sunflower seeds (30g)

Nutritional Information:
(per slice, assuming 12 slices)

130 calories, 4g protein, 5g fat, 21g carbs

Instructions:

Activate Yeast: Mix warm water and yeast in a bowl. Allow it to sit for 5 minutes until it becomes frothy.

Combine Wet Ingredients: Stir in honey (or stevia), olive oil, and salt.

Mix Dry Ingredients: In another bowl, mix pumpkin puree, gluten-free flour blend, and sunflower seeds.

Combine Ingredients: Mix the wet ingredients first, then introduce the dry ingredients gradually. Stir slowly after each addition to blend them well. Keep mixing until the batter reaches a smooth, consistent texture.

Select Setting: Choose the «Gluten-Free» setting.

Bake: Start the machine. Cool on a wire rack before slicing.

Bill's Tip:

Pumpkin puree can add moisture; adjust flour if needed for the dough consistency.

LOW-SODIUM BREAD FOR BREAD MACHINES: BILL'S TIPS

RESTRICTIONS AND RECOMMENDATIONS:

Salt: Reduce the amount of salt in the recipe or use a low-sodium salt substitute.

Cooking Ingredients: Avoid ingredients high in sodium, such as certain canned goods or processed foods.

Salt Alternatives: Use herbs and spices to enhance flavor without adding salt.

Label Checking: Carefully read labels when selecting ingredients to ensure they meet low-sodium requirements.

WHOLE GRAIN BREAD WITH FLAXSEEDS AND NUTS

Ingredients:

- 2 cups whole wheat flour (240g)
- 1 cup oat flour (120g)
- ¼ cup flaxseeds (30g)
- ½ cup chopped walnuts (60g)
- ¼ cup honey (85g)
- 1½ cups warm water (360ml)
- 2 tablespoons olive oil (30ml)
- 2 teaspoons yeast (7g)
- 1 teaspoon baking powder (5g)

Nutritional Information:

(per slice, assuming 12 slices)

Calories 140, Protein 5g, Carbs 22g, Fat 6g, Sodium 150mg

Instructions:

Activate Yeast: Combine warm water and yeast in a small bowl. Let sit for 5 minutes until frothy.

Combine Dry Ingredients: In the bread pan, mix whole wheat flour, oat flour, flaxseeds, walnuts, and baking powder.

Add Wet Ingredients: Add the yeast mixture, honey, and olive oil to the dry ingredients in the bread pan.

Mix and Knead: Select the «Whole Wheat» or «Whole Grain» setting on your bread machine. Start the machine, let it mix, and knead the dough.

First Rise: Let the machine complete the first rise.

Bake: The machine will bake the bread. Cool on a wire rack before slicing.

Bill's Tip:

Toast the flaxseeds lightly before adding them to the mix to enhance their nutty flavor.

CHICKPEA AND OAT FLOUR BREAD

Ingredients:

- 1 cup chickpea flour (120g)
- 1 cup oat flour (120g)
- ¼ cup olive oil (60ml)
- 1 tablespoon honey (21g)
- 1½ cups warm water (360ml)
- 2 teaspoons baking powder (10g)
- 1 teaspoon ground cumin (2g)

Nutritional Information:

(per slice, assuming 12 slices)

Calories 130, Protein 6g, Carbs 20g, Fat 4g, Sodium 120mg

Instructions:

Combine Dry Ingredients: In the bread pan, mix chickpea flour, oat flour, baking powder, and ground cumin.

Add Wet Ingredients: Pour in warm water, olive oil, and honey.

Mix and Knead: Turn on your bread machine and select the «Gluten-Free» setting. The machine will mix, knead, and raise the dough.

Bake: The machine will bake the bread. Cool on a wire rack before slicing.

Bill's Tip:

Add a pinch of black pepper or fresh herbs for extra flavor without increasing sodium.

RYE BREAD WITH CHIA SEEDS

Ingredients:

- 1½ cups rye flour (180g)
- 1 cup whole wheat flour (120g)
- ¼ cup chia seeds (30g)
- 2 tablespoons honey (42g)
- 1½ cups warm water (360ml)
- 2 teaspoons instant yeast (6g)

Instructions:

Activate Yeast: In a bowl, dissolve the yeast in warm water and let it sit for 5 minutes.

Combine Ingredients: In the bread pan, mix the rye flour, whole wheat flour, chia seeds, and honey.

Add Yeast Mixture: Pour the yeast mixture into the bread pan.

Mix and Knead: Start your bread machine and select the «Whole Grain» setting. The machine will mix, knead, and raise the dough.

Bake: The machine will bake the bread. Cool on a wire rack before slicing.

Nutritional Information:
(per slice, assuming 12 slices)

Calories 120, Protein 4g, Carbs 21g, Fat 5g, Sodium 130mg

Bill's Tip:

Soak chia seeds briefly before mixing to enhance their texture and distribution in the dough.

SUNFLOWER AND PUMPKIN SEED BREAD

Ingredients:

- 2 cups whole wheat flour (240g)
- ½ cup sunflower seeds (70g)
- ½ cup pumpkin seeds (70g)
- ¼ cup olive oil (60ml)
- ¼ cup honey (85g)
- 1½ cups warm water (360ml)
- 2 teaspoons instant yeast (6g)

Instructions:

Activate Yeast: In a bowl, dissolve the yeast in warm water and let it sit for 5 minutes.

Combine Ingredients: In the bread pan, mix the whole wheat flour, sunflower seeds, and pumpkin seeds.

Add Yeast Mixture: Pour the yeast mixture, olive oil, and honey into the bread pan.

Mix and Knead: Start your bread machine by selecting the «Whole Grain» setting. The machine will handle mixing, kneading, and rising.

Bake: The bread machine will bake the bread. Cool on a wire rack before slicing.

Nutritional Information:
(per slice, assuming 12 slices)

Calories 140, Protein 6g, Carbs 20g, Fat 7g, Sodium 110mg

Bill's Tip:

Lightly toast the seeds before adding them to the dough to deepen their flavor.

WHOLE GRAIN BREAD WITH NUTS AND BERRIES

Ingredients:

- 2 cups whole wheat flour (240g)
- ½ cup mixed nuts (e.g., almonds, walnuts) (60g)
- ½ cup dried berries (e.g., cranberries, blueberries) (70g)
- ¼ cup honey (85g)
- 1½ cups warm water (360ml)
- 2 teaspoons instant yeast (6g)

Nutritional Information:
(per slice, assuming 12 slices)

Calories 150, Protein 6g, Carbs 23g, Fat 6g, Sodium 120mg

Instructions:

Activate Yeast: In a bowl, dissolve the yeast in warm water and let it sit for 5 minutes.

Combine Ingredients: In the bread pan, mix the whole wheat flour, mixed nuts, and dried berries.

Add Yeast Mixture: Pour the yeast mixture and honey into the bread pan.

Mix and Knead: Start your bread machine by selecting the «Whole Grain» setting. The machine will handle mixing, kneading, and rising.

Bake: The bread machine will bake the bread. Cool on a wire rack before slicing.

Bill's Tip:

Sprinkle a few extra nuts on top of the dough before baking for added texture and flavor.

LOW-SODIUM MULTIGRAIN BREAD

Ingredients:

- 1 cup whole wheat flour (120g)
- 1 cup oat flour (100g)
- ½ cup barley flour (60g)
- ¼ cup sunflower seeds (30g)
- ¼ cup pumpkin seeds (30g)
- 1 tablespoon honey (21g)
- 1½ cups warm water (360ml)
- 2 teaspoons instant yeast (6g)

Nutritional Information:
(per slice, assuming 12 slices)

Calories 140, Protein 5g, Carbs 21g, Fat 5g, Sodium 115mg

Instructions:

Activate Yeast: In a bowl, dissolve the yeast in warm water and let it sit for 5 minutes.

Combine Ingredients: In the bread pan, mix the whole wheat flour, oat flour, barley flour, sunflower seeds, and pumpkin seeds.

Add Yeast Mixture: Pour the yeast mixture and honey into the bread pan.

Mix and Knead: Start your bread machine by selecting the «Whole Grain» setting. The machine will handle mixing, kneading, and rising.

Bake: The bread machine will bake the bread. Cool on a wire rack before slicing.

Bill's Tip:

Experiment with different multigrain blends to find your preferred flavor and texture.

WHOLE WHEAT & CHIA SEED BREAD

Ingredients:

- 2 cups whole wheat flour (240g)
- ¼ cup chia seeds (30g)
- ¼ cup honey (85g)
- 1½ cups warm water (360ml)
- 2 teaspoons instant yeast (6g)

Instructions:

Activate Yeast: In a bowl, dissolve the yeast in warm water and let it sit for 5 minutes.

Combine Dry Ingredients: Mix the whole wheat flour and chia seeds in the bread pan.

Add Wet Ingredients: Pour the yeast mixture and honey into the bread pan.

Mix and Knead: Start your bread machine by selecting the «Whole Wheat» or «Basic» setting. The machine will handle mixing, kneading, and rising.

Bake: The bread machine will bake the bread. Cool on a wire rack before slicing.

Nutritional Information:
(per slice, assuming 12 slices)

Calories 130, Protein 5g, Carbs 22g, Fat 5g, Sodium 120mg

Bill's Tip:

Soak chia seeds briefly before mixing to enhance their texture and distribution in the dough.

SPELT & ALMOND BREAD

Ingredients:

- 2 cups spelt flour (240g)
- ½ cup almond flour (50g)
- ¼ cup honey (85g)
- 1½ cups warm water (360ml)
- 2 teaspoons instant yeast (6g)

Instructions:

Activate Yeast: In a bowl, dissolve the yeast in warm water and let it sit for 5 minutes.

Combine Dry Ingredients: Mix spelled and almond flour in the bread pan.

Add Wet Ingredients: Pour the yeast mixture and honey into the bread pan.

Mix and Knead: Start your bread machine by selecting the «Whole Wheat» or «Basic» setting. The machine will handle mixing, kneading, and rising.

Bake: The bread machine will bake the bread. Cool on a wire rack before slicing.

Nutritional Information:
(per slice, assuming 12 slices)

Calories 140, Protein 6g, Carbs 20g, Fat 6g, Sodium 110mg

Bill's Tip:

Almond flour adds richness and flavor; combine it with a lighter flour, like spelt, for a balanced texture.

LOW-SODIUM OAT & RAISIN BREAD

Ingredients:

- 1 cup oat flour (120g)
- 1 cup whole wheat flour (120g)
- ½ cup raisins (80g)
- ¼ cup honey (85g)
- 1½ cups warm water (360ml)
- 2 teaspoons instant yeast (6g)

Nutritional Information:
(per slice, assuming 12 slices)

Calories 130, Protein 4g, Carbs 22g, Fat 5g, Sodium 115mg

Instructions:

Activate Yeast: In a bowl, dissolve the yeast in warm water and let it sit for 5 minutes.

Combine Dry Ingredients: In the bread pan, mix oat flour, whole wheat flour, and raisins.

Add Wet Ingredients: Pour the yeast mixture and honey into the bread pan.

Mix and Knead: Start your bread machine by selecting the «Whole Wheat» or «Basic» setting. The machine will handle mixing, kneading, and rising.

Bake: The bread machine will bake the bread. Cool on a wire rack before slicing.

Bill's Tip:

Soaking raisins in warm water before adding them to the dough can help them stay moist and distribute better.

WHEAT BREAD WITH GREEN HERBS

Ingredients:

- 2 cups whole wheat flour (240g)
- ¼ cup mixed fresh herbs, finely chopped (e.g., rosemary, thyme) (15g)
- ¼ cup olive oil (60ml)
- ¼ cup honey (85g)
- 1½ cups warm water (360ml)
- 2 teaspoons instant yeast (6g)

Nutritional Information:
(per slice, assuming 12 slices)

Calories 140, Protein 5g, Carbs 22g, Fat 6g, Sodium 115mg

Instructions:

Activate Yeast: In a bowl, dissolve the yeast in warm water and let it sit for 5 minutes.

Combine Ingredients: Mix whole wheat flour and chopped herbs in the bread pan.

Add Wet Ingredients: Pour the yeast mixture, olive oil, and honey into the bread pan.

Mix and Knead: Start your bread machine by selecting the «Whole Wheat» or «Basic» setting. The machine will handle mixing, kneading, and rising.

Bake: The bread machine will bake the bread. Cool on a wire rack before slicing.

Bill's Tip:

Experiment with herb combinations to find your favorite flavor profile.

CHAPTER 15:

DIET-FRIENDLY RECIPES: KETO & LOW-CARB BREADS

KETO BREADS FOR BREAD MACHINES: BILL'S TIPS

Keto and Low-Carb Bread share some similarities but have key differences based on dietary principles and restrictions.

Keto Bread's Primary Goal is to maintain ketosis by Minimizing carbs to an extremely low level (below 20–30g of carbs per serving). Fats are used as the primary energy source instead of carbs.

Ingredients:

The base consists of low-carb ingredients like almond flour, coconut flour, and flaxseeds.

Oils (such as coconut or olive oil) and high-fat products (like butter) are commonly used.

Incorporates low-carb or zero-calorie sweeteners like erythritol or stevia.

KETO ALMOND FLOUR BREAD

Ingredients:

- 1½ cups almond flour (150g)
- 1½ teaspoons baking powder (6g)
- ¼ teaspoon salt (1g)
- 4 large eggs
- ¼ cup melted butter (57g)
- 1 tablespoon apple cider vinegar (15ml)

Nutritional Information:
(per slice, assuming 12 slices)

Calories 150, Protein 6g, Carbs 2g, Fat 13g, Sodium 150mg

Bill's Tip:

Instructions:

Combine Dry Ingredients: In a large bowl, mix almond flour, baking powder, and salt.

Mix Wet Ingredients: In another bowl, whisk together eggs, melted butter, and apple cider vinegar.

Combine Ingredients: Add the wet mixture to the dry ingredients and stir until well combined.

Prepare for Baking: Pour the batter into the bread pan of your bread machine.

Select Setting: Use the «Quick Bread» setting on your bread machine.

To achieve a fluffier texture, separate the eggs and whip the egg whites before gently folding them into the batter.

KETO COCONUT FLOUR BREAD

Ingredients:

- ¾ cup coconut flour (75g)
- 1 teaspoon baking powder (4g)
- ½ teaspoon salt (2g)
- 6 large eggs
- ½ cup melted coconut oil (120ml)
- 1 teaspoon apple cider vinegar (5ml)

Instructions:

Combine Dry Ingredients: In a bowl, mix coconut flour, baking powder, and salt.

Mix Wet Ingredients: In a separate bowl, whisk together eggs, melted coconut oil, and apple cider vinegar.

Combine Ingredients: Mix the wet ingredients into the dry ingredients until well combined.

Prepare for Baking: Pour the mixture into the bread pan of your bread machine.

Select Setting: Use the «Quick Bread» setting on your bread machine.

Nutritional Information:

(per slice, assuming 12 slices)

Calories 120, Protein 5g, Carbs 3g, Fat 10g, Sodium 120m

Bill's Tip:

Coconut flour absorbs a lot of moisture, so don't skip the eggs—they provide the necessary liquid and structure.

KETO FLAXSEED BREAD

Ingredients:

- 1 ½ cups ground flaxseed (150g)
- 2 teaspoons baking powder (8g)
- ½ teaspoon salt (2g)
- 4 large eggs
- ½ cup water (120ml)
- 3 tablespoons olive oil (45ml)

Instructions:

Combine Dry Ingredients: In a bowl, mix ground flaxseed, baking powder, and salt.

Mix Wet Ingredients: Beat the eggs, then stir in water and olive oil.

Combine Ingredients: Add the wet ingredients to the dry ingredients and mix well.

Prepare for Baking: Pour the mixture into the bread pan of your bread machine.

Select Setting: Use the «Quick Bread» setting on your bread machine.

Nutritional Information:

(per slice, assuming 12 slices)

Calories 140, Protein 5g, Carbs 1g, Fat 12g, Sodium 130mg

Bill's Tip:

Flaxseed can give the bread a denser texture, so add a bit of baking soda for extra lift if needed.

187

KETO CHEESE BREAD

Ingredients:

- 1 ½ cups almond flour (150g)
- 1 teaspoon baking powder (4g)
- ½ teaspoon salt (2g)
- 1 cup shredded cheddar cheese (100g)
- 4 large eggs
- ¼ cup melted butter (60g)

Instructions:

Combine Dry Ingredients: In a bowl, mix almond flour, baking powder, salt, and shredded cheese.

Mix Wet Ingredients: Whisk together the eggs and melted butter.

Combine Ingredients: Add the wet and dry ingredients and mix until well combined.

Prepare for Baking: Pour the mixture into the bread pan of your bread machine.

Select Setting: Use the «Quick Bread» setting on your bread machine.

Nutritional Information:
(per slice, assuming 12 slices)

Calories 180, Protein 9g, Carbs 2g, Fat 15g, Sodium 220mg

Bill's Tip:

Want a little extra flavor? Add a pinch of garlic powder to the mix.

KETO PUMPKIN SEED BREAD

Ingredients:

- 1 cup almond flour (100g)
- ½ cup ground flaxseed (50g)
- 1 teaspoon baking powder (4g)
- ¼ teaspoon salt (1g)
- 4 large eggs
- ¼ cup pumpkin seeds (30g)
- ¼ cup melted butter (60g)

Instructions:

Combine Dry Ingredients: In a bowl, mix almond flour, ground flaxseed, baking powder, and salt.

Mix Wet Ingredients: Whisk together the eggs and melted butter.

Add Seeds: Stir in the pumpkin seeds.

Prepare for Baking: Pour the mixture into the bread pan of your bread machine.

Select Setting: Use the «Quick Bread» setting on your bread machine.

Nutritional Information:
(per slice, assuming 12 slices)

Calories 160, Protein 7g, Carbs 3g, Fat 13g, Sodium 150mg

Bill's Tip:

Add a sprinkle of pumpkin seeds on top for a crunchy crust.

KETO SUN-DRIED TOMATO BREAD

Ingredients:

- 1 ½ cups almond flour (150g)
- 1 teaspoon baking powder (4g)
- ½ teaspoon salt (2g)
- ½ cup chopped sun-dried tomatoes (oil-packed) (60g)
- 4 large eggs
- ¼ cup olive oil (60ml)

Instructions:

Combine Dry Ingredients: In a bowl, mix almond flour, baking powder, and salt.

Mix Wet Ingredients: Whisk together the eggs and olive oil.

Add Tomatoes: Stir in the chopped sun-dried tomatoes.

Prepare for Baking: Pour the mixture into the bread pan of your bread machine.

Select Setting: Use the «Quick Bread» setting on your bread machine.

Nutritional Information:

(per slice, assuming 12 slices)

Calories 170, Protein 6g, Carbs 3g, Fat 14g, Sodium 200mg

Bill's Tip:

Add a teaspoon of dried oregano for a Mediterranean twist.

KETO GARLIC HERB BREAD

Ingredients:

- 1 ½ cups almond flour (150g)
- 1 teaspoon baking powder (4g)
- ½ teaspoon salt (2g)
- 1 teaspoon garlic powder (2g)
- 1 teaspoon mixed dried herbs (e.g., rosemary, thyme, oregano) (1g)
- 4 large eggs
- ¼ cup melted butter (60g)

Instructions:

Combine Dry Ingredients: In a bowl, mix almond flour, baking powder, salt, garlic powder, and herbs.

Mix Wet Ingredients: Beat the eggs and melted butter together.

Combine Mixtures: Stir the wet ingredients into the dry ingredients until well combined.

Prepare for Baking: Pour the mixture into the bread pan of your bread machine.

Select Setting: Use the «Quick Bread» setting on your bread machine.

Nutritional Information:

(per slice, assuming 12 slices)

Calories 160, Protein 6g, Carbs 2g, Fat 14g, Sodium 170mg

Bill's Tip:

This bread pairs perfectly with a bowl of low-carb soup-comfort food, keto-style!

KETO ZUCCHINI BREAD

Ingredients:

- 1 ½ cups almond flour (150g)
- 1 teaspoon baking powder (4g)
- ½ teaspoon salt (2g)
- 1 cup grated zucchini (squeeze out excess moisture) (115g)
- 4 large eggs
- ¼ cup olive oil (60ml)

Instructions:

Combine Dry Ingredients: In a bowl, mix almond flour, baking powder, and salt.

Prepare Wet Ingredients: Whisk the eggs and olive oil together, then stir in the grated zucchini.

Combine Mixtures: Add the wet and dry ingredients and mix until well combined.

Prepare for Baking: Pour the mixture into the bread pan of your bread machine.

Select Setting: Use the «Quick Bread» setting on your bread machine.

Nutritional Information:

(per slice, assuming 12 slices)

Calories 150, Protein 5g, Carbs 3g, Fat 12g, Sodium 140mg

Bill's Tip:

Add a pinch of cinnamon and nutmeg for extra flavor.

KETO CHIA SEED BREAD

Ingredients:

- 1 cup almond flour (100g)
- ½ cup ground chia seeds (60g)
- 1 teaspoon baking powder (4g)
- ½ teaspoon salt (2g)
- 4 large eggs
- ¼ cup melted butter (60g)

Instructions:

Combine Dry Ingredients: In a bowl, mix almond flour, ground chia seeds, baking powder, and salt.

Prepare Wet Ingredients: Whisk the eggs and melted butter together.

Combine Mixtures: Add the wet and dry ingredients and mix until well combined.

Prepare for Baking: Pour the mixture into the bread pan of your bread machine.

Select Setting: Use the «Quick Bread» setting on your bread machine.

Nutritional Information:

(per slice, assuming 12 slices)

Calories 140, Protein 6g, Carbs 2g, Fat 11g, Sodium 130mg

Bill's Tip:

Chia seeds add a great texture—perfect for a breakfast sandwich!

KETO AVOCADO BREAD

Ingredients:

- 1 ½ cups almond flour (150g)
- 1 teaspoon baking powder (4g)
- ½ teaspoon salt (2g)
- 1 ripe avocado, mashed (about ½ cup)
- 4 large eggs
- ¼ cup olive oil (60ml)

Nutritional Information:
(per slice, assuming 12 slices)

Calories 160, Protein 5g, Carbs 3g, Fat 14g, Sodium 140mg

Instructions:

Combine Dry Ingredients: In a bowl, mix almond flour, baking powder, and salt.

Prepare Wet Ingredients: Mash the avocado and whisk it together with the eggs and olive oil.

Combine Mixtures: Add the wet and dry ingredients and mix until well combined.

Prepare for Baking: Pour the mixture into the bread pan of your bread machine.

Select Setting: Use the «Quick Bread» setting on your bread machine.

Bill's Tip:

Avocado adds creaminess—pair this with your favorite low-carb spread for a satisfying snack.

LOW-CARB BREAD BREADS FOR BREAD MACHINES: BILL'S TIPS

Low-Carb Bread's Primary Goal is to reduce carbs, but less drastically than the keto diet. Some carbs are allowed, especially complex carbs with a low glycemic index.

Ingredients:

Often a blend of low-carb flour, such as almond flour, coconut flour, and flaxseeds.

Natural sweeteners can be used in moderation.

Small amounts of low-carb vegetables or seeds (like pumpkin or sunflower seeds) may be included.

LOW-CARB ALMOND & FLAXSEED BREAD

Ingredients:

- 1 cup almond flour (100g)
- ½ cup ground flaxseed (50g)
- 1 teaspoon baking powder (4g)
- ½ teaspoon salt (2g)
- 4 large eggs
- ¼ cup melted butter (60g)

Instructions:

Combine Dry Ingredients: In a bowl, mix almond flour, ground flaxseed, baking powder, and salt.

Prepare Wet Ingredients: Whisk the eggs and melted butter together.

Combine Mixtures: Add the wet ingredients to the dry ingredients and mix well.

Prepare for Baking: Pour the mixture into the bread pan of your bread machine.

Select Setting: Use the «Quick Bread» setting on your bread machine.

Nutritional Information:
(per slice, assuming 12 slices)

Calories 130, Protein 6g, Carbs 3g, Fat 10g, Sodium 150mg

Bill's Tip:

To ensure the bread slices cleanly, let it cool completely before cutting. This helps in getting neat slices without crumbling.

LOW-CARB COCONUT FLOUR BREAD

Ingredients:

- ½ cup coconut flour (50g)
- 1 teaspoon baking powder (4g)
- ¼ teaspoon salt (1g)
- 6 large eggs
- ½ cup melted coconut oil (120g)
- 1 teaspoon apple cider vinegar (5ml)

Instructions:

Combine Dry Ingredients: In a bowl, mix coconut flour, baking powder, and salt.

Prepare Wet Ingredients: In a separate bowl, whisk together eggs, melted coconut oil, and apple cider vinegar.

Combine Mixtures: Add the wet ingredients to the dry ingredients and mix well.

Prepare for Baking: Pour the mixture into the bread pan of your bread machine.

Select Setting: Use the «Quick Bread» setting on your bread machine.

Nutritional Information:
(per slice, assuming 12 slices)

Calories 120, Protein 5g, Carbs 4g, Fat 9g, Sodium 140mg

Bill's Tip:

Coconut flour absorbs much liquid, so the eggs are crucial for keeping the bread moist and giving it structure. Mix thoroughly for a smooth batter.

LOW-CARB SUNFLOWER SEED & PUMPKIN SEED BREAD

Ingredients:

- 1 cup almond flour (100g)
- ½ cup ground sunflower seeds (50g)
- ½ cup pumpkin seeds (60g)
- 1 teaspoon baking powder (4g)
- ½ teaspoon salt (2g)
- 4 large eggs
- ¼ cup olive oil (60g)

Instructions:

Combine Dry Ingredients: In a bowl, mix almond flour, ground sunflower seeds, baking powder, and salt.

Prepare Wet Ingredients: Whisk the eggs and olive oil together, then stir in the pumpkin seeds.

Combine Mixtures: Add the wet ingredients to the dry ingredients and mix well.

Prepare for Baking: Pour the mixture into the bread pan of your bread machine.

Select Setting: Use the «Quick Bread» setting on your bread machine.

Nutritional Information:

(per slice, assuming 12 slices)

Calories 140, Protein 6g, Carbs 4g, Fat 12g, Sodium 160mg

Bill's Tip:

Top with extra seeds before baking for a crunchy crust that adds great texture and visual appeal.

LOW-CARB ZUCCHINI BREAD

Ingredients:

- 1 cup almond flour (100g)
- ½ cup grated zucchini, squeezed (50g)
- 1 teaspoon baking powder (4g)
- ½ teaspoon salt (2g)
- 4 large eggs
- ¼ cup olive oil (60g)

Instructions:

Combine Dry Ingredients: In a bowl, mix almond flour, baking powder, and salt.

Prepare Wet Ingredients: In another bowl, combine eggs, olive oil, and grated zucchini.

Combine Mixtures: Add the wet ingredients to the dry ingredients and mix well.

Prepare for Baking: Pour the mixture into the bread pan of your bread machine.

Select Setting: Use the «Quick Bread» setting on your bread machine.

Nutritional Information:

(per slice, assuming 12 slices)

Calories 110, Protein 4g, Carbs 5g, Fat 8g, Sodium 130mg

Bill's Tip:

Add a pinch of cinnamon and a sugar-free sweetener like stevia for sweetness.

LOW-CARB CHIA SEED BREAD

Ingredients:

- 1 cup almond flour (100g)
- ¼ cup chia seeds (40g)
- 1 teaspoon baking powder (4g)
- ½ teaspoon salt (2g)
- 4 large eggs
- ¼ cup melted butter (60g)

Instructions:

Combine Dry Ingredients: In a bowl, mix almond flour, chia seeds, baking powder, and salt.

Prepare Wet Ingredients: Whisk the eggs and melted butter together.

Combine Mixtures: Add the wet and dry ingredients and mix until well combined.

Prepare for Baking: Pour the mixture into the bread pan of your bread machine.

Select Setting: Use the «Quick Bread» setting on your bread machine.

Nutritional Information:

(per slice, assuming 12 slices)

Calories 130, Protein 6g, Carbs 4g, Fat 10g, Sodium 120mg

Bill's Tip:

Chia seeds add a delightful crunch—try this with some cream cheese for a tasty snack!

LOW-CARB HERB & GARLIC BREAD

Ingredients:
- 1 cup almond flour (100g)
- 1 teaspoon baking powder (4g)
- ½ teaspoon salt (2g)
- 1 teaspoon garlic powder (2g)
- 1 teaspoon mixed dried herbs (like rosemary, thyme, oregano) (2g)
- 4 large eggs
- ¼ cup olive oil (60ml)

Instructions:

Combine Dry Ingredients: In a bowl, mix almond flour, baking powder, salt, garlic powder, and dried herbs.

Prepare Wet Ingredients: Whisk the eggs and olive oil together.

Combine Mixtures: Add the wet and dry ingredients and mix until well combined.

Prepare for Baking: Pour the mixture into the bread pan of your bread machine.

Select Setting: Use the «Quick Bread» setting on your bread machine.

Nutritional Information:
(per slice, assuming 12 slices)

Calories 125, Protein 5g, Carbs 3g, Fat 10g, Sodium 150mg

Bill's Tip:

This ultimate sandwich bread—pairs well with fresh greens and low-carb fillings!

LOW-CARB NUT & SEED BREAD

Ingredients:

- 1 cup almond flour (100g)
- ¼ cup ground flaxseed (25g)
- ¼ cup chopped walnuts (30g)
- 2 tablespoons sunflower seeds (20g)
- 1 teaspoon baking powder (4g)
- ½ teaspoon salt (2g)
- 4 large eggs
- ¼ cup melted butter (60g)

Nutritional Information:

(per slice, assuming 12 slices)

Calories 150, Protein 6g, Carbs 4g, Fat 12g, Sodium 140mg

Instructions:

Combine Dry Ingredients: In a bowl, mix almond flour, ground flaxseed, chopped walnuts, sunflower seeds, baking powder, and salt.

Prepare Wet Ingredients: Whisk the eggs and melted butter together.

Combine Mixtures: Add the wet and dry ingredients and mix until well combined.

Prepare for Baking: Pour the mixture into the bread pan of your bread machine.

Select Setting: Use the «Quick Bread» setting on your bread machine.

LOW-CARB OLIVE & ROSEMARY BREAD

Ingredients:

- 1 cup almond flour (100g)
- ½ cup chopped olives (80g)
- 1 teaspoon baking powder (4g)
- ½ teaspoon salt (2g)
- 1 teaspoon dried rosemary (1g)
- 4 large eggs
- ¼ cup olive oil (60ml)

Nutritional Information:

(per slice, assuming 12 slices)

Calories 140, Protein 5g, Carbs 3g, Fat 11g, Sodium 160mg

Instructions:

Combine Dry Ingredients: In a bowl, mix almond flour, baking powder, salt, and dried rosemary.

Prepare Wet Ingredients: Whisk the eggs and olive oil together, then stir in the chopped olives.

Combine Mixtures: Add the wet and dry ingredients and mix until well combined.

Prepare for Baking: Pour the mixture into the bread pan of your bread machine.

Select Setting: Use the «Quick Bread» setting on your bread machine.

LOW-CARB SPINACH & FETA BREAD

Ingredients:

- 1 cup almond flour (100g)
- ½ cup crumbled feta cheese (75g)
- ½ cup chopped fresh spinach (15g)
- 1 teaspoon baking powder (4g)
- ½ teaspoon salt (2g)
- 4 large eggs
- ¼ cup olive oil (60ml)

Instructions:

Combine Dry Ingredients: In a bowl, mix almond flour, baking powder, and salt.

Prepare Wet Ingredients: Whisk the eggs and olive oil together, then stir in the crumbled feta cheese and chopped spinach.

Combine Mixtures: Add the wet and dry ingredients and mix until well combined.

Prepare for Baking: Pour the mixture into the bread pan of your bread machine.

Select Setting: Use the «Quick Bread» setting on your bread machine.

Nutritional Information:
(per slice, assuming 12 slices)

Calories 130, Protein 6g, Carbs 3g, Fat 10g, Sodium 180mg

Bill's Tip:

This bread is a Mediterranean delight! It is great on its own or as a base for a low-carb Greek-inspired sandwich.

LOW-CARB WHOLE GRAIN BREAD WITH NUTS & BERRIES

Ingredients:
- 1 cup almond flour (100g)
- ¼ cup ground flaxseed (30g)
- ¼ cup chopped walnuts (30g)
- ¼ cup mixed berries (raspberries, blueberries) (35g)
- 1 teaspoon baking powder (4g)
- ½ teaspoon salt (2g)
- 4 large eggs
- ¼ cup melted butter (60g)

Instructions:

Combine Dry Ingredients: In a bowl, mix almond flour, ground flaxseed, chopped walnuts, and baking powder.

Prepare Wet Ingredients: Whisk the eggs and melted butter together.

Combine Mixtures: Gently fold the berries into the wet ingredients, then mix the wet and dry ingredients until combined.

Prepare for Baking: Pour the mixture into the bread pan of your bread machine.

Select Setting: Use the «Quick Bread» setting on your bread machine.

Nutritional Information:
(per slice, assuming 12 slices)

Calories 160, Protein 7g, Carbs 5g, Fat 12g, Sodium 140mg

Bill's Tip:

The berries add a hint of sweetness—perfect for breakfast with a dollop of whipped cream!

CHAPTER 16:

DOUGH RECIPES

PRACTICALITY OF BREAD MACHINES FOR KNEADING DOUGH

Using a bread machine as a dough kneader can be quite practical, especially for those who want a hands-off approach to preparing dough.

HERE ARE SOME POINTS TO CONSIDER:

Consistency: Bread machines are excellent at providing consistent kneading results. They are programmed to mix and knead the dough thoroughly, ensuring even gluten development, which is crucial for good bread texture.

Hands-Off Approach: A major advantage is the convenience of setting the machine and letting it do all the work. You can focus on other tasks while the machine handles the kneading process.

Different Dough Settings: Many bread machines have various settings for different types of dough, such as pizza dough, sweet dough, whole wheat dough, and more. This makes them versatile and adaptable to various recipes.

Automatic Timers and Rest Periods: Bread machines typically have programmed rest periods (autolyze) and kneading cycles, which can enhance the dough's quality. These built-in features ensure the dough gets the right amount of work without over-kneading.

DIFFERENCES AMONG MACHINES

Kneading Blades: Some bread machines have one kneading blade, while others have two. Machines with two blades are generally better at kneading, especially for larger batches of dough.

Motor Power: The strength of the motor can affect how well the machine handles different types of dough. Sturdier, higher-powered machines are better for dense doughs like whole wheat or rye.

Bowl Shape: The shape and size of the bread machine's pan can influence how the dough is kneaded. Some machines may not knead as effectively in certain areas of the pan, potentially leading to uneven dough.

Dough Capacity: Bread machines vary in their dough capacity. If you're making a large batch, ensure your machine can handle it without overloading.

OVERALL EFFECTIVENESS

Good Alternative to Stand Mixers: While bread machines are not as powerful as dedicated stand mixers, they are a good alternative for those who don't want to invest in one or don't have the counter space.

Specific for Bread Dough: They are particularly well-suited for bread dough but might not perform as well with heavy or sticky doughs.

Timesaving: Bread machines save time and effort, particularly for those who frequently bake bread or other dough-based products.

Bread machines can be a very efficient and practical option for mixing dough, especially if you have a model that suits your specific needs and recipes.

Nutritional information for the dough is not relevant. It can only be a rough estimate. The dough will be baked and may undergo additional processing (such as adding fillings), which can significantly alter the final nutritional value of the finished product. Therefore, the final dietary value should only be provided for completed recipes (like pizza or rolls) in the relevant section.

CLASSIC PIZZA DOUGH

Ingredients:

- 4 cups bread flour (500g)
- 2 teaspoons salt (10g)
- 1 teaspoon sugar (5g)
- 2 tablespoons olive oil (30ml)
- 1 ½ cups warm water (360ml)
- 2 ¼ teaspoons active dry yeast (7g)

Instructions:

Mix Ingredients: Add warm water and yeast to the bread machine pan. Let it sit for 5 minutes until frothy. Add flour, salt, sugar, and olive oil.

Knead Dough: Select the dough setting on your bread machine and let it knead and rise the dough.

Rest Dough: After the cycle, let the dough rest for 30 minutes before rolling it out.

Prepare for Baking: Roll out the dough to your desired thickness and top with your favorite ingredients. Bake according to your pizza recipe.

Bill's Tip:

Add a touch of garlic powder and Italian herbs to the dough for an aromatic crust.

198

FRENCH BAGUETTE DOUGH

Ingredients:

- 3 ½ cups bread flour (440g)
- 2 teaspoons salt (10g)
- 1 ½ cups water (360ml), room temperature
- 2 teaspoons instant yeast (7g)

Instructions:

Mixing Ingredients: Add water and yeast to the bread machine pan. Follow with flour and salt.

Kneading: Select the dough cycle. Let the machine handle the kneading and first rise.

Shaping: After the cycle, shape the dough into baguettes, let them rise for 30 minutes, and then bake until golden brown.

Bill's Tip:

Place a steam tray in the oven during baking for a crispier crust. The steam will help develop that perfect crunchy exterior.

BUTTERY PIE DOUGH

Ingredients:

- 2 ½ cups all-purpose flour (320g)
- ½ teaspoon salt (2g)
- 1 tablespoon sugar (12g)
- 1 cup cold butter (225g), cubed
- ½ cup ice water (120ml)

Instructions:

Mixing Ingredients: Add flour, salt, sugar, and cold butter to the bread machine pan. Use the dough setting and mix until it forms coarse crumbs.

Adding Water: Add ice until the dough forms a ball.

Resting: Wrap in plastic and chill for 30 minutes before rolling.

Bill's Tip:

Substitute 2 tablespoons of water with vodka for a flakier crust.

WHOLE WHEAT PIZZA DOUGH

Ingredients:

- 2 cups whole wheat flour (240g)
- 1 cup bread flour (125g)
- 1 teaspoon salt (5g)
- 2 tablespoons olive oil (30ml)
- 1 tablespoon honey (15ml)
- 1 ¼ cups warm water (300ml)
- 2 teaspoons active dry yeast (7g)

Instructions:

Mixing Ingredients: Add warm water, honey, and yeast to the bread machine pan. Let it activate for 5 minutes, then add the flour, salt, and olive oil.

Kneading: Use the dough setting. Allow the machine to knead and rise the dough.

Using: Roll out and top as desired.

Bill's Tip:

Add 2 tablespoons of ground flaxseed for extra nutrition.

NEW YORK-STYLE PIZZA DOUGH

Ingredients:

- 4 cups bread flour (500g)
- 1 ½ teaspoons salt (8g)
- 1 teaspoon sugar (5g)
- 1 tablespoon olive oil (15ml)
- 1 ½ cups cold water (360ml)
- 1 teaspoon instant yeast (3g)

Instructions:

Mixing Ingredients: Place cold water and yeast in the bread machine pan, then add flour, salt, sugar, and olive oil.

Kneading: Select the dough cycle and let the machine handle the kneading and rising of the dough.

Resting: After the cycle, refrigerate the dough for 24 hours before using.

Bill's Tip:

Refrigerating the dough develops a richer flavor.

SWEET ROLL DOUGH

Ingredients:

- 4 cups all-purpose flour (500g)
- ½ cup sugar (100g)
- 1 teaspoon salt (5g)
- ¼ cup butter, softened (60g)
- 1 ¼ cups warm milk (300ml)
- 2 eggs
- 2 ¼ teaspoons active dry yeast (7g)

Instructions:

Mixing Ingredients: Add warm milk and yeast to the bread machine pan. Allow to foam, then add flour, sugar, salt, butter, and eggs.

Kneading: Select the dough setting and let the machine knead the dough.

Using: Roll out and use for sweet rolls or filled pastries.

Bill's Tip:

Add a touch of cinnamon to the dough for a warm aroma.

BAGEL DOUGH

Ingredients:

- 4 cups bread flour (500g)
- 1 tablespoon salt (15g)
- 1 tablespoon sugar (12g)
- 1 ¼ cups warm water (300ml)
- 2 teaspoons instant yeast (7g)

Instructions:

Mixing Ingredients: Add warm water and yeast to the bread machine pan. Let it bloom, then add flour, salt, and sugar.

Kneading: Select the dough cycle and let the machine knead and rise the dough.

Shaping: After the cycle, shape into bagels and boil before baking.

Bill's Tip:

Add a bit of malt syrup to the boiling water for an authentic bagel taste.

CINNAMON ROLL DOUGH

Ingredients:

- 4 cups all-purpose flour (500g)
- ½ cup sugar (100g)
- 1 teaspoon salt (5g)
- ¼ cup butter, softened (60g)
- 1 ¼ cups warm milk (300ml)
- 2 eggs
- 2 ¼ teaspoons active dry yeast (7g)

Instructions:

Mixing Ingredients: Add warm milk and yeast to the bread machine pan. After it foams, add flour, sugar, salt, butter, and eggs.

Kneading: Use the dough setting to knead the dough.

Using: Roll out, fill with cinnamon sugar, and bake.

Bill's Tip:

Drizzle with cream cheese frosting for extra richness.

CHALLAH BREAD DOUGH

Ingredients:

- 4 cups all-purpose flour (500g)
- ¼ cup sugar (50g)
- 1 teaspoon salt (5g)
- ¼ cup olive oil (60ml)
- 1 ¼ cups warm water (300ml)
- 2 eggs
- 2 ¼ teaspoons active dry yeast (7g)

Instructions:

Mixing Ingredients: Add warm water and yeast to the bread machine pan. Let it foam, then add flour, sugar, salt, olive oil, and eggs.

Kneading: Use the dough setting to knead the dough.

Using: Braid the dough and bake until golden.

Bill's Tip:

Add raisins or chocolate chips for a sweet variation.

PRETZEL DOUGH

Ingredients:

- 4 cups bread flour (500g)
- 2 teaspoons salt (10g)
- 1 tablespoon sugar (12g)
- 1 ¼ cups warm water (300ml)
- 2 teaspoons instant yeast (7g)

Instructions:

Mixing Ingredients: Add warm water and yeast to the bread machine pan. Let it bloom, then add flour, salt, and sugar.

Kneading: Select the dough cycle and let the machine knead and rise the dough.

Shaping: After the cycle, shape into pretzels and boil before baking.

Bill's Tip:

Sprinkle coarse sea salt on top before baking for an authentic taste.

CLASSIC DINNER ROLL DOUGH

Ingredients:

- 4 cups all-purpose flour (500g)
- 1 cup warm milk (240ml)
- 2 tablespoons sugar (30g)
- 1 teaspoon salt (6g)
- ¼ cup butter, softened (60g)
- 2 teaspoons yeast (7g)
- 1 large egg, lightly beaten

Instructions:

Mixing Ingredients: Add all ingredients to the bread machine pan in the order recommended by your manufacturer.

Kneading: Select the "Dough" setting and start.

Shaping and Baking: Once done, shape into rolls, let rise for 30-45 minutes, and bake at 350°F (175°C) for 15-20 minutes.

Bill's Tip:

Brush with melted butter right after baking for an extra-soft finish.

BASIC SWEET DOUGH

Ingredients:

- 3 ½ cups all-purpose flour (440g)
- ¾ cup warm milk (180ml)
- ⅓ cup sugar (65g)
- ½ teaspoon salt (3g)
- ¼ cup butter, softened (60g)
- 2 teaspoons yeast (7g)
- 2 large eggs

Instructions:

Mixing Ingredients: Place all ingredients in the bread machine pan.

Kneading: Select the "Dough" setting and start.

Using: Use the dough for cinnamon rolls, sweet buns, or fruit-filled pastries.

Bill's Tip:

To give the dough a warm, spiced flavor, add a hint of nutmeg or cinnamon.

BASIC PIE DOUGH

Ingredients:

- 2 ½ cups all-purpose flour (320g)
- 1 cup cold butter, cubed (225g)
- 1 teaspoon salt (6g)
- ¼ cup cold water (60ml)

Instructions:

Mixing Ingredients: Add flour and salt to the bread machine pan. Add cold butter and select the "Dough" setting.

Adding Water: Gradually add cold water until the dough forms.

Resting: Chill the dough in the fridge for at least an hour before rolling it out.

Bill's Tip:

To create an extra flaky crust, chill the dough for at least an hour before using it.

WHOLE WHEAT DOUGH

Ingredients:

- 3 cups whole wheat flour (390g)
- 1 cup warm water (240ml)
- 2 tablespoons honey (30ml)
- 1 teaspoon salt (6g)
- 2 tablespoons olive oil (30ml)
- 2 teaspoons yeast (7g)

Instructions:

Mixing Ingredients: Place all ingredients in the bread machine pan.

Kneading: Select the "Dough" setting and start.

Use the dough for whole wheat buns, loaves, or pizza crusts.

Bill's Tip:

Add a tablespoon of wheat gluten to improve texture and rise.

BASIC BRIOCHE DOUGH

Ingredients:

- 3 ½ cups all-purpose flour (440g)
- 3 large eggs
- 1 cup butter (225g), softened
- ¼ cup sugar (50g)
- 1 teaspoon salt (6g)
- 2 teaspoons yeast (7g)
- ¼ cup warm milk (60ml)

Instructions:

Mixing Ingredients: Add all ingredients to the bread machine pan.

Kneading: Select the "Dough" setting and start.

Using: Use the dough for brioche buns or loaves.

Bill's Tip:

This dough is rich buttery—perfect for sweet or savory fillings.

PUMPKIN SPICE ROLL DOUGH

Ingredients:

- 4 cups all-purpose flour (500g)
- 1 cup pumpkin puree (240g)
- ¼ cup warm milk (60ml)
- ¼ cup sugar (50g)
- 1 teaspoon salt (6g)
- ¼ cup butter (60g), softened
- 2 teaspoons yeast (7g)
- 1 teaspoon pumpkin pie spice (2g)

Instructions:

Mixing Ingredients: Add all ingredients to the bread machine pan.

Kneading: Select the "Dough" setting and start.

Shaping and Baking: Shape into rolls or braids, let rise, and bake at 350°F (175°C) for 15-18 minutes.

Bill's Tip:

Drizzle with a maple glaze after baking for a fall-inspired treat.

HERB & CHEESE BREAD DOUGH

Ingredients:

- 4 cups all-purpose flour (500g)
- 1 cup warm water (240ml)
- ¼ cup olive oil (60ml)
- 1 tablespoon sugar (15g)
- 1 teaspoon salt (6g)
- 2 teaspoons yeast (7g)
- 2 teaspoons mixed dried herbs (4g)
- ½ cup grated Parmesan (50g)

Instructions:

Mixing Ingredients: Place all ingredients in the bread machine pan.

Kneading: Select the "Dough" setting and start.

Using: Use for savory rolls, focaccia, or herb-infused bread.

Bill's Tip:

For added flavor, sprinkle sea salt and extra cheese on top before baking.

CHOCOLATE CHIP BRIOCHE DOUGH

Ingredients:

- 3 ½ cups all-purpose flour (440g)
- 3 large eggs
- 1 cup butter (225g), softened
- ¼ cup sugar (50g)
- 1 teaspoon salt (6g)
- 2 teaspoons yeast (7g)
- ¼ cup warm milk (60ml)
- 1 cup chocolate chips (175g)

Instructions:

Mixing Ingredients: Add all ingredients except chocolate chips to the bread machine pan.

Kneading: Select the "Dough" setting and start.

Adding Chocolate Chips: Add chocolate chips during the last kneading phase.

Using: Use for chocolate-filled buns or twists.

Bill's Tip:

Brush with egg wash before baking for a golden, shiny finish.

CINNAMON RAISIN DOUGH

Ingredients:

- 4 cups all-purpose flour (500g)
- 1 cup warm milk (240ml)
- ¼ cup sugar (50g)
- 1 teaspoon salt (6g)
- ¼ cup butter (60g), softened
- 2 teaspoons yeast (7g)
- 1 teaspoon ground cinnamon (2g)
- 1 cup raisins (150g)

Instructions:

Mixing Ingredients: Add all ingredients except raisins to the bread machine pan.

Kneading: Select the "Dough" setting and start.

Adding Raisins: Add raisins during the last kneading phase.

Using: Use for cinnamon raisin rolls or loaves.

Bill's Tip:

Add a sugar-cinnamon swirl inside the rolls for a sweet touch.

GARLIC & HERB PIZZA DOUGH

Ingredients:

- 3 ½ cups all-purpose flour (440g)
- 1 cup warm water (240ml)
- ¼ cup olive oil (60ml)
- 1 tablespoon sugar (15g)
- 1 teaspoon salt (6g)
- 2 teaspoons yeast (7g)
- 1 teaspoon garlic powder (2g)
- 1 teaspoon dried oregano (2g)

Instructions:

Mixing Ingredients: Place all ingredients in the bread machine pan.

Kneading: Select the "Dough" setting and start.

Using: Use for pizza crust, calzones, or garlic knots.

Bill's Tip:

Pre-bake the pizza crust for 5 minutes before adding toppings for a crispier base.

PUFF PASTRY DOUGH

Ingredients:

- 2 ½ cups all-purpose flour (320g)
- ½ teaspoon salt (2g)
- 1 cup cold butter (225g), cubed
- ½ cup very cold water (120ml)
- 1 teaspoon apple cider or white vinegar (5ml)

Instructions:

Mixing Ingredients: Place the flour and salt in the bread machine pan. Add the cold butter and vinegar. Set the bread machine to the dough setting and let it run for a few minutes until the butter is mixed with the flour and forms a crumbly texture.

Adding Water: Gradually add the very cold water until the dough becomes a ball.

Chilling: Remove the dough from the bread machine, wrap it in plastic wrap, and refrigerate for 30 minutes.

Rolling: Take the dough out of the refrigerator and roll it into a rectangle. Fold it into thirds like a letter, then roll it out again. Repeat this process 3 to 4 times.

Using: Your puff pastry dough is ready. You can make pies, croissants, or any other pastry..

Bill's Tip:

To improve the dough's texture and flavor, add lemon juice to the vinegar.

FRUIT PIE DOUGH

Ingredients:

- 2 ½ cups all-purpose flour (320g)
- 2 tablespoons sugar (25g)
- ½ teaspoon salt (2g)
- 1 cup cold butter (225g), cubed
- ½ cup very cold water (120ml)
- 1 teaspoon lemon juice (5ml)

Instructions:

Mixing Ingredients: Place the flour, sugar, and salt in the bread machine pan. Add the cold butter. Set the bread machine to the dough setting and let it run briefly until the butter is mixed with the flour to form a crumbly texture.

Adding Water: Gradually add the very cold water and lemon juice until the dough becomes a ball.

Chilling: Remove the dough from the bread machine, wrap it in plastic wrap, and refrigerate for 30 minutes.

Using: Take the dough out of the refrigerator, roll it out, and use it for your favorite fruit pie.

Bill's Tip:

Add a bit of grated lemon or orange zest to the dough for extra flavor.

CHAPTER 17:

NON-BREAD RECIPES

JAMS & PRESERVES

STRAWBERRY JAM

Ingredients:

- 2 ½ cups (500g) strawberries, chopped
- 1 ¼ cups (250g) sugar
- 2 tablespoons (30ml) lemon juice
- 1 tablespoon (15g) pectin

Nutritional Information:
(per tablespoon)

40 kcal, 0g fat, 10g carbs, 0g protein

Bill's Tip:

Add a vanilla extract at the end of the program for extra aroma.

Instructions:

Place all ingredients into the bread machine pan.

Select the "Jam" program.

After the cycle, pour the jam into sterilized jars.

BLUEBERRY JAM

Ingredients:

- 2 ½ cups (500g) blueberries
- 1 ¼ cups (250g) sugar
- 2 tablespoons (30ml) lemon juice

Nutritional Information:
(per tablespoon)

35 kcal, 0g fat, 9g carbs, 0g protein

Bill's Tip:

If fresh berries aren't available, use frozen ones and add 5 minutes to the program time.

Instructions:

Place the blueberries, sugar, and lemon juice into the bread machine pan.

Select the "Jam" program.

Once the cycle is finished, carefully pour the jam into sterilized jars.

APRICOT JAM

Ingredients:

- 2 cups (about 450g) fresh apricots, pitted and chopped
- 1 ¼ cups (250g) sugar
- 2 tablespoons (30ml) lemon juice
- 1 ½ tablespoons (12g) pectin (optional, for thicker consistency)

Nutritional Information:

(per tablespoon)

50 kcal, 13g carbs, 12g sugars

Instructions:

Place chopped apricots, sugar, and lemon juice into the bread machine pan.

Select the "Jam" setting on your bread machine.

Start the machine. The program will mix and cook the ingredients to the perfect consistency.

After the cycle, carefully pour the hot jam into sterilized jars. Seal immediately.

Bill's Tip:

Allow the apricots to macerate with sugar for a few hours before placing them in the bread machine. This draws out the juices and enhances the natural sweetness.

MIXED BERRY JAM

Ingredients:

- 2 cups (about 450g) mixed berries (strawberries, blueberries, raspberries), fresh or frozen
- 1 ½ cups (300g) sugar
- 2 tablespoons (30ml) lemon juice
- 1 ½ tablespoons (12g) pectin (optional, for thicker consistency)

Nutritional Information:

(per tablespoon)

55 kcal, 14g carbs, 13g sugars

Instructions:

Place the berries, sugar, and lemon juice into the bread machine pan. No need to thaw if using frozen berries.

Select the "Jam" setting on your bread machine.

Start the machine and let it work its magic.

Once the cycle is complete, carefully transfer the hot jam to sterilized jars and seal.

Bill's Tip:

Experiment with different ratios of berries to create unique flavors. For a twist, add a pinch of cinnamon or a splash of vanilla extract after cooking.

PEACH PRESERVES

Ingredients:

- 4 cups (about 800g) fresh peaches, peeled and diced
- 2 cups (400g) sugar
- 2 tablespoons (30ml) lemon juice
- 2 tablespoons (16g) pectin (optional, for thicker consistency)

Nutritional Information:

(per tablespoon)

50 kcal, 13g carbs, 12g sugars

Instructions:

Thoroughly wash the peaches, remove the skin and pits, and dice the flesh.

Place diced peaches in the bread machine pan. Add sugar, lemon juice, and pectin (if using).

Select the "Jam" or "Preserves" program on your bread machine, typically lasting 1-1.5 hours.

Once the program ends, carefully remove the hot preserves and pour them into sterilized jars. Seal immediately.

Bill's Tip:

Add 1 teaspoon of ground cinnamon or a pinch of nutmeg for a warm, spiced note. If the preserves seem too thin after the program ends, run the cycle again or add extra pectin.

PEACH JAM

Ingredients:

- 2 ½ cups (500g) peaches, diced
- 1 ¼ cups (250g) sugar
- 2 tablespoons (30ml) lemon juice

Nutritional Information:
(per tablespoon)

35 kcal, 9g carbs, 0g fat, 0g protein

Instructions:

Place the peaches, sugar, and lemon juice into the bread machine pan.

Select the "Jam" program.

After the cycle, pour the jam into sterilized jars.

Bill's Tip:

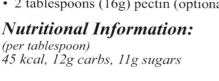

Add a pinch of ground ginger for a subtle kick.

APPLE-PLUM PRESERVES

Ingredients:

- 2 cups (300g) fresh apples, peeled and diced
- 2 cups (350g) fresh plums, pitted and chopped
- 2 cups (400g) sugar
- 2 tablespoons (30ml) lemon juice
- ½ teaspoon ground cinnamon (optional)
- 2 tablespoons (16g) pectin (optional)

Nutritional Information:
(per tablespoon)
45 kcal, 12g carbs, 11g sugars

Instructions:

Place diced apples and plums into the bread machine pan. Add sugar, lemon juice, and cinnamon (if using).

Select the "Jam" or "Preserves" program, typically lasting 1-1.5 hours.

Carefully transfer the hot preserves into sterilized jars once the program ends. Seal immediately.

Bill's Tip:

Experiment with spices like cloves or ginger to add a rich, warm flavor, perfect for autumn. Use sweet apple varieties and ripe plums for the best taste.

RICE AND GRAINS

CLASSIC OATMEAL (SMALL BATCH)

Ingredients:

- 1 cup (90g) rolled oats
- 2 cups (480ml) water
- ¼ teaspoon (1g) salt
- 2 tablespoons (30g) brown sugar
- 1 tablespoon (14g) butter
- ½ teaspoon (1g) cinnamon (optional)

Nutritional Information:
(per serving)

180 kcal, 29g carbs, 4g protein, 5g fat

Instructions:

Place all ingredients into the bread machine pan.

Select the «Porridge» or «Jam» setting and start the machine.

Once finished, let the oatmeal sit for a few minutes before serving.

Bill's Tip:

During the last 5 minutes of cooking, toss in a handful of nuts or dried fruit for added texture.

CREAMY POLENTA

Ingredients:

- 1 cup (160g) cornmeal
- 4 cups (960ml) water
- 1 teaspoon (6g) salt
- 2 tablespoons (28g) butter
- ½ cup (50g) Parmesan cheese, grated (optional)

Nutritional Information:
(per serving)

160 kcal, 31g carbs, 4g protein, 4g fat

Instructions:

Add water and salt to the bread machine pan, then gradually whisk the cornmeal.

Select the «Jam» or «Porridge» settings and start the machine.

Once finished, stir in the butter and Parmesan cheese.

Bill's Tip:

For an elevated dish, serve with a drizzle of olive oil and a sprinkle of fresh herbs.

APPLE CINNAMON RICE PUDDING

Ingredients:

- 1 cup (200g) Arborio rice
- 3 cups (720ml) milk
- ¼ cup (50g) sugar
- 2 tablespoons (28g) butter
- 1 medium apple, peeled and diced
- 1 teaspoon (2g) ground cinnamon

Nutritional Information:
(per serving)
230 kcal, 40g carbs, 5g protein, 6g fat

Instructions:

Place all ingredients into the bread machine pan.

Select the «Jam» or «Porridge» settings and start the machine.

Once finished, let it cool slightly before serving.

Bill's Tip:

Sprinkle with extra cinnamon or add a dollop of whipped cream for a dessert-like treat.

STEEL-CUT OATMEAL

Ingredients:

- 1 cup (180g) steel-cut oats
- 3 cups (720ml) water
- ¼ teaspoon (1g) salt
- 2 tablespoons (30ml) maple syrup
- 1 tablespoon (14g) butter

Nutritional Information:
(per serving)

190 kcal, 34g carbs, 5g protein, 5g fat

Instructions:

Place all ingredients into the bread machine pan.

Select the «Porridge» or «Jam» setting and start the machine.

Stir before serving for a smooth consistency.

Bill's Tip:

Top with fresh berries or chopped nuts to add flavor and texture.

BARLEY PORRIDGE

Ingredients:

- 1 cup (200g) pearl barley
- 4 cups (960ml) water
- ½ teaspoon (3g) salt
- 2 tablespoons (30g) honey
- 2 tablespoons (28g) butter

Nutritional Information:
(per serving)

210 kcal, 42g carbs, 4g protein, 5g fat

Instructions:

Add barley, water, and salt to the bread machine pan.

Select the «Porridge» or «Jam» setting and start the machine.

Once finished, stir in the honey and butter before serving.

Bill's Tip:

Add a splash of cream or milk at the end for a richer, creamier texture.

PAELLA (SPANISH RICE DISH)

Ingredients:

- 1 ½ cups (300g) Arborio rice
- 1 ½ cups (360ml) chicken broth
- ½ cup (120ml) white wine
- ½ lb (225g) shrimp, peeled and deveined
- ½ lb (225g) chicken breast, diced
- ¼ lb (115g) chorizo sausage, sliced
- ½ cup (80g) bell pepper, diced
- ½ cup (80g) tomatoes, chopped
- ½ cup (60g) peas, frozen
- 1 small onion, finely chopped
- 2 cloves garlic, minced
- ¼ teaspoon (1.2g) saffron threads
- 1 teaspoon (2g) smoked paprika
- Salt and pepper to taste
- 2 tablespoons (30ml) olive oil
- 1 lemon, cut into wedges (for serving)

Instructions:

Add olive oil, chicken, chorizo, onion, and garlic to the bread machine pan. Use the sauté or bake setting to cook until the chicken is browned and the onions are softened, for about 10 minutes.

Add the Arborio rice, chicken broth, white wine, saffron, smoked paprika, salt, and pepper to the pan. Stir to combine.

Close the lid and set the bread machine to the "Quick Bread" or "Cake" setting. Cook for 20 minutes.

After 20 minutes, open the lid and add the shrimp, bell pepper, tomatoes, and peas. Close the lid and continue cooking until the rice is tender and the shrimp are cooked through, about 20-25 more minutes.

Once the paella is done, let it sit for 5 minutes before serving. Garnish with lemon wedges.

Nutritional Information:
(per serving)

370 kcal, 40g carbs, 22g protein, 12g fat

Bill's Tip:

To enhance the flavor, soak the saffron threads in warm chicken broth before adding them to the bread machine. This will release more of the saffron's color and flavor into the dish.

PILAF (SAVORY RICE DISH)

Ingredients:

- 1 ½ cups (300g) basmati rice
- 2 cups (480ml) chicken or vegetable broth
- ½ cup (60g) carrots, diced
- ½ cup (80g) onions, finely chopped
- ½ cup (50g) peas, frozen
- ¼ cup (30g) slivered almonds
- ¼ cup (40g) raisins
- 2 cloves garlic, minced
- 1 bay leaf
- ½ teaspoon (1g) ground cumin
- ¼ teaspoon (0.5g) ground cinnamon
- Salt and pepper to taste
- 2 tablespoons (30ml) olive oil

Nutritional Information:
(per serving)

320 kcal, 52g carbs, 6g protein, 10g fat

Instructions:

Add olive oil, onions, garlic, and carrots to the bread machine pan. Cook on the sauté or bake setting until the onions are softened, about 5 minutes.

Add the basmati rice, chicken or vegetable broth, bay leaf, cumin, cinnamon, salt, and pepper to the pan. Stir to combine.

Close the lid and set the bread machine to the "Quick Bread" or "Cake" setting. Cook for 20 minutes.

After 20 minutes, open the lid and add the peas, slivered almonds, and raisins. Close the lid and continue cooking until the rice is tender and all the liquid is absorbed, about 15-20 more minutes.

Once the pilaf is done, let it sit for 5 minutes before serving. Remove the bay leaf before serving.

Bill's Tip:

Toast the almonds in a dry skillet before adding them to the pilaf for a richer, nutty flavor.

212

HOMEMADE YOGURT

Ingredients:

- 4 cups (950ml) whole milk
- 2 tablespoons (30ml) plain yogurt (for starter)

Nutritional Information:
(per ½ cup serving)

85 kcal, 9g carbs, 4g protein, 4g fat

Bill's Tip:

Use fresh yogurt as a starter – it improves the texture and flavor.

Instructions:

Pour the milk into the bread machine's container and select the "Yogurt" program (if available).

Heat the milk to 180°F (82°C), then cool it down to 110°F (43°C). Add the yogurt starter and stir well.

Start the program and let it run for 8-12 hours until the yogurt thickens.

Transfer the yogurt to a container and chill it in the refrigerator.

RICE PUDDING

Ingredients:

- ½ cup (100g) Arborio rice
- 4 cups (950ml) milk
- ½ cup (100g) sugar
- 1 tablespoon (14g) butter
- 1 teaspoon (5ml) vanilla extract
- Pinch of salt

Nutritional Information:
(per ½ cup serving)

200 kcal, 34g carbs, 5g protein, 6g fat

Bill's Tip:

Add a pinch of cinnamon or nutmeg for extra flavor.

Instructions:

Place all ingredients into the bread machine's container.

Select the "Pudding" or "Dessert" program and run for 1½-2 hours.

After the program finishes, stir the pudding and refrigerate it.

COCONUT YOGURT

Ingredients:

- 2 cups (475ml) coconut milk
- 2 tablespoons (30ml) coconut yogurt (for starter)
- 1 teaspoon (5g) agar-agar

Nutritional Information:
(per ½ cup serving)

150 kcal, 13g fat, 1g protein, 7g carbs

Bill's Tip:

Use full-fat coconut milk for a thicker consistency.

Instructions:

Mix coconut milk and agar-agar, boil in the bread machine, then cool to 110°F (43°C).

Add the yogurt starter and stir well.

Start the "Yogurt" program and let it run for 8-12 hours until the yogurt thickens.

Transfer to a container and chill in the refrigerator.

213

HOT CHOCOLATE

Ingredients:

- 2 cups (475ml) whole milk
- ½ cup (120ml) heavy cream
- ½ cup (85g) dark chocolate, finely chopped
- 1 tablespoon (15g) cocoa powder
- 2 tablespoons (25g) sugar
- Pinch of salt

Instructions:

Place all ingredients into the bread machine's container.

Select the "Beverage" or "Soup" program and run for 20-30 minutes until the chocolate melts and blends with the milk.

Pour the hot chocolate into mugs and enjoy.

Nutritional Information:
(per 1 cup serving)

300 kcal, 18g fat, 6g protein, 33g carbs

Bill's Tip:

Add a dash of cinnamon or peppermint extract for a unique twist.

HOMEMADE CIDER

Ingredients:

- 4 cups (950ml) apple juice
- 1 cinnamon stick
- 4 cloves
- 1 orange slice
- 1 tablespoon (12g) brown sugar

Instructions:

Place all ingredients into the bread machine's container.

Select the "Beverage" or "Soup" program and run for 1 hour.

Strain the cider and serve hot.

Nutritional Information:
(per 1 cup serving)

120 kcal, 0g fat, 0g protein, 31g carbs

Bill's Tip:

For a spiced aroma, add star anise or ginger.

CLASSIC MULLED WINE

Ingredients:

- 1 bottle (750ml) red wine, preferably a dry or semi-dry wine
- 1 orange, sliced into rounds
- ½ lemon, sliced into rounds
- 2 cinnamon sticks
- 6–8 cloves
- 2-star anise
- ¼ cup (60ml) honey or sugar, or to taste
- 1-inch piece of fresh ginger, peeled and sliced
- ¼ cup (60ml) brandy (optional)
- A pinch of freshly grated nutmeg

Instructions:

Preparation: Place all ingredients except brandy into the bread machine pan. If your bread machine has a delay start option, you can set it up in advance for a warm drink ready at the perfect time.

Select Program: Choose the «Jam» setting or another low-heat setting that gently warms the mixture without boiling it. Boiling will cause the alcohol to evaporate and alter the flavor.

Cook: Let the bread machine run the full cycle, which should be around 1-1.5 hours, allowing the flavors to meld together.

Finish: Carefully pour the mulled wine into heatproof glasses or mugs after the cycle. If you're adding brandy, stir it in just before serving.

Serve: Garnish with a slice of orange or a cinnamon stick for an extra touch of elegance.

Nutritional Information:
(per 5 oz. serving)

150 kcal, 15g carbs, 12g sugars, Alcohol: 12-15% (depending on the wine and added brandy)

Bill's Tip:

Adjust Sweetness: *Taste the mulled wine halfway through the cooking process. If it's not sweet enough, add more honey or sugar to your liking.*

Extra Spice: *Add a few extra cloves or another star anise for a more robust flavor. Just be careful not to overpower the wine with too many spices.*

No Alcohol Option: *If you prefer a non-alcoholic version, substitute the wine with a mix of grape and cranberry juice, adjusting the sweetness as needed.*

HEARTY CHICKEN SOUP

Ingredients:

- 1 large chicken breast (about 250g), diced
- 2 medium carrots, sliced
- 2 stalks celery, sliced
- 1 small onion, diced
- 2 cloves garlic, minced
- 4 cups (1 liter) chicken broth
- 1 cup (85g) egg noodles
- Salt & pepper to taste
- 2 tablespoons fresh parsley, chopped

Nutritional Information:
(per serving)

250 kcal, 20g protein, 25g carbs, 7g fat

Instructions:

Preparation: Add the diced chicken, carrots, celery, onion, garlic, and chicken broth to the bread machine pan.

Select Program: Choose your bread machine's «Soup» or «Stew» setting.

Cook: Let the machine run its cycle, which should last about 1-2 hours. Add the egg noodles in the last 30 minutes of cooking.

Finish: Season with salt and pepper to taste and garnish with fresh parsley once the cycle is complete.

Bill's Tip:

For a richer flavor, use homemade chicken broth and add a bay leaf during cooking. Remove the bay leaf before serving.

BEEF STEW

Ingredients:

- 1 lb. (450g) stew beef, cubed
- 2 medium potatoes, diced
- 2 medium carrots, sliced
- 1 large onion, chopped
- 4 cups (1 liter) beef broth
- 2 tablespoons (30g) tomato paste
- 1 tablespoon (15ml) Worcestershire sauce
- 1 bay leaf
- Salt & pepper to taste

Nutritional Information:
(per serving)
350 kcal, 30g protein, 28g carbs, 12g fat

Instructions:

Preparation: Place the beef, potatoes, carrots, onion, beef broth, tomato paste, and Worcestershire sauce into the bread machine pan.

Select Program: Use the «Stew» setting.

Cook: Let the machine work for 2-3 hours until the beef is tender and the vegetables are cooked.

Finish: Season with salt and pepper and discard the bay leaf before serving.

Bill's Tip:

To thicken the stew, mix 1 tablespoon of flour with 2 tablespoons of water and add it to the last 20 minutes of cooking

TOMATO BASIL SOUP

Ingredients:

- 4 cups (1 liter) canned crushed tomatoes
- 1 medium onion, chopped
- 2 cloves garlic, minced
- 2 cups (500 ml) vegetable broth
- ¼ cup (10 g) fresh basil, chopped
- ½ cup (120 ml) heavy cream
- Salt & pepper to taste
- 2 tablespoons (30 ml) olive oil

Instructions:

Preparation: Place the crushed tomatoes, onion, garlic, vegetable broth, and olive oil into the bread machine pan. Select Program: Choose the «Soup» setting.

Cook: Let it cook for 1-2 hours, stirring occasionally.

Finish: Add the fresh basil and heavy cream in the last 10 minutes of cooking. Season with salt and pepper.

Nutritional Information:
(per serving)

220 kcal, 4g protein, 18g carbs, 15g fat

Bill's Tip:

For a smoother texture, blend the soup using an immersion blender directly in the bread machine pan before adding the cream.

THAI COCONUT CHICKEN SOUP

Ingredients:

- 1 large (250 g) chicken breast, thinly sliced
- 2 cups (500 ml) coconut milk
- 2 cups (500 ml) chicken broth
- 1 stalk lemongrass, chopped
- 1-inch piece ginger, sliced
- 2 cloves garlic, minced
- 1 cup (100 g) mushrooms, sliced
- 2 tablespoons (30 ml) fish sauce
- 2 tablespoons (30 ml) lime juice
- 1 red chili, sliced
- ¼ cup (10 g) fresh cilantro, chopped

Instructions:

Preparation: Add the chicken, coconut milk, chicken broth, lemongrass, ginger, garlic, and mushrooms to the bread machine pan.

Select Program: Use the «Soup» or «Stew» setting.

Cook: Let it cook for 1-2 hours, allowing the flavors to meld.

Finish: Stir in the fish sauce, lime juice, and red chili. Garnish with fresh cilantro before serving.

Nutritional Information:
(per serving)

300 kcal, 20g protein, 8g carbs, 20g fat

Bill's Tip:

To make the soup spicier during cooking, add more chili or a spoonful of Thai red curry paste.

MOROCCAN LAMB STEW

Ingredients:

- 1 lb. (450 g) lamb shoulder, cubed
- 2 medium sweet potatoes, diced
- 1 cup (150 g) cooked chickpeas
- 1 large onion, chopped
- 1 cup (240 g) diced tomatoes
- 2 cups (500 ml) chicken broth
- ½ cup (80 g) dried apricots, chopped
- 1 teaspoon (5 g) ground cumin
- ½ teaspoon (2.5 g) ground cinnamon
- ½ teaspoon (2.5 g) ground coriander
- Salt and pepper to taste

Nutritional Information:

(per serving)

400 kcal, 25g protein, 35g carbs, 15g fat

Instructions:

Preparation: Place the lamb, sweet potatoes, chickpeas, onion, diced tomatoes, chicken broth, and spices into the bread machine pan.

Select Program: Choose the «Stew» setting.
Cook the stew for 2-3 hours until the lamb is tender and the flavors are well combined.

Finish: In the last 30 minutes of cooking, stir in the dried apricots and season with salt and pepper.

Bill's Tip: *Serve with couscous or flatbread for a complete Moroccan-inspired meal.*

TOM YUM SOUP

Ingredients:

- 4 cups (960 ml) chicken stock
- 2 stalks lemongrass, trimmed and smashed
- 1-inch piece (2.5 cm) galangal, sliced
- 4 kaffir lime leaves torn into pieces
- 2-4 Thai bird's eye chilies, smashed (adjust to taste)
- 12 oz (340 g) shrimp, peeled and deveined
- 1 cup (100 g) mushrooms, sliced (straw mushrooms or button mushrooms)
- 2 tablespoons (30 ml) fish sauce
- 2-3 tablespoons (30-45 ml) lime juice (to taste)
- ½ cup (100 g) tomatoes, chopped
- 2 tablespoons cilantro, chopped (for garnish)
- ½ cup (120 ml) coconut milk (optional, for a creamy version)

Nutritional Information:

(per serving)

150 kcal, 7 g carbs, 20 g protein, 4 g fat

Instructions:

Preparation: Place the chicken stock, lemongrass, galangal, and kaffir lime leaves into the bread machine pan.

Program: Set your bread machine to the «Jam» or «Soup» setting. This will allow the ingredients to simmer and blend their flavors.

Cooking: Start the machine and let the stock simmer for about 20-30 minutes.

Add Shrimp and Mushrooms: Add the shrimp, mushrooms, fish sauce, and tomatoes to the soup. Continue cooking for another 5-10 minutes until the shrimp are cooked through and the mushrooms are tender.

Finish: Carefully open the bread machine and remove the pan once the cycle is complete. Stir in the lime juice, adjusting to taste. If you prefer a creamier version, add the coconut milk at this stage.

Serve: Ladle the hot soup into bowls and garnish with chopped cilantro. Serve immediately.

Bill's Tip:

Adjust the Heat: *If you prefer a spicier soup, increase the chilies or add a touch of chili oil at the end.*

Traditional Twist: *Serve with jasmine rice to balance the spicy and sour flavors.*

MUSHROOM SOUP

Ingredients:

- 2 tablespoons (28 g) butter
- 1 small onion, finely chopped
- 2 cloves garlic, minced
- 12 oz (340 g) mixed mushrooms, sliced (button, cremini, shiitake)
- 4 cups (960 ml) chicken or vegetable stock
- ½ cup (120 ml) heavy cream
- 1 teaspoon (2 g) thyme, dried or fresh
- 1 bay leaf
- Salt and pepper to taste
- 2 tablespoons chopped parsley for garnish

Nutritional Information:
(per serving)

190 kcal, 8 g carbs, 4 g protein, 16 g fat

Instructions:

Preparation: Add the butter, onions, and garlic to the bread machine pan. Set to the «Jam» or «Soup» setting and let it sauté for about 5 minutes until the onions are translucent.

Add Mushrooms: Add the sliced mushrooms to the pan, cooking for 5-7 minutes until they soften and release their juices.

Stock and Herbs: Add the stock, thyme, and bay leaf. Simmer the soup in the bread machine for 30-40 minutes.

Finish: Remove the bay leaf and stir in the heavy cream after the cooking cycle—season with salt and pepper to taste.

Serve: Ladle the soup into bowls and garnish with chopped parsley.

Bill's Tip:

Intensify Flavor: Use a variety of mushrooms for a deeper, richer flavor profile.

Creamy Option: If you prefer a thicker soup, blend half of the cooked mushrooms before adding the cream.

CHAPTER 18:

TROUBLESHOOTING AND TIPS

COMMON BREAD MACHINE ISSUES AND THEIR SOLUTIONS

Common bread machine issues and their solutions are often found in the device's manuals, but general recommendations apply to many models. These tips will help you avoid common errors and ensure a comfortable, high-quality bread-baking experience.

BREAD DOESN'T RISE

Cause: Insufficient yeast, old yeast, lack of sugar, incorrect water temperature.

Solution: Ensure the yeast is fresh and use the correct amount. The water temperature should be warm but not hot (around 110°F or 43°C). Add a pinch of sugar to help activate the yeast.

BREAD IS TOO DENSE

Cause: Not enough liquid, too much flour, or incorrect setting.

Solution: Check the correct proportions of ingredients. Ensure the bread machine setting matches the type of bread (e.g., use the whole grain setting for whole wheat bread).

BREAD COLLAPSES IN THE MIDDLE AFTER RISING

Cause: Too much yeast or liquid or too high a temperature during rising.

Solution: Reduce the amount of yeast or liquid. Avoid using the bread machine in an overly warm environment.

BREAD IS DRY AND CRUMBLY

Cause: Lack of liquid or too long baking time.

Solution: Add more liquid (1–2 tablespoons of water or milk). Check the baking time settings and reduce them if necessary.

BREAD IS STICKY OR UNCOOKED IN THE CENTER

Cause: Insufficient baking time or too much liquid.

Solution: Extend the baking time by 5–10 minutes or reduce the amount of liquid in the recipe.

CRUST IS TOO DARK OR TOO LIGHT

Cause: Incorrect crust setting or too high temperature.

Solution: Choose a different crust setting on the bread machine (light, medium, dark) or reduce the temperature if possible.

KNEADING BLADE STAYS IN THE BREAD AFTER BAKING

Cause: This is a fairly common issue.

Solution: To avoid this, carefully remove the blade before the final kneading cycle if the bread machine allows. Or, after baking, immediately remove the bread from the pan, let it cool slightly, and then remove the blade.

BREAD DOESN'T COME OUT OF THE PAN

Cause: Bread is sticking to the pan walls.

Solution: Gently run a knife along the edges of the pan before removing the bread. Ensure the pan is well greased before adding ingredients.

UNEVEN MIXING (INGREDIENTS DON'T MIX PROPERLY)

Cause: Incorrect ingredient loading or worn kneading blade.

Solution: Ensure ingredients are added correctly (liquids first, then dry), and check the blade condition, replacing it if necessary.

BREAD MACHINE DOESN'T START

Cause: Possible electrical issues or improperly installed pan.

Solution: Ensure the pan is securely placed in the machine and plugged into a functional outlet. If the issue continues, reach out to the service center.

INCONSISTENT RESULTS WITH AUTOMATIC PROGRAMS

Cause: Ingredients were measured by eye or habit instead of being accurately weighed.

Solution: Always weigh your ingredients carefully when using automatic programs. Precise measurements are crucial for consistent and successful results. Avoid estimating or relying on habit.

TIPS FOR IMPROVING THE QUALITY OF BAKING

USE HIGH-QUALITY INGREDIENTS:

Fresh Flour: Store flour in a cool, dry place and always check the expiration date.

Natural Sweeteners: Consider replacing regular sugar with honey or maple syrup for a richer flavor.

Oils and Fats: Use butter or olive oil instead of margarine for a more robust taste.

ADJUST DOUGH MOISTURE:

If the dough is too dry, add 1-2 tablespoons of water or milk. Continue adjusting until you reach the desired consistency.

If the dough is too sticky, gradually add a small amount of flour, being careful not to add too much.

EXPERIMENT WITH BAKING MODES:

Try using the delayed start mode to give the dough more time to rise before baking.
If your bread machine offers a crust setting, try experimenting with different levels (light, medium, dark) to find the perfect texture.

ADD FLAVORS AND SPICES:

Add spices (such as cinnamon, cardamom, or cumin) to the dough to give the bread a new aroma.
Incorporating fresh or dried herbs, like rosemary and thyme, into the dough can enhance flavor.

221

USE THE BREAD MACHINE FOR KNEADING COMPLEX DOUGHS:

Doughs for baguettes, focaccia, or brioche require extended kneading. The bread machine can simplify this process, allowing you to control the dough's texture and achieve the perfect rise.

MONITOR AMBIENT TEMPERATURE:

In hot weather, yeast may work faster, producing over-proofed dough. In this case, the amount of yeast or the rising time should be reduced.

TRY DIFFERENT TYPES OF FLOUR:

Experiment with whole wheat, rye, or gluten-free flours to create new textures and flavors.

COOKING MEASUREMENT TABLE CHART

COOKING MEASUREMENT CHART

WEIGHT

IMPERIAL	METRIC
1/2 oz	15 g
1 oz	29 g
2 oz	57 g
3 oz	85 g
4 oz	113 g
5 oz	141 g
6 oz	170 g
8 oz	227 g
10 oz	283 g
12 oz	340 g
13 oz	369 g
14 oz	397 g
15 oz	425 g
1 lb	453 g

MEASUREMENT

CUP	ONCES	MILLILITERS	TABLESPOONS
8 cup	64 oz	1895 ml	128
6 cup	48 oz	1420 ml	96
5 cup	40 oz	1180 ml	80
4 cup	32 oz	960 ml	64
2 cup	16 oz	480 ml	32
1 cup	8 oz	240 ml	16
3/4 cup	6 oz	177 ml	12
2/3 cup	5 oz	158 ml	11
1/2 cup	4 oz	118 ml	8
3/8 cup	3 oz	90 ml	6
1/3 cup	2.5 oz	79 ml	5.5
1/4 cup	2 oz	59 ml	4
1/8 cup	1 oz	30 ml	3
1/16 cup	1/2 oz	15 ml	1

TEMPERATURE

FARENHEIT	CELSIUS
100 °F	37 °C
150 °F	65 °C
200 °F	93 °C
250 °F	121 °C
300 °F	150 °C
325 °F	160 °C
350 °F	180 °C
375 °F	190 °C
400 °F	200 °C
425 °F	220 °C
450 °F	230 °C
500 °F	260 °C
525 °F	274 °C
550 °F	288 °C

CONCLUSION

And so, we've reached the end of our culinary journey! In this world where time is precious, let your bread machine be your faithful ally, freeing you from the routine and allowing you to focus on the true joy of baking. Each book page invites you to explore the world of bread from a fresh perspective and maximize your bread machine's potential.

This book is more than just a collection of recipes—it opens up a world of culinary possibilities. We hope you've discovered inspiration here to create dishes that will bring joy to you and your loved ones.

May everything you bake with your bread machine become a meal and a work of art, reflecting your taste and culinary creativity. Instead of spending time on complex processes, savor the results and take pride in each culinary masterpiece from your kitchen.

Thank you for embarking on this delicious adventure with me. We wish you success, joy, and many delightful moments on your journey to culinary greatness. May your love of baking always warm your home and lift your spirits!

USEFUL RESOURCES AND REFERENCES

RESEARCH AND CLINICAL INSIGHTS:

Peter H. R. Green, MD, Benjamin Lebwohl, MD, MS, and Ruby Greywoode, MD «Celiac Disease»
Detailed insights into celiac disease and its management.

Abdalla, S. Abdel-Gawad; Mohamed, N. Elghazali; Abdullah, K. Elliby, Amna, A. A. Osman
«Influence of Legumes Flour on Physical and Sensory Attributes of Gluten-Free Bread»
Explore how legume flours affect the texture and flavor of gluten-free bread.

Suneil A. Raju, Anupam Rej, and David S. Sanders
«The Truth About Gluten!»
Understanding gluten and its implications for health.

Iqra Kalsoom Sughra
«Wheat-Based Gluten and Its Association with Pathogenesis of Celiac Disease: A Review»
A review of how wheat-based gluten contributes to celiac disease.

Edurne Simón, Marta Molero-Luis, Ricardo Fueyo-Díaz, Cristian Costas-Batlle, Paula Crespo-Escobar, and Miguel A. Montoro-Huguet
«The Gluten-Free Diet for Celiac Disease: Critical Insights to Better Understand Clinical Outcomes»
Key insights into the effectiveness of a gluten-free diet.

Thomas J Littlejohns, Amanda Y Chong, Naomi E Allen, Matthew Arnold, Kathryn E Bradbury, Alexander J Mentzer, Elizabeth J Soilleux, Jennifer L Carter
«Genetic, Lifestyle, and Health-Related Factors»
An exploration of various factors affecting health and genetic predispositions.

Paoli, A., Rubini, A., Volek, J.S., Grimaldi, K.A. (2013). «Beyond weight loss: a review of the therapeutic uses of very-low-carbohydrate (ketogenic) diets.» European Journal of Clinical Nutrition, 67(8), 789-796.

BREAD MACHINE MANUFACTURER INSTRUCTIONS:

Hamilton Beach Bread Machine
Hamilton Beach Bread Machine Manual
https://useandcares.hamiltonbeach.com/files/840194100.pdf

Cuisinart Bread Machine
Cuisinart Bread Machine Instruction Manual
https://www.cuisinart.ca/on/demandware.static/-/Sites-ca-cuisinart-Library/en_CA/dwc9677e12/Instruction%20 Booklet/CBK-200C_en.pdf.

KitchenAid BreadMaker
KitchenAid BreadMaker User Manual
https://www.kitchenaid.com/pinch-of-help/stand-mixers/tips-for-making-bread-with-stand-mixer.html

Zojirushi Bread Machine
Zojirushi Bread Machine Instruction Manual
https://www.zojirushi.com/support/manuals_breadmakers.html

Panasonic Bread Machine
Panasonic Bread Machine User Guide

https://tda.panasonic-europe-service.com/docs/2z66c85613z1z4153fz656ez706466z21zd38d 669703a93df3d660d721528db88b6400ab0c/pgrp005/pcat003/sdyr2550/984956/OI3_en_SD-YR2550%20SERIES%20EU_M1_20210205.pdf

BOOKS BY THIS AUTHOR

CRAFTING ARTISAN BREAD MADE EASY: A SOURDOUGH COOKBOOK FOR BEGINNERS
https://www.amazon.com/dp/B0D5H5MFQ7/

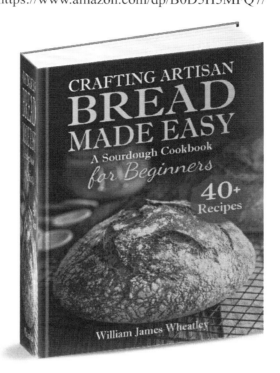

THE PERFECT ARTISAN GLUTEN-FREE BREAD: FLOUR BLENDS, SOURDOUGH TECHNIQUES, RECIPES, TIPS, AND MORE
https://www.amazon.com/dp/B0CJLLLTWH

EL PAN ARTESANO SIN GLUTEN PERFECTO: MEZCLAS DE HARINAS, TÉCNICAS DE MASA MADRE, RECETAS, CONSEJOS Y MÁS
(Spanish Edition)
https://www.amazon.com/dp/B0D8JT8S9S

Made in United States
Orlando, FL
18 April 2025

60633798R00125